The Resurrection of Jesus

New Considerations
for Its Theological Interpretation

KENAN B. OSBORNE, O.F.M.

D1004509

PAULIST PRESS
New York/Mahwah, N.J.

Cover design by Chiu-Man Chu

ACKNOWLEDGMENTS
The Publisher gratefully acknowledges use of the following materials:
Excerpts from *The New Jerusalem Bible*. Copyright © 1985 by Doubleday, a division of Bantam Doubleday Dell Publishing Group, Inc. and Darton, Longman & Todd, Ltd. Used by permission of Doubleday, a division of Bantam Doubleday Dell Publishing Group, Inc.
Quotations from the Greek New Testament: *Novum Testamentum Graece,* Nestle-Aland 27th Edition © 1898 and 1993 by Deutsche Bibelgesellschaft, Stuttgart. Used by permission.

Library of Congress Cataloging-in-Publication Data

Osborne, Kenan B.
   The Resurrection of Jesus : new considerations for its theological
interpretation / Kenan B. Osborne.
      p.   cm.
   Includes bibliographical references.
   ISBN 0-8091-3703-8 (alk. paper)
   1. Jesus Christ—Resurrection.   I. Title.
BT481.0824   1997
232'.5—dc21   97-1669
                                                      CIP

Published by Paulist Press
997 Macarthur Boulevard
Mahwah, New Jersey 07430

Printed and bound in the
United States of America

Contents

Introduction   1

1 Contemporary Theological Research
   on the Resurrection of Jesus   7

2 The Many Voices of the New Testament   30

3 A Theology of the Resurrection   105

4 The Resurrection and a Unified Christology   141

Notes   174

Index   191

Introduction

During most of this present century, discussion and reflection about the resurrection of Jesus have moved in two different ways. First of all, the current research by both systematic theologians and biblical scholars on this theme has moved toward a new understanding of the resurrection, but, second, the understanding of the resurrection found in catechetics, in sermons, and at times in liturgical prayers has moved in a different direction, namely, one that appears unaffected by the scholarly research. It is almost as though the intellectual life and the pastoral life of the church, both Roman Catholic and Protestant, have moved in increasingly polar ways as regards the resurrection of Jesus. The following pages are intended to do three things: first, to assemble in a readable and understandable way the contemporary scholarly research on the resurrection of Jesus; second, on the basis of this scholarly research, to formulate at some length an aspect of the resurrection that hopefully will further the field of discourse—that is, the aspect of religious experience as central to an understanding of the resurrection; third, to indicate in a brief way a possibility to develop a more unified christology than one generally finds in christological discussion.

The first chapter will provide an overview or exposition of the contemporary research: namely, What are contemporary Roman Catholic and Protestant theologians saying as regards the resurrection of Jesus? Studies by various theologians of this century provide us with details and insights touching on both the theological and biblical sides of the issue. On the other hand, there are the current catechetical and liturgical descriptions of the resurrection of Jesus: namely, the way in which the ordinary contemporary Roman Catholic and Protestant Christian

1

generally understands the resurrection of Jesus. A few pages will be devoted to this pastoral and catechetical side of the issue. There are reasons why these two groups of Christians appear to be moving along different lines and I will mention these reasons at the conclusion of the first chapter.

As regards the views of biblical and systematic theologians, one finds that in the twentieth century the amount of work that Roman Catholic and Protestant theologians have dedicated to the study of Jesus' resurrection surpasses almost all other theological study that these same authors have devoted to christological themes. The resurrection of Jesus has indeed earned the lion's share of theological time and effort; however, one notes also that most of this research on the resurrection of Jesus has affected the ordinary Christian, whether Catholic or Protestant, in only a superficial way. The disparity between theologian and ordinary Christian is, on this theme of the resurrection, rather acute.

From the Roman Catholic point of view, popular works on Jesus as well as sermons delivered in the Easter season have often presented the resurrection in an apologetic way, that is, in a defensive way. All that Jesus did, all that he prophesied, and all that he claimed were validated by his return to life "on the third day."[1] In an extremely popular book of mid-twentieth century, *The Faith of Millions,* John O'Brien wrote:

> Even if there remained any traces of uncertainty in the minds of any of the disciples as to the deity of Jesus after witnessing the numerous miracles He had wrought, surely those vestiges must have been dispelled by the stupendous miracle of the Resurrection. This occurrence, confirmed by such an abundance of testimony, including that of the Apostles who spoke with the Master after his Resurrection, would seem to have removed the last vestiges of uncertainty from the minds of the disciples as to the divine Sonship of Jesus.[2]

In this quotation we see that the resurrection is viewed as a "miracle" that dispelled all doubt regarding the divinity of Jesus. O'Brien's characterization of the resurrection is typical of the popular Catholic understanding of the risen Lord during the first half of this century. Jesus was God Incarnate; Jesus died for our salvation; the resurrection proves the divinity of Jesus and verifies his salvific sacrifice. In such works as the one cited above the resurrection accounts of the New Testament are taken at face value; their historicity is never questioned;

Jesus after his death once again walked this earth and spoke with his disciples, although in a glorified way.

We also find some tendency toward a literal, even fundamentalist interpretation of the resurrection in liturgical books. For instance, in the *Vatican II Sunday Missal,* a book meant to be used today by ordinary Catholics attending the eucharist, we find the following introductory comment made by the editors of this missal for the early eucharistic liturgy on Easter Sunday morning:

> The physical resurrection from the grave of Jesus Christ is the basic belief of Christianity, the reason for Christian faith, hope and courage. The Feast of the Resurrection is our greatest feast. Every Sunday is a "little Easter." The Gospel of today is the original "Good News"—Jesus of Nazareth, crucified, is risen and is present with us.[3]

There is much that is correct in this statement, but there is also a question about the meaning of "physical resurrection," which could be interpreted in a very realistic and fundamentalist way. The resurrection of Jesus is presented as the "reason for Christian faith," which raises enormous questions, since the resurrection of Jesus by itself is not the central belief of Christians. Rather, belief in God is far more central than belief in the resurrection of Jesus.

Even in the liturgical texts, however, there is a tendency toward a physical and fundamentalist approach to the resurrection of Jesus. In the liturgy for the early Easter morning eucharist, the alternate opening prayer states:

> This is the morning on which the Lord appeared to men who had begun to lose hope and opened their eyes to what the scriptures foretold: that first he must die, and then he would rise and ascend into his Father's glorious presence.[4]

The reference to Luke's gospel and the narrative about the two disciples' trip to Emmaus is clear, but there is a very strong overtone of an apologetic meaning of the resurrection of Jesus. The risen Lord opened the eyes of the disciples, proving the scriptures to be correct.

In the liturgical celebration of the Easter vigil, the *Exultet* is a magnificent hymn about our salvation through the death and resurrection of Jesus. In this song of the Easter night there are such phrases as:

> Christ has ransomed us with his blood and paid
> for us the price of Adam's sin to our eternal Father.
>
> This is the night when Jesus Christ broke the chains of
> death and rose triumphant from the grave.
>
> To ransom a slave you gave away your Son
>
> O happy fault, O necessary sin of Adam which gained
> or us so great a Redeemer.

Just prior to the many readings used in this Easter Vigil service, the introductory prayer says: "Through this Easter celebration may God bring to perfection the saving work he has begun in us."

In these citations we see that salvation or redemption is connected to the Easter event. A connection is made between the death of Jesus on the cross and the resurrection. In line with the letter to the Romans, one could say: we are saved by the death and the resurrection of Jesus. This connection of the resurrection of Jesus to our "salvation" is theologically quite correct, but it raises questions about the meaning of the death of Jesus and its connection to the meaning of the resurrection. The *Exultet* clearly unites the two, but once more, as we will see, there is an understanding of the death that one finds in the pastoral and catechetical area of church life, which stresses the teaching that Jesus died for our sins, and which leaves little room for a teaching that the resurrection is also part of the salvation-event. Not all is of a piece on this matter of "salvation," "redemption," "justification." This issue will be taken up in chapter 4.

This present study will proceed as follows: in chapter 1 there is a presentation and some comment on the state of current theological research on the resurrection of Jesus from Roman Catholic, Anglican, and Protestant scholarship. This chapter is meant to provide a background for further discussion of the meaning of the resurrection of Jesus. In the second chapter, there is a fairly in-depth study of the main New Testament voices on the resurrection of Jesus. The renewed research on the resurrection of Jesus actually began with a renewed biblical analysis, which is vital for any further theological speculation on the resurrection. One must understand as clearly as possible both the texts and contexts of the various New Testament passages that specifically deal with the resurrection before one draws together a theological statement. In chapter 3 there is an effort to provide a theology of the resurrection that brings into the center area of the discussion of the resurrection the issue of the action of God and the consequent human religious experience of this divine action. In the final chapter there are some observations on the need for a unified christology, in which the resurrection of Jesus is presented in a way that has a basic relationship to the preexistence/ infancy sections of the New Testament; to the public ministry of Jesus, including his arrest, trial, and death. This final chapter attempts to draw together at least in outline form a unified christology and a christology that also is congruent with the church's teaching on grace.

Contemporary Theological Research on the Resurrection of Jesus

In this chapter I would like to present an overview of the theological research on the resurrection of Jesus that has taken place during the past eighty years. The research began slowly but then mushroomed into a major area of christological study. Indeed, as far as christological research is concerned, the resurrection of Jesus became one of the most profoundly studied issues in christology that this century has experienced. The published material is both comprehensive and intensive.

It must be noted, however, that this christological interest in the resurrection of Jesus began slowly, and only in the course of the twentieth century did it reach its major development. At the beginning of the twentieth century not all Roman Catholic nor all Protestant theologians and biblical scholars shared this interest in the resurrection of Jesus. At that time, Roman Catholic theology was by and large still dominated by the so-called manuals of theology, used extensively in seminary education. When one reviews these manuals of theology, two major items concerning the resurrection of Jesus emerge. First, in the sections devoted specifically to christology the authors generally spent only a few paragraphs on the resurrection. This paucity of discussion indicates that the resurrection of Jesus did not at that time serve as a major focus of christological synthesis, a christological synthesis in which the major focus was almost exclusively the divinity of Jesus. Often the few remarks on the resurrection were consigned in these books to a "scholion," that is, a brief mention—and this more often than not of very meager length. Second, outside of the specific chapters on christology in these text books, the pages dedicated to apologetics offered a somewhat more extensive explanation of the resurrection. Nonetheless, in these christological sections of theological apologetics the resurrection of Jesus was considered primarily as a proof both of his divinity and of the claims and prophecies that Jesus himself had made during his earthly life.[1]

One example might serve as typical. I select this example, because of all the textbooks that were used from the late 1800s to the mid-century of the 1900s, this four-volume work ranks as one of the best.[2] In 1961, on the very eve of the Second Vatican Council, the Jesuit theologians from various universities and colleges in Spain produced a four-volume work on Roman Catholic theology entitled, *Sacrae Theologiae Summa*. The section on christology was developed by I. Solano.[3] In his presentation of christology, the resurrection is considered in the paragraphs dealing with the ministry and the arrest/suffering of Jesus. In typical scholastic fashion, Solano assembles his material around various theses, and the single thesis within which the resurrection is treated reads as follows: "Jesus Christ, through his most holy passion, effected our redemption."[4]

As one readily sees, the thesis itself is focused directly not on the resurrection but on the passion of Christ and on the redemption it effected. Within such an overarching theme, Solano turns to his only discussion of the resurrection, located in a small scholion.[5] Solano's entire treatise on christology numbers some 315 pages; however, out of this large number of pages, the resurrection of Jesus merits but a single page.

In the same set of volumes, *Sacrae Theologiae Summa,* Miguel Nicolau is the author of the fundamental or apologetic section on revelation. In his presentation we find some twenty pages on the resurrection, primarily in the form of a "proof" for Jesus' claims.[6] His thesis states: "Jesus, after his predicted resurrection, confirmed his divine testimony through a splendid proof by truly dying and truly rising."[7] Nicolau begins his task by enumerating all the adversaries to the truth of Jesus' resurrection, that is, those who see the resurrection as a fraud, as only apparent death, as a myth, as a symbol, and so on. He then proceeds to the doctrine of the church and divides his material into three sections:

1. *Jesus foretold his resurrection* (Jn 2:13–22; Mt 26:61; 27:40; Mk 14:58; also Mt 12:38–40; Lk 11:29ff.; Mk 8:30–32; Mt 16:20–22; Lk 9:21ff.).

2. *Jesus truly died.* The gospel material on the actual death of Jesus is enumerated, and the various people who attest to the actuality of Jesus' death, both disciples and adversaries, are mentioned.

3. *Jesus truly rose.* In this section, Nicolau begins first with the attestations from the various people to whom the Easter apparitions occurred and then with the data on the empty tomb. All of the resurrection material confirms, in Nicolau's approach, that Jesus is the Son of God. The resurrection of Jesus has meaning primarily because of its apologetic value.

In the *Manual of Dogmatic Theology* by A. Tanquerey, a volume used extensively in many American seminaries of the pre–Vatican II era, the situation is quite the same.[8] Tanquerey dedicates not quite six pages to the resurrection of Jesus, and his argument for all these pages is stated as follows: "If Jesus of Nazareth actually arose from the dead, we must believe that He has been really sent by God in order to teach us the true Religion."[9] Once more the apologetic character of the presentation of the resurrection of Jesus is evident.

Perhaps the reason for this rather narrow approach to the resurrection of Jesus in that period of our church history can be sought in the still prevalent siege mentality that the Roman Catholic Church had steadily maintained. Given all of this, it is not surprising that both the research and the theologians concerned with the resurrection of Jesus which this current century has experienced began with Protestant biblical and systematic scholars, and that Roman Catholic biblical and systematic scholars entered into the discussion only at a much later date.

For organizational reasons, we will review this material from the following three foci: an overview of the history of this research; contemporary methodological approaches; and contemporary christological emphases by both systematic and biblical scholars.

AN OVERVIEW OF THE HISTORY OF THIS RESEARCH

In the late eighteenth and early nineteenth centuries, the awakening of critical-historical biblical scholarship had indeed shaken the Protestant theological world, particularly in Germany.[10] Samuel Reimarus, through the posthumous publication of the *Wölfenbuttel Fragmente,*[11] and later in the nineteenth century David Friedrich

Strauss, with his critical methodological considerations of the New Testament in *Das Leben Jesu,*[12] and F. C. Baur with his *Geschichte der christlichen Kirche*[13] had created among Protestants not only a strong storm of protest but also a wave of support.[14] The Baur-Strauss period proved to be a turning point in Protestant theology, although the shadow of Friedrich Schleiermacher remained strong throughout the nineteenth and early twentieth centuries.

Roman Catholic scholars who moved in this historical-critical direction were seen by the church leadership of that period as followers of modernism, a movement that this same leadership denounced with anathema.[15] In Catholic circles of that time, creative biblical thinking was not acceptable; the status quo had to be maintained. The nineteenth century and the first half of the twentieth were threatening to the leadership of the Catholic Church, which had as yet not found a way to deal positively and creatively with the new currents of thought that had been emerging since the Enlightenment.

Moreover, the First Vatican Council abruptly ended its sessions with the takeover of the papal states by Garibaldi in 1870. At that period of time this was considered a major defeat for the Catholic Church, and as a result the papal leadership moved even more strongly into a siege mentality, trying with all its might to regain a position of papal power and prestige throughout the Christian world. In such an atmosphere, interchange with Protestant scholars was viewed as a weakening of "catholic substance." In the quite popular book of J. A. O'Brien cited above, we find such statements as: "All forms of Protestantism are man-made" and "they are without any divine sanction or approval."[16] Of course, there was in this same period an anti-Catholic stance as well, as was evident in 1928 when a Catholic was proposed for the presidency of the United States by a major national party, as well as the openly anti-clerical stance of many major figures throughout France and northern Italy. The prevailing effect of all this was that the majority of Catholics tried to maintain a conservative, that is, traditional and apologetic approach to theology; and Catholic theology at that time was almost the exclusive preserve of Catholic seminaries, in which only future priests were students. In these seminaries, Catholic theological tradition meant "the scholastic and Tridentine" approach to theology, rather than a historical-critical, biblical approach.

Protestantism, during this same period, however, was not in an enviable position. Walter Künneth[17] reminds us of the strong influence on

European Protestant thought that came from Schleiermacher, who had written: "The facts of the resurrection and the ascension of Christ . . . cannot be taken as an authentic part of the doctrine of his person."[18] Künneth goes on to cite in this same vein A. Ritschl and H. Stephan.[19] It was the criticism of Schleiermacher, begun by R. Frank and continued by L. Ihmels and C. Stange, that began to move Protestant thought in Germany away from this depreciation of the resurrection and into its more positive valency for Christian thought.[20] M. Kähler, P. Althaus, K. Heim, K. Barth, E. Brunner, and F. Gogarten all took an anti-Schleiermacher approach and offered a more positive evaluation of the resurrection.[21] Künneth writes:

> This brief glance at the history of theological discussion on the subject of the resurrection makes it clear that in itself there is no lack of valuable approaches towards a theological formulation of the problem, and in particular that contemporary theological reflection shows the time is ripe for a new start in this field.[22]

Künneth wrote in 1933, and many of the authors just cited wrote in the period of 1920–1930, which indicates that the contemporary interest in the resurrection, as far as German Protestant theology was concerned, really began around the second decade of the current century.

By the middle of the twentieth century, a wide variety of scholarly research had been developed by Protestant theologians, particularly in Germany but also in England. It was the publication of F.-X. Durwell's book *La résurrection de Jesus, mystère du Salut* in 1963 that truly inaugurated the Catholic contribution to the study of the resurrection.[23] Durwell admits his dependence on such authors as J. Schmitt (*Jesus ressuscité dans la prédication apostolique*), Künneth (*Theologie der Auferstehung*), A. M. Ramsey (*The Resurrection of Christ*), and, from a Catholic biblical standpoint, F. Prat (*La Théologie de Saint Paul*).[24] This scholarly book by Durwell, though somewhat conservative in approach and at times fairly redundant, broke the apologetic mold into which Catholic thought had encased the resurrection of Jesus and began a Roman Catholic theological presentation on the multidimensionality of this mystery of our faith.

Some twenty years later, an international symposium was held at Rome under the presidency of Edouard Dhanis, S.J., with mostly Catholic scholars contributing, but also a small number of Protestant scholars.[25] This symposium, held under Roman Catholic—that is,

Vatican—auspices, in a way signified the rapid and strong entry of the Catholic scholar into the field of the theological research on the resurrection of Jesus. Unsurprisingly, a major part of this symposium was the contributions of biblical scholars, since so much of the theology of the resurrection of Jesus is based on New Testament data. The proceedings of this symposium, the *Acta,* included significant monographs by systematic theologians as well. The *Acta* were subsequently published, and the contribution of G. Ghiberti deserves special mention.[26] In a most thorough way, Ghiberti developed a bibliography on the resurrection of Jesus, with books, monographs, and articles from all major languages between the years 1920 and 1973. Ghiberti tabulated 1,510 entries. This large number of entries alone indicates that since 1920 Protestant scholars and, somewhat later, Catholic scholars have devoted a major portion of their time and effort to the theme of the resurrection of Jesus. One could almost say that in our own century the major christological subject of study by theologians has been the resurrection of Jesus.

Around mid-century, Protestant and Catholic writers produced a growing number of influential volumes such as *Der Ablauf der Osterereigniße und das leere Grab* by H. von Campenhausen (1952); *Ostergeschehen und Osterberichte* by H. Graß (1956); *Die Bedeutung der Auferstehungsbotschaft für den Glauben an Jesus Christus* by W. Marxsen, U. Wilckens, G. Delling, H. B. Geyer, G. Mohn (1966); *Passion et résurrection du Seigneur* by P. Benoit (1966); *Die Auferstehung Jesu in der Botschaft der Evangelisten* by Ph. Seidensticker (1967); *Die Auferstehung Jesu: Form, Art und Sinn der urchristlichen Botschaft* by K. Rengstorf (1967); *The Resurrection of Christ as History and Experience* by H. Hooke (1967); *Die Auferstehung Jesu von Nazareth* by W. Marxsen (1968); *La résurrection* by J. Daniélou (1969); *Résurrection de Jésus et message pascal* by X. Léon-Dufour (1971); *The Formation of the Resurrection Narratives* by R. H. Fuller (1971); *Dieu l'a ressuscité* by B. Rigaux (1973); *The Resurrection of Jesus Christ* by G. O'Collins (1973).

More recently there has occurred a formal debate on the issue "Did Jesus Rise from the Dead?" by Gary R. Habermas and Anthony G. N. Flew, held on May 2, 1985, at Liberty University, a debate that was subsequently made into a book edited by T. L. Miethe.[27] P. Perkins's *Resurrection: New Testament Witness and Contemporary Reflection* is also important, particularly for the issue of the empty tomb tradition.[28] The contemporary research in Germany by Ingo Broer should also be a noted.[29]

What began as an interest in the exegetical issues involved in the resurrection narratives of the New Testament gradually took on wider significance. The systematic theologians, particularly of Europe, saw in this biblical development an even greater value, so that many of them at mid-century began to consider the resurrection of Jesus the very starting point *(Ausgangspunkt)* for all christology.[30] This concentration on the resurrection of Jesus as the starting point for christology has continued down to the present day; however, this position is not without its critics. Latin American theologians, such as Jon Sobrino and Leonardo Boff, have taken issue with this starting point for christology. Nonetheless, the centrality of the resurrection of Jesus remains a formidable focus, if not the most dominant focus, of contemporary christological research.

All of this theological interest and research, however, has not generally permeated the common piety of Christians, whether Protestant or Catholic, nor has it influenced strongly the pastoral work of the churches. In noting this discrepancy between theological thought on the one hand and general Christian belief on the other, one might find some parallels between the contemporary *theological* studies on the infancy narratives and the *general understanding* of these infancy narratives by Christians at large.[31] Earlier on in this present century, the exegetical and theological hesitations about the historicity of many details in the infancy narratives did filter down to the parochial areas of church life, and there were serious concerns and even outcries by many Christians when they heard that some details regarding the birth of Jesus might not stand up to literal and historical verification. For these Christians the visual image of the crèche was far more conclusive than any academic, historical, critical conclusion. This same pattern holds true for the resurrection of Jesus. That the literal, historical approach must be maintained as regards the details of Jesus' resurrection remains strong in the common Christian mind. In this view, what the gospels portray must have actually and historically happened in the precise way it is described. Any diminution of this historicity is seen as threatening. O'Brien, as we saw above, clearly accepted the historical reality of the apostles' talking with the risen Lord on many occasions in the same way that Jesus had spoken with them during his earthly life. The reason for this fairly adamant stand on the literal and historical meaning of the resurrection narratives is not difficult to find, and the standpoint of the leadership of the Roman Catholic Church on this matter during the nineteenth and twentieth centuries assuredly provides the clue. If for so long the resurrection of Jesus, interpreted in a strictly historical manner, was presented as the proof or, better, the main proof for all that Jesus stood for, then any meddling with this proof might easily undermine all that Jesus stood for and validated. The church itself would be invalidated if the resurrection were anything else than an actual event in history. This emphasis continues even into the present time at the popular level.[32] In all of this "proof" material from the resurrection chapters of the four gospels, the emptiness of the tomb was paramount, as also the fact that there were people such as Thomas who actually touched the risen Jesus and put his hands into the very wounds of the Lord. The stark physical reality of the risen Lord provided that rock of Gibraltar for Christian faith. Meddle with the rock, and the faith will crumble. There clearly remains an understandable resistance to anything that alters this touchstone of our faith.

Nonetheless, such widespread Christian concern about the foundations of faith has not discouraged scholars from delving more carefully into the theological and exegetical aspects of the resurrection of Jesus. Slowly a deeper and more nuanced view of the meaning of this resurrection is beginning to evolve, not only in the scholarly world but, it may be hoped, also in the rank and file of the Christian people.

CONTEMPORARY METHODOLOGICAL APPROACHES

There is no easy approach to the resurrection of Jesus, and the contemporary writings on this theme present us with a variety of methodologies and stances, all of which must simply be seen as an introduction to contemporary thought on the resurrection of Jesus. Method is highly important, not only on the issue of understanding the resurrection of Jesus but in all issues of theological endeavor. Since the methodological positions of contemporary theologians are not identical, the results or conclusions on the resurrection of Jesus cannot help but be slightly different. Conservative theologians will employ certain methodologies and disallow others; more liberal theologians will employ certain methodologies but disallow a nonscholarly, fundamentalist approach to the biblical texts. Since the conclusions are often the result of the use or nonuse of methodologies, let us take a moment to consider what current methodologies on the resurrection of Jesus have been developed.

In 1967 Bertold Klappert edited a sourcebook on various theological positions concerning the resurrection of Jesus, *Diskussion um Kreuz und Auferstehung,* which he hoped would be of wide benefit for the pastoral activity of Protestant ministers in Germany.[33] Included in this publication are essays on the resurrection by such leading theologians as Karl Barth, Rudolf Bultmann, Werner Georg Kümmel, Joachim Jeremias, Wolfhart Pannenberg, Jürgen Moltmann, and others. All of these major Protestant scholars have taken a position on the resurrection of Jesus that opposed the long-standing influence of Schleiermacher and applied, although in differing ways, the historical-critical method of biblical studies to the New Testament resurrection material.[34] In addition, Klappert prepared a small introductory essay in which he divided his own material on the resurrection of Jesus methodologically into the following headings:

1. The resurrection as an actual event in history: the historical aspect of the resurrection of Jesus.
2. The resurrection as the activation of forgiveness: the soteriological aspect of the resurrection of Jesus.
3. The resurrection as the commencement of the new future: the future-eschatological aspect of the resurrection of Jesus.
4. The resurrection as the establishment of the kerygma: the kerygmatic aspect of the resurrection of Jesus.
5. The resurrection as the grounding of faith: the anthropological aspect of the resurrection of Jesus.[35]

Klappert concludes this schematization with a brief section on the multidimensionality of the resurrection accounts.[36] His entire schematization offers a helpful example of a theological approach to the understanding of the resurrection that draws into the field of discourse a multiplicity of voices. The various aspects of his methodology could be formulated as questions:

1. The historical question: What actually happened?
2. The soteriological question: How are we saved?
3. The eschatological question: In what do we hope?
4. The kerygmatic or ecclesiological question: What do we preach?
5. The anthropological question: Who is a person of Christian faith?

The Kantian overtones of these questions are evident, but perhaps the key word that Klappert utilizes is *multidimensionality*. The resurrection of Jesus, theologically considered, cannot be approached from a single standpoint; rather, it must be approached from a number of vantage points. Clearly, the resurrection is not only a complex issue but a multidimensional complex issue. No single dimension can possibly provide us with an adequate understanding of this mystery of our faith. In some ways this may sound like *déjà vu;* however, in reality, many Christian people never go beyond the first question, the historical question: What actually happened? They simply ask: What factually took place? So concerned are they about the reality of the risen body of Jesus, about Jesus' eating honey or fish, about Thomas touching Jesus' wounds, and all the other sundry "historical" details of the appearance narratives, that the depth of the resurrection remains quite unexplored. For this reason, Klappert's schematization offers a helpful pedagogical tool or methodological framework, since it makes one go beyond the historical data and ask far more profound theological questions about the resurrection of Jesus.

This methodological framework does not resolve all the issues, but it places all the key issues on the table. Let us for a moment utilize Klappert's methodological approach, but add to it some details.

The Historical Question: What Can We Know?

From a factual, historical, physical viewpoint, how can one understand the New Testament data? There are various answers to this question:

1. One can simply accept the data at face value as historical, just as one accepts other historical data (e.g., Kähler and other nineteenth-century Protestant and most Roman Catholic scholars).

2. It is not the historical issues that are of vital importance but the action of God, that is, a revelatory new action of God in history through Jesus which is the controlling factor in any interpretation of the resurrection of Jesus (e.g., Barth, Moltmann).

3. The veracity of such historical data is only of secondary importance. The existential challenge of the Word of God speaking to us through such accounts and our response—a yes or no—to this existential Word of God is ultimately what is important (e.g., Bultmann, Marxsen, and to some degree Käsemann).

4. One is able through historical methodology to "prove" the resurrection of Jesus, but this proof must also include the mystery of eschatology, which is a new spatio-temporal form of existence. The resurrection must be affirmed as a historical event as such, but it must also be affirmed as an eschatological event (e.g., Pannenberg).

The Soteriological Question: In What Have We Been Saved?

In Romans 4:25, the resurrection of Jesus is united to the death of Jesus as God's instrument of salvation: "Our faith, too, will be considered if we believe in him who raised Jesus our Lord from the dead, Jesus who was put to death for our sins and raised to life to justify us." On this point, J. Fitzmyer notes:

> Since the cross and the resurrection are two intimately connected phases of the same salvific event, their juxtaposition here is the result of the rhetoric of antithetical parallelism. It is not to be pressed as if Christ's death were destined only for the removal of human sin and his resurrection for justification. Paul does not always explicitly relate justification to the resurrection. The affirmation of the part played by Christ's death and resurrection in the objective redemption of humanity forms a fitting conclusion to this part A of the doctrinal section of Romans.[37]

If we have been saved by the death and resurrection of Jesus, then there is an urgent need to rethink the entire theological meaning of such terms as *salvation, redemption, justification, sacrifice,* and so on. In both Roman Catholic and Protestant circles, the death of Jesus has been presented as the vicarious sacrifice through which God has saved, redeemed, and justified all men and women. The death of Jesus is the victory over Satan, sin, and death which has gained salvation, redemption, justification for all men and women (G. Aulén). Even more close to home is the understanding, especially in Roman Catholic areas, that the eucharist is the unbloody sacrifice of the bloody sacrifice of the cross. If we have been saved, however, by the death *and* resurrection of Jesus, then all such terms—*salvation, redemption, justification, sacrifice*—must be rethought in terms of *cross-and-resurrection* and not simply in terms of the crucifixion. Already one sees that this renewed understanding of the resurrection of Jesus could and does engender a radical rethinking of what salvation, redemption, and justification are all about.

The resurrection is not simply a "proof" that Jesus' death was salvific. That is not the meaning either in Paul or in the contemporary research on the resurrection. Rather, the resurrection, like the death of Jesus, is central to the salvific act of God. I will return to this theme in the final chapter of this volume when I will consider the need for a unified christology.

The Kerygmatic Question: What Do We Preach?

As we shall see in the third chapter, there is a mission and commissioning connected to the appearances of Jesus to his disciples, both men and women. The resurrection is an essential part to what is described analogically as the "birth of the church." The church was not born when the body of Jesus, hanging on the cross, was pierced with a lance and blood and water flowed. The church was not born when Jesus died. The "birth" of the new Israel, eventually called church, arose because of the total incarnation, an incarnation that includes *the life, the death, and the resurrection* of Jesus.

There are consequences to this view. H. Küng has continually stressed that one cannot speak of "church" until one arrives at a post-resurrection situation. Only after the resurrection can one begin to speak about the new Israel, the church. In other words, during his lifetime Jesus did not "institute" a church. He did not establish the Twelve as bishops, nor did he establish a new priesthood. All of this hierarchical development arose in a postresurrection milieu and was brought about because of Easter faith. Once again, because of this methodological approach, a "shaking of foundations"—to borrow a phrase from Paul Tillich—emerges. A new approach to the resurrection of Jesus will not and cannot leave the fabric of Christian life untouched. A new approach to the resurrection of Jesus impacts on the entire theological structuring of Christian life.

The Anthropological Question:
What Does It Mean to Be Human?

As far as the human condition is concerned, the resurrection of Jesus that is connected to our own resurrection (cf. Romans 15) opens up the question of what it really means to be a human person. In the faith-stance of our Christian life, human life is ultimately defined by risen life, a totally new way of being human. This does not devalue our earthly life, since risen life has already begun while we are on this earth.

Risen life, just like our ordinary human life, must be seen as a process, not as a single moment. Incarnation is a process that begins with creation and finds its completion in the final stage of resurrection.

The Eschatological Question:
In What Can We Hope?

We are called on by this methodological question to understand our human situation against the horizon of hope (cf. Moltmann), as well as against the horizon of our current social and political situation (cf. Metz and Segundo). The eschaton is not only in the future, but is also realized to certain degree in the "now" of our Christian life. There is a proleptic situation at work in our current existential living (cf. Pannenberg).

This brief usage of Klappert's multidimensional methodology for the resurrection indicates that the very raising of these multidimensional questions impacts on a theoretical or theological understanding not only of the resurrection but also of many other areas of our Christian faith. In turn, such theoretical and theological views impact on the actual structuring of our Christian life. In other words, all of this renewed research and evaluation of the resurrection of Jesus do not remain in an ivory tower of exegetical and theological discourse. There are major effects on the actual life of the church, and this undoubtedly will cause much concern. In many ways, the reentry of the resurrection of Jesus into the very core of our Christian thought and life—not simply as a "proof" event—can be seen as the beginning of a radical paradigm shift for Christian theology and practice.

In a rather similar way, J. Sobrino, in *Cristología desde américa latina,* first discusses the theological positions on the resurrection of Jesus taken by Bultmann, Marxsen, Pannenberg, and Boff. He indicates that all of them are, in his view, limited and inadequate.[38] He then offers his own position, not as the final word but as a possibly better hermeneutic:

> Now I should like to propose another focus for understanding the resurrection of Jesus. Let us assume that the resurrection is not simply the resuscitation of a cadaver or some great "miracle" performed by God. Let us assume that it is the event that reveals God. In that case our talk about the resurrection and our hermeneutics of the resurrection bring us to the same set of problems we face with

regard to knowledge of God in general. In other words, we cannot assume at the start that we already know who God is and move from there to an understanding of the resurrection. As was the case with the cross of Jesus, we can only learn who God is from the cross and the resurrection of Jesus.[39]

Sobrino proceeds in a way that reminds one of Klappert, developing a hermeneutic for the resurrection of Jesus by asking three basic questions:

1. What may I hope for?
2. What can I know?
3. What should I do?

In using these questions, Sobrino indicates, in his own way, the multidimensionality of the resurrection of the Lord. Eschatology, history, and discipleship are the dimensions Sobrino utilizes.

Neither Klappert nor Sobrino, however, meant that the various aspects their questions involved exhausted the approaches to the resurrection of Jesus. Indeed, other aspects, and therefore other questions, might be added to their lists, for instance:

1. **The pneumatological question:** What is the role of the Spirit in the resurrection?
2. **The ecclesiological question:** How is the Christian community an Easter community?
3. **The sacramental question:** In what way is the risen Lord the primordial sacrament?
4. **The cosmological question:** How is the resurrection of Jesus the omega or ecological point of our universe?

This listing of questions could go further, but the issue I want to stress at this juncture is this: both from a theological, especially a methodological, viewpoint and from a faith viewpoint, the resurrection of the Lord must be seen as a multidimensional reality. To approach the resurrection only through a single viewpoint impoverishes our understanding of this saving reality. Indeed, such a single-lens approach ultimately makes the resurrection of Jesus a noncredible doctrine.

Since the knowledge that we have of the resurrection of Jesus is found primarily in the New Testament, part of the methodology must include a textual analysis of the gospel passages, as well as other New

Testament passages. This means, first of all, that the Greek text itself needs to be firmly established. In our day and age, the Nestle-Aland edition of the Greek text of the New Testament provides us with the best Greek text available to date, and yet even with this text one must carefully note the numerous textual variants that the editors of this Greek text provide in the apparatus.[40] No translation can possibly take the place of this Greek original.

Besides this basic textual material, detailed commentaries on the resurrection passages are also necessary. Fortunately, contemporary scholarship has provided us with some notable commentaries. In 1969 C. F. Evans in his *Resurrection and the New Testament* provided the English-speaking world with just such a commentary.[41] Almost at the same time, Reginald H. Fuller published his first edition of *The Formation of the Resurrection Narratives*.[42] In his introduction, Fuller mentions that this kind of exegetical study had not occurred in English since the early part of this century with the publication of Kirsopp Lake's ground-breaking *The Historical Evidence for the Resurrection of Jesus Christ*,[43] and a few years later that of P. Gardner-Smith, *The Narratives of the Resurrection*.[44] Maurice Goguel, in 1933, published his own study: *La foi a la résurrection de Jesus dans la christianisme primitif*.[45] A shorter and less detailed presentation is that of R. Brown in the introductory section to the Johannine resurrection account in his commentary *The Gospel According to John*.[46] The more pressing difficulties and differences of the various gospel accounts are quite clearly elaborated in these pages by Brown. Methodologically, the systematic theologian must begin with this textual and contextual material.

Beyond the textual and contextual data, there is, nonetheless, an ecclesiological issue. Willi Marxsen writes:

> In all the discussions which at present occupy our churches and our theology, the question of Jesus' resurrection plays a decisive part: one might even say the decisive part. This is understandable, particularly if we remember the Pauline statement so often quoted in this connection: "If Christ has not been raised, then our kerygma (our message) is in vain and your faith is in vain." (1 Cor. 15, 14) According to this, talking about the resurrection means talking about the faith of the church.[47]

Marxsen admits that almost all Christians agree with the statement that Jesus is risen, but the interpretation of this fundamental sentence is not that unanimous. The one who utters such a statement already has an interpretation, out of which he or she explains it. The one to whom the statement is addressed likewise has an interpretation, through which it is heard. These various interpretations are grounded, Marxsen notes, in different courts of appeal: for example, in the New Testament itself as the word of God; or in "modern thinking"; or in the creeds of the church. Most of these appeals, Marxsen observes, end up, however, in a sort of cul-de-sac, and the only way out, he maintains, is to turn back.

However, this turning back in itself is not an easy matter, since new difficulties almost immediately begin to appear. For example, the very term *is,* in the statement "Jesus is risen" might mean something present: that is, Jesus is alive right now. Or it might mean that Jesus has risen, in which the emphasis is on the past. However one might temporally emphasize the statement "Jesus is risen," there is still another issue connected with this: namely, To what degree is the speaker personally involved in this statement? This personal involvement is very much an ecclesiological consideration. To profess that Jesus is risen is, of course, a faith statement, but one made in the context of a faith community, that is, in the context of the church. Whether one considers the resurrection of Jesus more in terms of a resuscitation of the body, or in a more spiritual fashion, or in an existential way, there is still a faith commitment, both personally and *ecclesially.* Jesus is risen not only for me; Jesus is actually risen for us. Christian faith in the resurrection is not totally or exclusively a personal situation; it is a communal and ecclesial situation. For this reason one must ascertain what kind of faith community might validate not only the statement "Jesus is risen" but also the interpretation of that statement, that is, the meaning the community speakers intend to give to this statement.[48]

A further issue arises, but one connected intrinsically to the profession of faith in the resurrection of Jesus. In the matter of the resurrection of Jesus, experience cannot be discounted, since our present experience of the resurrection is also the beginning of our interpretation. Marxsen and to an even stronger degree E. Schillebeeckx are correct in seeing this inescapable connection between experience and interpretation.[49] There is no "neutral experience"; there is always an "interpreted experience" as well as an "interpreting experience." One does not first experience something and only later, through reflection, interpret what was experienced. Rather, in the very experiencing, interpretation is going on. Experience itself presents us with some sort of information on the "what" which we are experiencing. Most often we are not totally satisfied with such interpretive material, so we look elsewhere for collaboration or additional information. We look to others, and, in the issue of the resurrection, these "others" might be church authorities or theological authorities. In the course of the Christian tradition, solemn church statements on the resurrection have been relatively modest, most often repeating biblical phrases. As far as the resurrection of Jesus is concerned, there are no official church documents, comparable to those on the divinity of Jesus, that is, the documents from the councils of Nicaea, Ephesus, and Chalcedon on the one person/two natures of Jesus. It is primarily in creeds (see Denz. 2, 13, 16, 20, 40, 42, 54, 86, 286, 344) and in professions of faith (see Denz. 255, 422, 429, 462, 709, 994, 1463) that we find the solemn statements of the church on the resurrection of Jesus. The various creeds the church uses most often simply restate biblical terms and phrases, such as "on the third day he rose again from the dead." Some variations, at times, do occur. For example, in the Ninth Council of Toledo (675 C.E.) the framers added that Jesus rose *virtute sua,* that is, by his own power. In 1053, in *Congratulamur vehementer,* his letter to Peter, the patriarch of Antioch, Leo IX placed a great deal of emphasis on the actuality of the body of the risen Lord. Jesus ate, not because of any need but only because he willed it, and he did so to confirm that he had actually risen with the same body that he had had during his lifetime. In 1208, Innocent III wrote a letter, *Eius exemplo,* to the archbishop of Tarragona, in which there is a profession of faith prescribed for the Waldensians. In this profession there is mention of a resumption of the soul to the body at the resurrection of Jesus. It is interesting to see in official church statements the amazing length and depth in which the one person/two natures of Jesus is spelled out, whereas there is little in dogmatic church documents on the resurrection of Jesus itself.

In the Roman Catholic theological tradition of modern—not contemporary—times, the common teaching on the resurrection of Jesus, as found in pre–Vatican II, or Counter-Reformation theological manuals, is for the most part a collection of scholastic opinions, appended to these brief creedal and scriptural statements. In these volumes, the authority presented to validate a given interpretation of Jesus' resurrection involves: (a) New Testament passages; and (b) church pronouncements, which as was noted are meager. However, New Testament passages need to be exegetically understood in order to be interpreted correctly, and the few solemn church pronouncements are, for the most part, cautious reiterations of New Testament passages. The cul-de-sac situation, mentioned by Marxsen, is evident.

More often than not, Marxsen notes, the "other" to whom Protestants go for interpretation is the New Testament. Again, however, this is a return to that area with which the present essay begins. What does the New Testament actually state? (the text), and in what way should it be interpreted? (the context).

X. Léon-Dufour approaches the issue in a way different from that of either Marxsen or Schillebeeckx.[50] He begins with the New Testament texts themselves but immediately moves back beyond the canonical texts we now possess. These canonical texts, he argues, are themselves the end result of a lengthy process that took place in various Christian communities. Léon-Dufour schematizes his genesis and development of the New Testament texts as follows:[51]

First Stage: The various categories of thought underlying the resurrection formulae and the developments of these categories. At first different kinds of statements were separated—for example, exaltation statements, risen body statements, empty tomb statements, which were the diverse ways used by the various early Christian communities to speak of the risen Lord. This stage is important since in certain Jesus communities "exaltation" was the primary analogue used to interpret the postdeath living of Jesus. The Old Testament story of Elijah was an example of this kind of interpretation. This "exaltation" motif lingers on in the eventual canonical texts, namely, in the "ascension" episodes. Exaltation and resurrection are correlative interpretive terms; one without the other diminishes one's understanding of the meaning of the event.

Second Stage: The literary category of the Easter narratives and the origin of the traditions that underlie them. In this period the Christian communities begin to develop various ways of communicating the Easter kerygma in some uniform way. These are the traditions immediately below the surface of the canonical texts. Here again we notice that both the exaltation motif and the resurrection motif are present.

Third Stage: The actual New Testament texts themselves and the different perspectives in them. In this stage, *category* is no longer the operative word; rather it is *kerygma,* or message. The gospels are all professions of Christian faith.

Fourth Stage: The subsequent problem of hermeneutics and communication, which centers on the problem of faith and historical knowledge. In this stage the communities subsequent to New Testament times have attempted to proclaim and interpret the resurrection message to their contemporaries.

The value of Léon-Dufour's approach is that it gives us some indication of the way in which the earliest groups of Christians understood the resurrection (first stage) and the ways in which these Christian communities attempted to communicate the Easter message in an organized way (second stage). The later expressions of this message, as found in the various canonized texts, indicate to us the distinctive theological approaches to the resurrection of the various New Testament authors (third stage). It should be noted in this regard that the New Testament texts provide us not only with "history" but also with theological interpretations of the resurrection of Jesus. To see the New Testament accounts of the resurrection of Jesus as merely historical narrative is to misinterpret the accounts. Finally (fourth stage), the Christian communities, over the centuries, have had to rethink and reinterpret the Easter message and to proclaim it anew to their respective generations, so that the resurrection becomes a centering point of one's faith. The genetic quality of Léon-Dufour's approach or methodology is extremely helpful and indicates clearly that the Easter message is both historical and has a history of its own.

The thrust of this entire section has been an attempt to indicate that one cannot rush into the resurrection accounts as found in the New Testament and expect clear-cut pictures. Nor can one simply ask such simplistic questions as, What actually happened? Did Thomas really touch Jesus? Did Jesus really eat grilled fish? expecting that the answers to such questions will indicate precisely what the resurrection of Jesus is truly about. Such questions indeed have validity, but only within a context that includes faith and the theological dimensions of the resurrection. The resurrection of Jesus is truly a multidimensional reality; as such it must be approached in a multidimensional way.

CONTEMPORARY CHRISTOLOGICAL EMPHASES BY BOTH SYSTEMATIC AND BIBLICAL SCHOLARS

The bibliography on the resurrection of Jesus which Ghiberti compiled extended from 1920 to 1973, as we noted above. What has happened to the research on the resurrection of Jesus since 1973? Can we still say today that the resurrection of Jesus is the major focus of New Testament and systematic theological endeavors? An affirmative answer to this last question might be difficult to sustain, for some additional factors have played major roles in shaping the christological thought during the last quarter of the second millennium.

The Second Vatican Council

When the Second Vatican Council had promulgated all of its decrees, the major focus of Roman Catholic theologians was on the explanation, interpretation, and integration of these documents. Excellent commentaries were drawn up by theological *periti* (experts) who had personally taken part in the council. Such commentaries include the volumes in German edited by H. Vorgrimler; the work by Gérard Philips on *Lumen Gentium;* the two volumes by G. Baraúna and S. Olivieri; and the volume by B. Kloppenburg.[52] Many other authors could be cited. In all of this material the focus was primarily on the church, more specifically the Roman Catholic Church. From this ecclesiological and ecclesial center, discussion moved to worship and liturgy; to ecumenism with Orthodox, Anglican, and Protestant churches as well as with other world religions; to religious freedom; to the lay/clergy distinction; to mariology; and to many other related themes included in the conciliar documents. As one might notice, research on the resurrection of Jesus was not central in any of these efforts.

The Ecumenical Movement

Although the many dialogues that the ecumenical movement inspired did not focus on resurrection research, the issues these dialogues did raise have steadily asked each of the churches to delve into its ultimate meaning as a "Jesus" church. If all our churches proclaim the message of Jesus, what is this message that so unites us? Naturally, this includes the very meaning of the life, death, and resurrection of Jesus. If the churches agree on this basic and fundamental gospel message, why do institutional and structural differences continue to be obstructive? Where are the priorities for the establishment of unity? Only here and there have ecumenical dialogues begun to face this ecumenical interfacing of christology and ecclesiology.

Liberation Theology

The amount of literature on liberation theology has increased dramatically. Liberation theology is a multifaceted reality that includes the following:

1. The liberation theology of Central and South America, guided by such scholars as G. Gutierrez, L. Boff, J. Sobrino, J. Segundo, and others. Often the term *liberation theology* is used only for this group of thinkers.

2. Feminist theology, also a liberation theology, is not limited to North America. There is a strong development of feminist theology in South America, in Asia, and in Europe, and a growing feminist theology in Africa. There is already a significant amount of feminist christological literature, including a profound rethinking of the life, death, and resurrection of Jesus.

3. There is in the United States a form of theology called *black theology*. In essence this is a very strong exposition of liberation theology that is unique to the United States, since it is rooted in the non-Christian, non-gospel experience of slavery. This liberation theology has and continues to develop an understanding of the life, death, and resurrection of Jesus.

4. There is a burgeoning African liberation theology, even beyond its feminist aspect. The Christian faith has many strong pockets throughout the various areas of Africa, each of which has its own ethnic and cultural distinctiveness. At times the political boundaries are at odds with cultural boundaries, and at times interpretations of Christian values imported from the northern hemisphere run counter to the ways in which African groups themselves interpret the gospel. There is, then, a current searching for a deeper understanding—although clearly in a way that respects the pluralism of the African peoples—of an African interpretation of the gospel. This does and will include several African interpretations of the life, death, and resurrection of Jesus.

5. There is also a small but growing Asian liberation theology. Here too one realizes that the term *Asian* is overbroad. There are diverse Asian liberation theologies, which variously interpret the life, death, and resurrection of Jesus.

In all of this liberation theology, an emphasis on ecclesiological structures was perhaps a beginning point, since the structures both of the church and of society were the nonliberating elements. Gradually, there was and continues to be a liberation from theological structures themselves, and this includes a liberation from "accepted" theological interpretations of the life, the death, and the resurrection of Jesus.

The Jewish Jesus

A major christological issue has become part of the discussion of Jesus in this last quarter of the second millennium, namely, the intensive study of the Jewishness of Jesus by authors such as E. P. Sanders, J. Charlesworth, D. Crossan, and J. Meier, to name only some of the major figures. This work by Christian scholars is in step with work by Jewish scholars on Second Temple Judaism, namely, such authors as J. Neusner and G. Vermes.

Although this issue may appear at first blush to be somewhat far from any research on the resurrection of Jesus, this is hardly the case. All of this material has provided a major rethinking of the historical Jesus, but also a rethinking of the historical Jesus movement and the people who were involved in this movement. These latter people include Paul and the writers of the four gospels, who were all Jewish people. The more we learn about the worldview they shared, the better we will understand and interpret their writings, which include passages that focus on the resurrection of Jesus. In other words, in Paul and in the gospel writers we must hear their words with Jewish ears, not with Chalcedonian ears or any other type of Christian ears. We must see their vision with Jewish eyes, not with Chalcedonian eyes or with any other type of Christian eyes. This does not mean that once we do this kind of hearing and seeing we will understand the meaning of the resurrection of Jesus, for there is still the ongoing fourth stage of Léon-Dufour, namely, the continuous need to make the gospel message meaningful to generation after generation, including those of our own times.

It is in these four areas in particular that current christology has its major foci. Nonetheless, all four of these emphases affect the way we will interpret the life, death, and resurrection of Jesus, and to do so we must move slowly and methodically. As mentioned above, the text and the context of the New Testament passages on the resurrection are the gateway to our interpretation, and this leads us to chapter 2.

SUMMARY OF CHAPTER ONE

1. Until the middle of this century, Roman Catholics in the late Counter-Reformation period approached the resurrection of Jesus primarily from the standpoint of apologetics. The resurrection of Jesus was seen as the major proof for the claim to his divinity.

2. From 1950 to the present, Roman Catholic theology of the resurrection has opened itself in a strong way to the theological depths of the resurrection. Indeed, discussion of the resurrection of Jesus dominates the research material of contemporary Catholic christology.

3. Protestant theological discussion of the resurrection in modern times was at first highly influenced by Schleiermacher, who was perceived, rightly or wrongly, by a majority of Protestant theologians in the late nineteenth century as belittling the import of the resurrection for christology. Many Protestant theologians tended to agree with Schleiermacher.

4. From 1920 onward Protestant theologians have developed a more profound and more nuanced theological understanding of the resurrection of Jesus. Protestant literature on the subject of Jesus' resurrection plays a dominant role in contemporary Protestant writings on christology.

5. Contemporary authors, both Protestant and Catholic, have developed methodologies for the study of the resurrection of Jesus. These methodologies move scholars out of an apologetic framework and out of a purely historical or factual consideration of the resurrection of Jesus. These methodologies also indicate the multidimensionality of the resurrection of Jesus and its multiple relationships to all of christology.

6. In contemporary theology, thorough exegetical studies have appeared that analyze in depth the genre of the resurrection accounts of the New Testament and provide a genetic approach to their eventual form in the canonical texts.

7. The interpretation factor, which involves a faith statement and an ecclesial statement, is seen as a central issue by contemporary scholars. This interpretation factor has become part of both the textual and the contextual analysis, as well as of the theological and christological discussion.

2

The Many Voices
of the New Testament

In the New Testament we find that there are many different authors who speak to us about the resurrection of Jesus. Their voices and accounts, however, are not always the same. Variations occur because of the differing theological perspectives and pastoral emphases of each author. Efforts to arrange the New Testament texts about the resurrection chronologically have not been successful. One cannot select some details from Mark, then some from Matthew, then some from Luke, then some from John, then some from Paul and order them in a "historical" sequence. The New Testament material cannot be harmonized in such a fundamentalist way. Rather, one must acknowledge clearly that there are different voices in the New Testament and that these different voices, though focused on the resurrection, are not saying exactly the same thing as far as the individual details are concerned. It is also important to acknowledge that all of the New Testament material is revelation, or God's Word, including this disparate material on the resurrection of Jesus. One cannot opt for one author and bypass or play down another. In some way all these varying voices must be heard, each in its own way, as expressive of the revelatory Word of God.

In this chapter we shall look, first of all, at these voices one by one. As each voice from the New Testament is cited, there will be a brief comment on some key issues involved in both the text and the context. By no means are these comments intended to be a full explanation of either the text or the context. Rather, they are meant to highlight some significant issues that a systematic theologian needs to take into account in discussing the resurrection. At the end of this task, however, we will still have only the pieces, not a synthesis. My attempt to reach some sort of synthesizing understanding of these disparate voices will occupy chapter 3.

In the New Testament the main voices that speak of the resurrection of Jesus can be classified as follows:

1. MARK I

   This "Mark" is the author of the Marcan gospel itself, including the first eight verses of the final chapter, namely, 16:1–8. The author and place of composition remain unknown, and biblical scholars are not of one mind on either issue.[1] There is sufficient evidence to have serious doubts that the title "according to Mark"—which was added to the text—refers to the John Mark mentioned in Acts, Colossians, and 1 Peter. The date of composition is also disputed. Was the gospel written after 70 C.E., that is, after the destruction of the temple in Jerusalem?

2. MARK II

   This "Mark" is an unknown author who appended early on, perhaps at the beginning of the second century, the ending of the gospel, 16:9–19. Since both Tatian and Irenaeus know of this secondary ending, an early-second-century date for its addition is generally acknowledged. However, no Greek manuscripts prior to the fifth century contain this short ending of Mark's gospel.

3. MARK III

   This "Mark" is likewise from an unknown source. In various bibles it is simply called "a shorter ending of Mark," or "another ending of Mark," or the so-called Freer Logion. In certain bibles it is mentioned only in a footnote. It seems to be a Western addition, although this too is not completely verified.

4. MATTHEW

   The writer of the gospel known to us as "Matthew" does not seem to be the apostle named Matthew. "Since the author of the final Gk text seems to have copied with modifications the whole Gospel according to Mark, it is now commonly thought that it is improbable that in its present form it is the work of an eyewitness apostle. Why would an eyewitness need to copy from someone who was not? The Gospel as we have it is best understood as a work of mature synthesis, combining the earliest Gospel, Mark, with an early collection of sayings of Jesus (the so-called *Logion-Quelle* or *Q*) which it shares with the Gospel according to Luke."[2] The author seems to be a Greek-speaking Jew, perhaps a scribe or a rabbi, residing perhaps at Antioch or Caesarea Maritima. The gospel is written after the gospel of Mark, but cannot be dated later than 110 C.E., since it is cited by Ignatius of Antioch.[3]

5. LUKE

This man is the author of both the gospel of Luke and the Acts of the Apostles. In both writings there are important statements on the resurrection of Jesus. The precise identity of this Luke, however, remains unknown. Still, the gospel appears to have been written after that of Mark, sometime between 70 and 85 C.E. The Acts of the Apostles was written shortly after the composition of the gospel itself.[4]

6. JOHN I

This is the author of the gospel of John, but as with the gospel of Matthew, we cannot be certain that the actual author was named John. This John, however, is not to be identified with the John of the Twelve, nor, it seems, with the "one whom Jesus loved."[5] The gospel was probably written no earlier than 80 to 90 C.E. and no later than the end of the first century.

7. JOHN II

This is the author of the final chapter of the gospel according to John, namely, chapter 21. This author not only added this section to the gospel but also might have edited many parts of the gospel. The added chapter focuses on the resurrection of Jesus and the role of Peter.

8. PAUL

We will consider here only the authentic letters of Paul. In many bibles there are other letters that are ascribed to Paul, but contemporary scholarship has in most instances disproved such attributed authorship. Two textual foci are important as regards the Pauline understanding of the resurrection of Jesus: first, the statements he makes in 1 Corinthians 15 on the resurrection; second, the scattered references to his own encounter with the risen Christ.

There are, of course, other New Testament authors who mention in a brief way the resurrection of Jesus, but these eight are the voices who present us with a substantive message on the resurrection. Let us look at these voices in detail and rethink both their content and their import.

1. MARK I

Text

16 Καὶ διαγενομένου τοῦ σαββάτου Μαρία ἡ Μαγδαληνὴ καὶ Μαρία ἡ Ἰακώβου καὶ Σαλώμη ἠγόρασαν ἀρώματα ἵνα ἐλθοῦσαι ἀλείψωσιν αὐτόν. 2 καὶ λίαν πρωῒ τῇ μιᾷ τῶν σαββάτων ἔρχονται ἐπὶ τὸ μνημεῖον ἀνατείλαντος τοῦ ἡλίου. 3 καὶ ἔλεγον πρὸς ἑαυτάς, Τίς ἀποκυλίσει ἡμῖν τὸν λίθον ἐκ τῆς θύρας τοῦ μνημείου; 4 καὶ ἀναβλέψασαι θεωροῦσιν ὅτι ἀποκεκύλισται ὁ λίθος, ἦν γὰρ μέγας σφόδρα. 5 καὶ εἰσελθοῦσαι εἰς τὸ μνημεῖον εἶδον νεανίσκον καθήμενον ἐν τοῖς δεξιοῖς περιβεβλημένον στολὴν λευκήν, καὶ ἐξεθαμβήθησαν. 6 ὁ δὲ λέγει αὐταῖς, Μὴ ἐκθαμβεῖσθε· Ἰησοῦν ζητεῖτε τὸν Ναζαρηνὸν τὸν ἐσταυρωμένον· ἠγέρθη, οὐκ ἔστιν ὧδε· ἴδε ὁ τόπος ὅπου ἔθηκαν αὐτόν. 7 ἀλλὰ ὑπάγετε εἴπατε τοῖς μαθηταῖς αὐτοῦ καὶ τῷ Πέτρῳ ὅτι Προάγει ὑμᾶς εἰς τὴν Γαλιλαίαν· ἐκεῖ αὐτὸν ὄψεσθε, καθὼς εἶπεν ὑμῖν. 8 καὶ ἐξελθοῦσαι ἔφυγον ἀπὸ τοῦ μνημείου, εἶχεν γὰρ αὐτὰς

16 After the Sabbath day was over, Mary Magdalene, Mary the mother of James, and Salome bought spices to go and anoint the body of Jesus. 2Very early on Sunday morning, at sunrise, they went to the grave. 3-4On the way they said to one another, "Who will roll away for us the stone from the entrance to the grave?" (It was a very large stone.) Then they looked up and saw that the stone had already been rolled back. 5So they entered the grave, where they saw a young man sitting at the right, wearing a white robe—and they were filled with alarm.

6"Don't be alarmed," he said. "I know you are looking for Jesus of Nazareth, who was nailed to the cross. He is not here—he has been raised! Look, here is the place where they placed him. 7Now go and give this message to his disciples, including Peter: 'He is going to Galilee ahead of you; there you will see him, just as he told you.'"

τρόμος καὶ ἔκστασις· καὶ οὐδενὶ οὐδὲν εἶπαν, ἐφοβοῦντο γάρ.

⁸So they went out and ran from the grave, because fear and terror were upon them. They said nothing to anyone, because they were afraid.

Comments

When one looks at this section of the gospel (16:1–8), one sees that three women are named and that these three women are the same as those mentioned in the preceding chapter (15:40), namely, Mary Magdalene, Mary the mother of both the younger James and Joses, and Salome. In Mk 15:47, however, only two of these women are mentioned: Mary of Magdala and Salome. In 16:1–8 the three women are again referred to, once again by name. This repetition has caused some authors to conclude that 16:1–8 is either based on another source which Mark I has used and appended to the death and burial account or is an addition made by Mark I himself. In many ways, because of this naming of the women, chapter 16 does seem to start over again.

The sabbath had ended and these women were now free to perform some tasks connected with the burial of Jesus. Both the buying of the spices and the journey to the tomb were done "very early on the first day after the sabbath." The three women are presented as rather unthinking, since they are going to the tomb but they do not know how they might find someone to roll the stone back, for it is too large or heavy for them to move.

One cannot help noticing that this entire narrative is somewhat contrived. First of all, the reasons for the anointing are not well considered, nor is the issue of the large stone well thought out. These traditional data are all mentioned but not well integrated into the account. Second, there is a dramatic formalism to the speech by the young man. Finally, the women depart in confusion and fear, and nothing more is said, leaving a sort of unfinished quality about the passage. One has the impression that the eight verses focus on certain central issues and that details are mentioned but with no integration. It is the central issues that dominate the construction of these few verses: (a) the message of the young man *(neaniskos);* (b) the role of the women at the tomb and their connection with Joseph of Arimathea; and (c) the mention of Galilee.

THE MESSAGE OF THE YOUNG MAN (*NEANISKOS*)

Mark presents us in a terse way with the Christian kerygma of the resurrection: *Jesus has been raised. He is not here.* Let us reflect on this kerygma message by the young man.

When the women arrived at the tomb, they saw that the stone had been rolled back, and so they entered the grave, a sort of cave that had been dug out of the rock (15:46). There they saw a "young man" *(neaniskos).* In Matthew's account this young man will be called an "angel" *(aggelos),* but in Mark I the Greek simply has *neaniskos,* a young man. The intent, however, by Mark I is clearly to describe some sort of heavenly messenger. He is described in simple terms: he is seated and is wearing a white robe. Again, Matthew will enhance these details, but in both gospels a messenger from God is certainly intended. Note that the focus is on a messenger not from Jesus but from God. In Mark I the main figure of these eight verses is certainly the "young man," the messenger of Yahweh. The women are secondary to him and, even more significantly, secondary to his message. For Mark I, the resurrection of Jesus must be seen as God's action, God's grace, God's work. It is the announcement of this marvelous action of God that is center stage in these eight verses. To miss this emphasis would be to miss what the author is trying to say.

The young man's message indicates that fundamentally faith in the resurrection does not come from one's "seeing" or "touching" Jesus; rather, faith comes from above, from the one who sent the messenger—God. Just as the raising of Jesus is an action of God, a gift of God, so too is the message about this action a gift of God. And the response one might make to this message, faith, is likewise a gift of God. This messenger of God emphasizes that the one who has been raised is the very Jesus who came from Nazareth and who was crucified. There is no split between a "Jesus of history" and a "Christ of faith"—to use a vocabulary of much later exegesis. The historical Jesus is the very one who has been raised by God from the dead. Mark I goes out of his way to emphasize both Nazareth and the cross in connection with the risen Lord. Nonetheless, it is not so much the action of the human Jesus or the relationship of Jesus to Nazareth or even his crucifixion that is central. God's action on this Jesus of Nazareth who was crucified is the central focus.

"He has been raised" *(ēgerthē)*. The verb is in the third person singular first aorist passive, which means that the emphasis in the context of Mark I is on the work of God. God has already raised Jesus in his humanity from death. Other voices in the New Testament will at times speak differently, for example: "On the third day Jesus rose from the tomb," indicating the activity of Jesus himself rather than the action of God. One might pose the question on this differing verb form as follows: Is God the agent or is Jesus the agent? We will come back to this issue, but for the moment it is important to see that Mark I employs the aorist passive with God as the agent. Resurrection faith is ultimately a God-centered response. The more one focuses on the touching, the eating, the seeing, and other secondary issues, the further one is from the very heart of faith in the resurrection of Jesus—namely, God in a free and gracious action has raised Jesus from the dead, freely and graciously announced this to us, and again freely and graciously assisted us to respond in faith to this action of God and its revelatory message.

The women are given a task: "Go and give a message." This relationship between the Easter event and a mission should not be overlooked. It is a characteristic of almost all the Easter apparitions mentioned in the gospels. The Easter event is portrayed not as a private matter but as an event that includes a public task. As we shall see later, almost every resurrection account of an apparition contains a social dimension.

THE ROLE OF THE WOMEN AT THE TOMB
AND THEIR CONNECTION WITH JOSEPH OF ARIMATHEA

These two traditions, namely, the women at the tomb and the role of Joseph of Arimathea, are distinct but nonetheless have become interrelated in the course of history, including the prehistory to the writing of the gospel of Mark. Let us consider first the role of the women at the tomb, and then turn to the role of Joseph.

Mark I remains a solid witness to an earlier Easter tradition which involved women at the tomb of Jesus on the day after the sabbath. This tradition is mentioned in some way or another also by the other New Testament voices, with the exception of Paul. Mark I, as also these other New Testament writers, has inherited this tradition from sources, and each writer has recounted it in his own distinctive way and has adapted it to the needs of his respective community, which is the primary intended readership of their respective gospels. The variety of these accounts as well as the persistence of these accounts in each of the gospels indicates that the presence of women to the Easter event has a solid substrate in historical actuality. The role of women in the Easter event belongs to the Easter event itself. It is not a tangential issue added at a later time for whatever reason.

In the course of church history, the role of the twelve apostles has been developed, to some extent been mythologized, and at times even been overemphasized. This later emphasis on the apostles and their witness value to the resurrection of Jesus has tended to crowd out the role of the women and their witness value to the resurrection. The women in Mark I, however, are key to his entire gospel message. In other words, by itself, this pericope about the women at the tomb on the morning of the first day of the week has little meaning. It derives its true meaning only when taken within the context of the entire gospel of Mark I.

In the early chapters of Mark's gospel, we see Jesus calling disciples: first are Simon and Andrew, then James and John. Then there is Simon's mother-in-law. There is Levi, the toll collector. In the section on Levi, we read also that there were many disciples *(polloi mathētai).* There is the listing of the Twelve. With the exception of Simon's mother-in-law, it is male disciples who are singled out for special mention. The role of the woman disciple is not emphasized. In chapter 8 of Mark I, however, a strange thing happens. Jesus mentions for the first time that he will suffer and die, and the immediate response of the male disciples is disbelief, a disbelief that is intensified as the gospel moves toward the actual arrest, trial, and death of Jesus. When Jesus is arrested, the male disciples abandon Jesus. Peter disavows Jesus. Throughout the gospel, Mark I is attempting to tell his community what discipleship is about. All the male disciples, including the twelve, are ultimately presented as failures. Mark I is saying to his readership: "Do not imitate the male disciples. They are failures. They did not understand what discipleship of the Lord is all about."[6]

Against this background of discipleship—and a failed discipleship at that—one should consider the role of the women who in chapters 15 and 16 come to center stage. When the women hear the message and see the empty tomb, they are deeply frightened, rush away, and say nothing to anyone. With this rushing away and with this fear and silence, the gospel of Mark I comes to an end. Again, the author is saying to his own community, his own readership: "Do not imitate these women in your efforts at discipleship. They, too, just like the men, failed to understand what discipleship of Jesus really means."

However, it is not just the author's admonition: "Do not imitate either the male or female disciples," that is his ultimate focus. Rather, Mark I urges: If you want to be a disciple of Jesus, keep your eyes on Jesus alone. It is Jesus whom God raised from the dead. It is in Jesus that you will see the true action of God on your behalf.

Mark I places no emphasis, then, on either the men, including the Twelve, or the women, as the "foundation of one's faith," as the "foundation on which the Church stands." The later emphasis on the apostolic foundation, that is, a church built on the Twelve apostles, is totally absent from Mark's gospel. Neither the apostles nor the other men and women who followed Jesus are presented as the foundation. Jesus alone is presented as the foundation, or, even better, Yahweh acting with and in the human Jesus remains the only foundation. We are disciples because of God's action not because of our action, even our imitative action of other followers of Jesus, whether male or female.

Another but secondary issue is found in this brief chapter on the resurrection. The women in Mark I are portrayed as filled with alarm and fear. They are not presented as people who, upon seeing an empty tomb, believe that Jesus was raised. Rather, they are profoundly frightened and give no indication of faith in the risen Lord. According to Mark I, belief in the resurrection is not a logical conclusion based on an empty tomb. There is no indication that an empty tomb by itself is a "proof" for the risen Lord. These women saw an empty tomb, but they did not thereby begin to believe in the resurrection of Jesus. Resurrection faith is not fundamentally faith in an empty tomb. It is faith in the action of God. The empty tomb tradition must be seen as a secondary and tangential issue. It cannot be made the "basis" or the "proof" for one's belief, nor is it at the center of what the resurrection of Jesus is all about.

Let us now turn to the role of Joseph of Arimathea. It should be noted that the women at the tomb are associated with the burial, and therefore with Joseph of Arimathea. In Mark I, Joseph is simply called "a prominent member of the Council, who himself lived in the hope of seeing the kingdom of God." In Matthew, this same Joseph is described as a rich man and a "disciple of Jesus." In Luke, Joseph is an "upright and virtuous man," who "had not consented to what the others had planned and carried out." In John, Joseph is a secret disciple of Jesus, since he was afraid of the Jews. One can hardly miss the heightening of Joseph by the various evangelists. Benoit notes: "It is possible that the Christians embellished him and made him out to be more of a Christian than he actually was; there are analogous cases in the gospel, and Pilate [for example] is later almost turned into a saint."[7]

Goguel, early on in this century, proposed that Jesus had not been buried by Joseph of Arimathea, but rather by some of the Jews. Indeed, in Acts 13:29, one does read: "They [the people of Jerusalem and their rulers] took him down from the tree and buried him in a tomb." This "alternate tradition" on the burial of Jesus further complicates the way in which we today might interpret the role of Joseph of Arimathea.

There are many details connected to the Joseph of Arimathea tradition that raise questions. The presence of the women at the tomb is connected to the burial of Jesus' body, so that in some way the interpretation of the Joseph material will, in turn, determine the interpretation of the women at the tomb, and vice versa, the interpretation of the women at the tomb will determine to some degree the interpretation of Joseph of Arimathea. All we can draw from Mark's gospel, however, is that already by the mid-70s of the first century some connection of these two traditions had already begun to develop, and this interconnection becomes further entangled as the writing of the other canonical gospels and even the writing of the noncanonical gospels moves forward. The gospel of Mark I, however, does not go out of its way to draw any conclusions on this connection. We simply find the relationship stated in the gospel, perhaps because this is the way the material came down to the author. Joseph is also not portrayed as an ideal, exemplary disciple. He buried a dead person. Later traditions will enhance Joseph, but these enhancements are foreign to Mark I.

THE MENTION OF GALILEE

Consonant with the theological geography of Mark's entire gospel, the author indicates that Galilee is the place for the appearance of Jesus himself. For Mark I, Galilee represents the place least likely to engender the messiah. There is a sort of "surprise" element in the Galilee. R. Brown mentions that Galilee is "an area which figures surprisingly little in OT history."[8] Galilee was at the time of Jesus "treated with disdain." It was the "Galilee of the Gentiles" in which "people walked in darkness." Throughout Mark's gospel, Jesus is presented as preaching and healing in the southern Galilee area. Clearly, this is not the locale from which the majority of Jewish scholars at that time expected to see a messianic leader arise. For Mark I Jesus is continually presented as the "maverick" messiah.

Matthew will follow Mark I in this matter of geography, at least insofar as Matthew emphasizes the locale of Galilee. Both Luke and John, however, will make Jerusalem the place for the appearances. The discrepancy between Galilee and Jerusalem as the locus for the apparitions cannot be seen simply as a historical problem, namely, Did Jesus actually or historically appear in Galilee or did he appear in Jerusalem? Given all that Galilee means for the theology of Mark's gospel and all that Jerusalem means for the theology of Luke's gospel, it is clear that these two places are used primarily for their theological importance, not for their historical validity. Whether one can interpret Galilee as the "Galilee of the Gentiles" and bypass the Palestinian, Jewish area of Galilee, as Weiss, Hoskyns, and Evans do, might stretch the material too far. Other writers, such as E. Lohmeyer, R. H. Lightfoot, O. Michel, and W. Marxsen, see in the Galilee a symbol of the parousia rather than a geographical site—a parousia that is neither Jewish nor Gentile. The wording in Mark I is terse and does not readily of itself substantiate either of these two views.

Mark I in this mention of Galilee does give witness to some sort of previous Galilean tradition as regards the resurrection. In the pre-Marcan material there was already a relationship between the Easter event and Galilee. Even Luke, in his own way, alludes to it. There is some connection between the disciples' belief in the resurrection and Galilee, and this connection antedates Mark I. It is simply part of the earliest resurrection tradition. In this sense, then, one can speak of some sort of historical connection between the resurrection event on the one hand, and an area called Galilee on the other.

Another aspect from the traditional source material is the emphasis on Peter. Peter is singled out, whereas the other disciples are spoken of generally. In the volume *Peter in the New Testament,* the authors remark: "Perhaps when Mark was being completed, the evangelist's community was already familiar with a narrative of how Jesus had appeared to Peter and to the Twelve."[9] Mark I seems to allow for this tradition, namely, that in Galilee both the disciples and Peter will see the risen Lord. In Luke 24:34 and in Paul (1 Cor 15:5) it seems that Peter was the first to experience an appearance of the risen Lord. In Mark I, however, the disciples are named first, and then, in second place, Peter. Some biblical scholars would say that Mark I is aware of a first or special appearance of the Lord to Peter, while others would say that the risen Lord will appear to the disciples, including but especially to Peter in Galilee. Others suggest that there might also be the nuance that even though Peter had denied the Lord, he too will see the risen Lord.[10] On the basis of Mark I alone a position of Peter in the early community cannot be developed to any great extent, but the many Petrine passages in the New Testament, both in these resurrection accounts and in other segments of the New Testament, do allow for a Petrine position in the early community. Thus, this section of Mark I contributes to a larger and stronger picture of Peter in the New Testament, even though by itself such a developed position of Peter in Mark I would be difficult to maintain.[11]

2. MARK II

For the gospel of Mark, most contemporary bibles complete chapter 16 with vv. 9–19. This is an appended account that is omitted by the Sinaiticus and Vaticanus manuscripts as well as the Greek minuscule 2386, dating from the twelfth century. The Syriac s and the Armenian manuscript from the fourth or fifth century also omit this section. Clement, Origen, Eusebius, Jerome, and Ammonius do not have this text; however, the Alexandrinus, Ephraem, Beza, and many others do include it. Generally, scholars suggest a date of origin for these verses sometime in the second century. Still, it is commonly recognized today that this section is an addition, and therefore we have here another distinct voice in the New Testament speaking to us about the resurrection of Jesus.[12]

Text

The Appearance
to Mary Magdalene
(Mt 28:9–10; Jn 20:11–18)

[9 Ἀναστὰς δὲ πρωῒ πρώτῃ ἐφάνη πρῶτον Μαρίᾳ τῇ Μαγδαληνῇ, παρ᾽ ἧς ἐκβεβλήκει ἑπτὰ δαιμόνια. 10 ἐκείνη πορευθεῖσα ἀπήγγειλεν τοῖς μετ᾽ αὐτοῦ γενομένοις πενθοῦσι καὶ κλαίουσιν· 11 κἀκεῖνοι ἀκούσαντες ὅτι ζῇ καὶ ἐθεάθη ὑπ᾽ αὐτῆς ἠπίστησαν.

Jesus Appears
to Mary Magdalene
(Also Mt 28:9–10; Jn 20:11–8)

[9After Jesus rose from death, early on Sunday, he appeared first to Mary Magdalene, from whom he had driven out seven demons. 10She went and told it to his companions. They were mourning and crying; 11and when they heard her say that Jesus was alive and that she had seen him, they did not believe her.

The Appearance
to Two Disciples
(Lk 24:13–35)

12 Μετὰ δὲ ταῦτα δυσὶν ἐξ
αὐτῶν περιπατοῦσιν ἐφανερώθη ἐν
ἑτέρᾳ μορφῇ πορευομένοις εἰς
ἀγρόν· 13 κἀδεῖνοι ἀπελθόντες
ἀπήγγειλαν τοῖς λοιποῖς· οὐδὲ
ἐκείνοις ἐπίστευσαν.

14 Ὕστερον [δὲ] ἀνακειμένοις
αὐτοῖς τοῖς ἕνδεκα ἐφανερώθη, καὶ
ὠνείδισεν τὴν ἀπιστίαν αὐτῶν καὶ
σκληροκαρδίαν ὅτι τοῖς θεασα-
μένοις αὐτὸν ἐγηγερμένον οὐκ
ἐπίστευσαν. 15 καὶ εἶπεν αὐτοῖς,
Πορευθέντες εἰς τὸν κόσμον
ἅπαντα κηρύξατε τὸ εὐαγγέλιον
πάσῃ τῇ κτίσει. 16 ὁ πιστεύσας
καὶ βαπτισθεὶς σωθήσεται, ὁ δὲ
ἀπιστήσας κατακριθήσεται. 17
σημεῖα δὲ τοῖς πιστεύσασιν ταῦτα
παρακολουθήσει· ἐν τῷ ὀνόματί
μου δαιμόνια ἐκβαλοῦσιν, γλώσ-
σαις λαλήσουσιν καιναῖς, 18 [καὶ
ἐν ταῖς χερσὶν] ὄφεις ἀροῦσιν, κἂν
θανάσιμόν τι πίωσιν οὐ μὴ αὐτοὺς
βλάψῃ, ἐπὶ ἀρρώστους χεῖρας
ἐπιθήσουσιν καὶ καλῶς ἕξουσιν.

The Ascension of Jesus
(Lk 24:50–53; Acts 1:9–11)

19 Ὁ μὲν οὖν κύριος [Ἰησοῦς]
μετὰ τὸ λαλῆσαι αὐτοῖς ἀνελήμφθη
εἰς τὸν οὐρανὸν καὶ ἐκάθισεν ἐκ
δεξιῶν τοῦ θεοῦ. 20 ἐκεῖνοι δὲ
ἐξελθόντες ἐκήρυξαν πανταχοῦ,
τοῦ κυρίου συνεργοῦντος καὶ τὸν
λόγον βεβαιοῦντος διὰ τῶν ἐπα-
κολουθούντων σημείων.]]

Jesus Appears
to Two Disciples
(Also Lk 24:13–35)

[12]After this, Jesus appeared in a different manner to two of them while
they were on their way to the country. [13]They returned and told it to the
others, but they would not believe it.

[14]Last of all, Jesus appeared to the
eleven disciples as they were eating.
He scolded them, because they did
not have faith and because they were
too stubborn to believe those who
had seen him alive. [15]He said to
them, "Go to the whole world and
preach the gospel to all mankind.
[16]Whoever believes and is baptized
will be saved; whoever does not believe will be condemned. [17]Believers
will be given these signs of power:
they will drive out demons in my
name; they will speak in strange
tongues; [18]if they pick up snakes or
drink any poison, they will not be
harmed; they will place their hands
on the sick, who will get well."

Jesus Is Taken up to Heaven
(Also Lk 24:50–53; Acts 1:9–11)

[19]After the Lord Jesus had talked
with them, he was taken up to heaven
and sat at the right side of God. [20]The
disciples went and preached everywhere, and the Lord worked with
them and proved that their preaching
was true by giving them the signs of
power.]

Comments

As the reader has noticed, this text treats of three resurrection events: the first is that of an appearance to Mary Magdalene; the second is an appearance to the two disciples; and the last is the commissioning of the disciples. Let us consider these three separately.

THE APPEARANCE TO MARY MAGDALENE

In the account concerning Mary Magdalene, the clear connection this passage has with a similar section from John (20:11–18) is unmistakable. Mark II merely abbreviates the account. Besides this connection to John, Mark II serves as an additional witness to the involvement of women in the resurrection tradition. Similar to the Johannine account, Mark II presents not three women but only one; nonetheless, the connection of the risen Lord with a woman or women is a well-attested tradition and is fundamental to any interpretation of the resurrection. Any presentation of belief in the resurrection by the early followers of Jesus that does not include this male–female dimension is missing a fundamental issue of the resurrection material. A one-sided and male-dominated interpretation overlooks an issue that will surface on several occasions in the total New Testament material, namely, the equality of men and women in the kingdom of God. The passages on baptism, for instance, which in the Pauline material stress "neither male nor female," bear witness to a kingdom that breaks down the barriers of gender. Luke's presentation of women as disciples of Jesus is yet another New Testament indication of this equalization of gender roles in the kingdom of God. In Mark II, all we have is the mention that Jesus appeared to Mary Magdalene. There is no theological development in Mark II about the kingdom of God and the role of women. This is clearly not the focus of Mark II.

THE APPEARANCE TO THE TWO DISCIPLES

In the account concerning the two disciples and the appearance of the risen Lord, the connection of this passage with a similar section from Luke (24:13–35) is unmistakable. Mark II abbreviates the account, but the relationship between the Lucan narrative and this section of Mark II is clear.

THE COMMISSIONING OF THE DISCIPLES

In the account of the commissioning of the disciples, there is a relationship to Mt 28:16–20; Lk 24:36–39; Jn 20:19–23; and Acts 1:6–8. Moreover, the signs of power given to the believers also have relationships with passages in the New Testament: speaking in tongues can be found in Acts 2:4; 2:11; 10:46; 19:6; 1 Cor 14:2–4; taking up serpents relates to Lk 10:19; Acts 28:3–6; laying on of hands to heal is found often in the gospel accounts of Jesus' healings and in Acts 4:30; 5:16; 8:7; as also Jas 5:14–15. The ascension also has Old Testament overtones, which we shall consider at a later date. In all of these connections with other New Testament and even Old Testament passages, Mark II is a strong witness to the widespread awareness within the Jesus communities to these various traditional details. The commissioning in Mark II exhibits some independence from the commissioning in either Matthew or Acts so that one must acknowledge, along with Goguel and Dodd, that the author, Mark II, has freely adapted material and given it supplementary interpretations.[13]

All in all, the voice of Mark II summarizes material that other New Testament authors had developed more at length. In this sense, Mark II continues several traditions of resurrection material; however, there is something quite special about these passages which indicates the focus of Mark II and tells us something about the community to which he belonged. This distinctive focus is *disbelief.* One notices how often the issue of unbelief is mentioned by Mark II:

v. 11   But they [Jesus' disciples] *did not believe her* [Mary Magdalene]

v. 13   They [two disciples] went back and told the others, *who did not believe them* either.

v. 14   He [Jesus] reproached them *for their incredulity* and obstinacy, because they were *too stubborn to believe* those who had seen him alive.

Evidently, there was a pastoral problem in the community of Mark II. In that Jesus community men and women were finding it quite difficult to believe in the resurrection. The author, Mark II, solicitous for these men and women, had a pastoral goal in mind as he wrote this section. He emphasized that even the first disciples of Jesus, even the twelve, found belief in the resurrection difficult. Jesus himself upbraided his own disciples for their lack of faith in the resurrection. If the first disciples had such difficulty, this should encourage Mark II's own community in their struggle to believe in the resurrection. The author is indicating that belief in the resurrection of Jesus is not something easy to come by, since the resurrection is a mystery at the very heart of faith in Jesus as messiah and lord. Such belief is, consequently, no simple human act. This pastoral concern of Mark II is more than evident in these few verses and gives us a small window into one of the early second-century Jesus communities and into a problem that it apparently had: hesitation to believe that God had raised Jesus from the dead. That belief in the resurrection was central to one's faith in Jesus is clear in Mark II; that such belief is not an easy thing to do is also eminently clear.

Against this background of disbelief of both the first disciples and then the community of Mark II, the remainder of the passage is also pastoral. Even after the reproach by Jesus, the doubting disciples were commissioned to go out and preach the good news, to baptize, to speak in tongues, to cast out devils, to pick up snakes, and to cure the sick. This the early disciples did (16:20). The implication is clear: if the doubting disciples of Jesus' own time became such wonderful preachers of the good news, so too the doubting community of Mark II can become believers and be commissioned by the Lord as well. This appears to be the pastoral intent of 16:9–20.[14]

3. MARK III

There is still another ancient ending for Mark's gospel, which in some manuscripts replaces Mark II. We can call this ending Mark III. It is not found in any of the major manuscripts, but only in some minor manuscripts. In addition, there is more textual certainty for v. 9 than for v. 10 of this ending, and there are even some manuscripts that have both added texts: Mark II and Mark III.[15]

Text

[[Πάντα δὲ τὰ παρηγγελμένα τοῖς περὶ τὸν Πέτρον συντόμως ἐξήγγειλαν. Μετὰ δὲ ταῦτα καὶ αὐτὸς ὁ Ἰησοῦς ἀπὸ ἀνατολῆς καὶ ἄχρι δύσεως ἐξαπέστειλεν δι᾽ αὐ-

[9The women went to Peter and his friends and gave them a brief account of all they had been told. 10After this, Jesus himself sent out through his disciples, from the east

τῶν τὸ ἱερὸν καὶ ἄφθαρτον κήρυγμα τῆς αἰωνίου σωτηρίας. ἀμήν.]]

to the west, the sacred and ever-living message of eternal salvation.]

Comments

Contrary to the actual ending of Mark I, Mark III has the women in v. 9 go to Peter and his friends and give an account of what had happened to them. Mark III reverses the entire direction of Mark I. Still, this ending has been deliberately added by some unknown author to the material of Mark I as a corrective; in other words, it appears to have been written so as to continue the abrupt ending of Mark I. Without Mark I, Mark III makes little sense.[16]

In Mark III, we once more see a continued attestation of two traditions connected to the resurrection of Jesus: namely, the appearance to women and the singling out of Peter.

In v. 10 we find an attestation of the growth of the early community of believers in Jesus: "from the east to the west." The message or kerygma regarding Jesus is one of unending salvation. This connection of salvation, explicitly called *sōtēria,* with the resurrection is a point that Paul often makes in his letters. Not only have we been saved by the death of Jesus but also by the resurrection of the Lord. Perhaps there is some historical or factual connection between Mark III and the theological stance of Paul, but this would be hard to verify. For Mark III, salvation has a universal significance (from the east to the west), which is a theme rather common in the second century. A worldwide mission of salvation has begun through the Jesus event, which includes his resurrection.

4. MATTHEW

In general, Matthew utilized Mark's gospel when he wrote his own gospel. This is evident when one compares the two full gospel texts, but also when one compares the resurrection text of Matthew with the resurrection text of Mark I.[17] Matthew, of course, adapts, changes, and adds to the material he received from Mark's gospel.

Text

28 Ὀψὲ δὲ σαββάτων, τῇ ἐπιφω-σκούσῃ εἰς μίαν σαββάτων, ἦλθεν Μαρία ἡ Μαγδαληνὴ καὶ ἡ ἄλλη

28 After the Sabbath, as Sunday morning was dawning, Mary Magdalene and the other Mary went to

Μαρία θεωρῆσαι τὸν τάφον. 2 καὶ ἰδοὺ σεισμὸς ἐγένετο μέγας· ἄγγελος γὰρ κυρίου καταβὰς ἐξ οὐρανοῦ καὶ προσελθὼν ἀπεκύλισεν τὸν λίθον καὶ ἐκάθητο ἐπάνω αὐτοῦ. 3 ἦν δὲ ἡ εἰδέα αὐτοῦ ὡς ἀστραπὴ καὶ τὸ ἔνδυμα αὐτοῦ λευκὸν ὡς χιών. 4 ἀπὸ δὲ τοῦ φόβου αὐτοῦ ἐσείσθησαν οἱ τηροῦντως καὶ ἐγνήθησαν ὡς νεκροί. 5 ἀποκριθεὶς δὲ ὁ ἄγγελος εἶπεν ταῖς γυναιξίν, Μὴ φοβεῖσθε ὑμεῖς, οἶδα γὰρ ὅτι Ἰησοῦν τὸν ἐσταυρωμένον ζητεῖτε· 6 οὐκ ἔστιν ὧδε, ἠγέρθη γὰρ καθὼς εἶπεν· δεῦτε ἴδετε τὸν τόπον ὅπου ἔκειτο. 7 καὶ ταχὺ πορευθεῖσαι εἴπατε τοῖς μαθηταῖς αὐτοῦ ὅτι Ἠγέρθη ἀπὸ τῶν νεκρῶν, καὶ ἰδοὺ προάγει ὑμᾶς εἰς τὴν Γαλιλαίαν, ἐκεῖ αὐτὸν ὄψεσθε· ἰδοὺ εἶπον ὑμῖν. 8 καὶ ἀπελθοῦσαι ταχὺ ἀπὸ τοῦ μνημείου μετὰ φόβου καὶ χαρᾶς μεγάλης ἔδραμον ἀπαγγεῖλαι τοῖς μαθηταῖς αὐτοῦ. 9 καὶ ἰδοὺ Ἰησοῦς ὑπήντησεν αὐταῖς λέγων, Χαίρετε. αἱ δὲ προσελθοῦσαι ἐκράτησαν αὐτοῦ τοὺς πόδας καὶ προσεκύνησαν αὐτῷ. 10 τότε λέγει αὐταῖς ὁ Ἰησοῦς, Μὴ φοβεῖσθε· ὑπάγετε ἀπαγγείλατε τοῖς ἀδελφοῖς μου ἵνα ἀπέλθωσιν εἰς τὴν Γαλιλαίαν, κἀκεῖ με ὄψονται.

The Report of the Guard

11 Πορευομένων δὲ αὐτῶν ἰδού τινες τῆς κουστωδίας ἐλθόντες εἰς τὴν πόλιν ἀπήγγειλαν τοῖς ἀρχιερεῦσιν ἅπαντα τὰ γενόμενα. 12 καὶ συναχθέντες μετὰ τῶν πρεσβυτέρων συμβούλιόν τε λαβόντες ἀργύρια ἱκανὰ ἔδωκαν

look at the grave. [2]Suddenly there was a strong earthquake; an angel of the Lord came down from heaven, rolled the stone away, and sat on it. [3]His appearance was like lightning and his clothes were white as snow. [4]The guards were so afraid that they trembled and became like dead men.

[5]The angel spoke to the women. "You must not be afraid," he said. "I know you are looking for Jesus, who was nailed to the cross. [6]He is not here; he has been raised, just as he said. Come here and see the place where he lay. [7]Quickly, now, go and tell his disciples, 'He has been raised from death, and now he is going to Galilee ahead of you; there you will see him!' Remember what I have told you."

[8]So they left the grave in a hurry, afraid and yet filled with joy, and ran to tell his disciples.

[9]Suddenly Jesus met them and said, "Peace be with you." They came up to him, took hold of his feet, and worshiped him. [10]"Do not be afraid," Jesus said to them. "Go and tell my brothers to go to Galilee, and there they will see me."

The Report of the Guard

[11]While the women went on their way, some of the soldiers guarding the grave went back to the city and told the chief priests everything that had happened. [12]The chief priests met with the elders and made their plan; they gave a large sum of money

τοῖς στρατιώταις 13 λέγοντες, Εἴπατε ὅτι Οἱ μαθηταὶ αὐτοῦ νυκτὸς ἐλθόντες ἔκλεψαν αὐτὸν ἡμῶν κοιμωμένων. 14 καὶ ἐὰν ἀκουσθῇ τοῦτο ἐπὶ τοῦ ἡγεμόνος, ἡμεῖς πείσομεν αὐτὸν καὶ ὑμᾶς ἀμερίμνους ποιήσομεν. 15 οἱ δὲ λαβόντες τὰ ἀργύρια ἐποίησαν ὡς ἐδιδάχθησαν. Καὶ διεφηρίσθη ὁ λόγος οὗτος παρὰ Ἰουδαίοις μέχρι τῆς σήμερον [ἡμέρας].

to the soldiers [13]and said, "You are to say that his disciples came during the night and stole his body while you were asleep. [14]And if the Governor should hear of this, we will convince him and you will have nothing to worry about."
[15]The guards took the money and did what they were told to do. To this very day that is the report spread around by the Jews.

The Commissioning
of the Disciples
(Mk 16:14–18; Lk 24:36–49;
Jn 20:19–23; Acts 1:6–8)

Jesus Appears to His Disciples
(Also Mk 16:14–18;
Lk 24:36–49;
Jn 20:19–23; Acts 1:6–8)

16 Οἱ δὲ ἕνδεκα μαθηταὶ ἐπορεύθησαν εἰς τὴν Γαλιλαίαν εἰς τὸ ὄρος οὗ ἐτάξατο αὐτοῖς ὁ Ἰησοῦς, 17 καὶ ἰδόντες αὐτὸν προσεκύνησαν, οἱ δὲ ἐδίστασαν. 18 καὶ προσελθὼν ὁ Ἰησοῦς ἐλάλησεν αυτοῖς λέγων, Ἐδόθη μοι πᾶσα ἐξουσία ἐν οὐρανῷ καὶ ἐπὶ γῆς. 19 πορευθέντες οὖν μαθητεύσατε πάντα τὰ ἔθνη, βαπτίζοντες αὐτοὺς εἰς τὸ ὄνομα τοῦ πατρὸς καὶ τοῦ υἱοῦ καὶ τοῦ ἁγίου πνεύματος, 20 διδάσκοντες αὐτοὺς τηρεῖν πάντα ὅσα ἐνετειλάμην ὑμῖν· καὶ ἰδοὺ ἐγὼ μεθ᾽ ὑμῶν εἰμι πάσας τὰς ἡμέρας ἕως τῆς συντελείας τοῦ αἰῶνος.

[16]The eleven disciples went to the hill in Galilee where Jesus had told them to go. [17]When they saw him they worshiped him, even though some of them doubted. [18]Jesus drew near and said to them, "I have been given all authority in heaven and on earth. [19]Go, then, to all peoples everywhere and make them my disciples: baptize them in the name of the Father, the Son, and the Holy Spirit, [20]and teach them to obey everything I have commanded you. And remember! I will be with you always, to the end of the age."

Comment

Matthew is writing for his own community, and as a result not only are we presented with material on the resurrection of Jesus, but also this chapter of Matthew offers us a sort of window into the community itself, with its difficulties and its vision of faith. For the sake of analysis, let us divide the material as follows:

a. The essential message of Matthew on the resurrection of Jesus
b. The role of women in the resurrection event
c. The apologetic issues
d. The promise/fulfillment aspect of the risen Jesus

THE ESSENTIAL MESSAGE OF MATTHEW
ON THE RESURRECTION OF JESUS

The angel's message to the women has similarities to that of the young man in Mark I: there is an emphasis on the humanity of Jesus. There is no distinction between a Jesus of history and a Christ of faith. "He has been raised" *(ēgerthē),* the same term we found in Mark I. The emphasis in Matthew is on the agency of God. God has acted. God has raised Jesus. Belief in the resurrection is primarily and fundamentally a belief in God's action. It is not a belief caused by touching, seeing, hearing. It is not a belief caused by seeing an empty tomb. God has acted; the disciple believes. The author, Matthew, time and again evidences a very Jewish approach to sacred issues, so much so that the author himself might have been a Jewish scribe or rabbi who has accepted Jesus as messiah and lord, *kyrios.* For the Jewish people the action of God in Egypt, the action of God in the Sinai, the action of God in Moses, the action of God in David were all fundamental to Jewish faith. Matthew is similar. Just as there was an action of God in all of these events, so too Yahweh has acted in Jesus of Nazareth, who was crucified and who died and was buried. Yahweh has raised Jesus from the dead and Jesus is now with Yahweh.

This relationship to Jewish descriptions of a divine appearance is further emphasized by Matthew's use of angel, *aggelos,* rather than simply a young man, *neaniskos.* There is a divine revelation, a theophany, but mediated through a messenger, namely, an angel. The activity of this angel, a messenger and legate of God himself, further emphasizes the work of God in this resurrection. The angel is described in typical apocalyptic imagery: an appearance like lightning, clothes white as snow. Matthew in typical Jewish fashion is describing an angelophany, such as we find, for instance, in Daniel 10. It is an angel of God who comes down from heaven and rolls away the stone from the tomb. When the angel rolled away the stone from the tomb, the tomb was already empty. It was not the angel who caused the resurrection of Jesus; it was God. The angel and the empty tomb are simply revelatory of what God has already done.

It has often been noted that none of the New Testament writers describes the actual resurrection of Jesus. The second-century apocryphal *Gospel of Peter* does give an account of the actual resurrection, but such a description is not even hinted at in the four canonical gospels. The canonical gospels focus on the effect of the actual resurrection of Jesus: the sending of an angel, the apparitions of Jesus himself, the empty tomb, etc. In the silence of these authors about the actual rising of Jesus himself we can hear a powerful message. This silence and this message will be considered later in the discussion of the theological significance of the resurrection.

This divine revelatory overtone is further enhanced by the earthquake that Matthew adds. Only in Matthew is there such an earthquake. In 27:51 Matthew had already described an earthquake at the time of Jesus' death; now at his resurrection there is another shaking of the earth. In the Old Testament earthquakes can be found in the psalms and other writings, indicating the "walking of Yahweh." Such a religious interpretation of this natural phenomenon expresses the idea that God has entered our world, and therefore the world shakes at the presence and power of God's footsteps. Throughout his gospel, Matthew builds on Old Testament themes. In this detail of the earthquake, Matthew uses the religious view of earthquakes common in Jewish piety to indicate that at the resurrection of Jesus, God himself has entered once again into our world. Both the earthquake and the mention of an angel have apocalyptic overtones as well, since in the Jewish apocalyptic writings earthquakes and apparitions by angels are used to indicate God's intervention at the end of the world. Matthew's mention of an earthquake, then, has much more a theological and symbolic significance than a historical one.

THE ROLE OF WOMEN IN THE RESURRECTION EVENT

In Matthew's account there are only two women, not three, who go to the tomb early on the day after the sabbath. These two are Mary Magdalene and the "other" Mary, without any further specification. In the previous chapter of this gospel (27:61), Matthew had enumerated the same two women: Mary Magdalene and the "other" Mary, called the mother of James and Joseph. In 12:55 the text notes that "many women" from afar watched the death of Jesus, and these women "had followed Jesus from Galilee and helped him." "Among them were Mary Magdalene, Mary the mother of James and Joseph, and the wife of

Zebedee" (12:56). This threefold repetition of these women strengthens the tradition that women disciples were an essential part of the death-resurrection of Jesus. Their reason for going to the tomb is modified from that found in Mark I: they are going simply to look at the tomb, not to anoint the body. In all of this, Matthew attests to the tradition of an involvement of women with the resurrection of Jesus. Although Matthew distances himself from Mark as regards the anointing of the body of Jesus, this does not mean that there is a separation in this gospel between the burial by Joseph of Arimathea and the women's presence at the tomb. Joseph is still present in Matthew, for in 12:61 Mary and the "other Mary" had watched Joseph bury Jesus. The presence of the women at the tomb of Jesus again must be understood in connection with the role of Joseph of Arimathea. This appears to be the inherited tradition, and Matthew does not make any further elaboration.

Quite opposite to Mark I, the women in Matthew are afraid but filled with joy and obey the command: they fulfill their mission to bring the message to the disciples. The message of the angel does not, however, have a specific reference to Peter, perhaps a deliberate deletion by Matthew.

In Matthew's account, Jesus then appears directly to the women. In John, Jesus appears directly to Mary Magdalene. Neither Mark I nor Luke includes this tradition. Matthew and John, however, have women not only connected with the empty tomb but also presented as first recipients of an appearance of the risen Lord. Scholars are at odds as to the source of this difference: Is this from some earlier source that Matthew had, but Mark I and Luke did not, or is it a free composition of Matthew himself? Fuller thinks that an original angelophany has been converted into a Christophany, because of the Galilean appearance material influencing the empty tomb Jerusalem material.[18] The appearance of Jesus to the women is portrayed in a rather physical way, a detail that is indicative also of an interpretive meditation that developed subsequent to the resurrection of Jesus. The message the women were to bring to the disciples is, nonetheless, the same as the message of the angel.

The appearance of Jesus to the women once again includes a message and a mission: "Go and tell. . . ." The social or public aspect of Easter is evident. The appearance was not a private vision simply for the devotion and edification of the women involved. The women, as loyal disciples of Jesus, have been entrusted with a message of reconciliation, that is: even though the male disciples had fled and some had even rejected Jesus, Jesus now takes the initiative to meet them in Galilee and thus be reconciled with them. In the text, Jesus even calls them "brothers," a term indicative of reconciliation (28:10). D. Senior notes that this appearance to the women might have the quality of a reward about it. After all, the women had been faithful disciples of Jesus, standing by the cross of Jesus during his final agony, whereas the male disciples had fled. A "reward," however, tends to be at odds with Matthew's emphasis on the gratuitous action of Yahweh: God alone raised Jesus from the dead and God alone communicates this message to all. The angel, the women, and the disciples generally are at best messengers of this grace-filled action of Yahweh.

The presence, commission, and special placement of women in the resurrection tradition must be seen within the postresurrection role of women generally and therefore a role within the various Jesus communities of the late first century. That the role of the Twelve came to be more operational and influential cannot be denied. The deemphasizing of the role of women is, however, a later development. In the gospels, the role of women at the resurrection event is not devalued but rather is enhanced.

THE APOLOGETIC ISSUES

After the burial of Jesus by Joseph of Arimathea, Matthew, and only he, has added the setting of a guard (27:62–66). Senior notes that "it is likely that Matthew himself has composed this scene rather than drawing on specific historical information about this secret meeting."[19] In the resurrection account (28:4 and 28:11–15) Matthew continues his narration of the Roman guards. They are afraid; they tremble; and they become like dead men. They go back to the chief priests, receive money, and are told to give a report that the body was stolen. They are assured of the backing of the chief priests and elders as far as the Romans were concerned. Consequently, they spread their own version of what happened.

The key to this entire narration about the Roman guards in both chap. 27 and chap. 28 lies in 28:15: "To this very day that is the report spread around by the Jews." Such a statement raises the question, To what very day? *Eis to sēmeron?* The answer, of course, is the time contemporary with Matthew himself and with his community in Antioch. Even in the years shortly after 70 C.E. there were in Antioch some Jewish people who claimed that Jesus' body had been stolen and that the entire description of a resurrection of Jesus was a fabrication. Matthew is attempting to counteract this contemporary interpretation of Jesus' resurrection; he is fighting a contemporary rumor alive "to this very day" in Antioch.[20] Both Justin (ca. 165) and Tertullian (ca. 155–220) repeat this detail of a "Jewish rumor" that the body had been stolen.[21]

As a result, the description of the guard in these two chapters of Matthew can only be interpreted as apologetic and defensive. It would be hard to verify that this detail of guard setting and alibi giving has a historical basis at the very time of Jesus' death and the subsequent resurrection event. Its historicity lies in an Antioch (or Caesarea Maritima) setting in a time shortly after the destruction of the temple. One might also note that even in its formulation, which appears to be a literary creation by Matthew but with a factual foundation in some sort of rumor, there is a presumption of an empty tomb. On the one hand, the Jesus community proclaimed that God had raised Jesus from the dead and that the tomb was empty; on the other hand, those who were spreading the rumor that the body had been stolen also presumed an empty tomb. In Matthew both the belief in the resurrection of Jesus and the spreading of a rumor of stealing presume an empty tomb. Clearly, the tradition of an empty tomb antedated Matthew's writing of the gospel. The fact that the opponents as well, although indirectly and for quite different reasons, attest to an empty tomb is itself an attestation of this tradition.[22]

Some Jewish leaders are portrayed in Matthew as the culprits for this kind of rumor. Senior makes several references to the use of this gospel over the centuries as an anti-Semitic work.[23] But the author of this gospel, Matthew, was probably a Jew, perhaps a scribe or a rabbi who was now part of the Jesus community. In Antioch, where the gospel seems to have originated, the believers in Jesus were still strongly Jewish, although some Gentile converts were also a part of the Antiochene community. With the destruction of the temple in the year 70 C.E., a pharisaic Jewish leadership group had moved out of Jerusalem and relocated at Jamnia. At the same time, the leadership of the basically Jewish Jesus community had also moved out of Jerusalem, and some of these Jewish leaders had settled in Antioch. Peter seems to have been among this group of leaders who had resettled in Antioch.[24] With the destruction of the temple and its aftermath, the harsh Roman domination of Jerusalem did not bode well for any Jewish leadership — either that of the Jesus group or that of various other Jewish groups. Antioch, one of the larger Roman cities in that area, in which the Jesus people had already been well established, became one of the major leadership centers for those Jews who believed that Jesus was the messiah and that he was the fulfillment of the Torah, the prophets, and the writings. Matthew, it seems, was part of such a Jewish community. Eventually, pharisaic Jewish leaders, probably influenced by the Jamnia leadership, frequented Antioch, and in the course of time some sort of antagonism developed between these two groups of Jewish people. This is an important consideration, for in the gospel of Matthew much of the antagonism with the "Jewish leaders" must be seen as an intra-Jewish dispute, not as an anti-Semitic situation.[25] We will see later that the early followers of Jesus had no identity other than a Jewish identity. Any early insertion of a "Christian identity" into the first phases of the Jesus community, any early insertion of a "church-distinct-from-the-temple" identity cannot be verified. As Jacob Neusner notes, there were many Judaisms at the time of the second temple, and the Jesus community in its beginnings is simply another of these Judaisms.

A further puzzling part of the presentation of this particular detail about guard setting and alibi making were it to be taken not as a literary creation by the author but as something historical is as follows. On the sabbath day itself, the chief priests and the pharisees came to Pilate and asked that a guard be posted at the sepulcher of Jesus. Jesus is referred to as an impostor or liar, *planos*. The preaching of the resurrection is seen by these Jewish leaders as a second deception, even worse than the first. Oddly enough, a night had already passed with no guard at the tomb. If the chief priests and pharisees were fearful of someone stealing the body at night, they had not been very quick to act. Such an activity on the sabbath, given all the research a scholar such as Jeremias has done on the issue of what can and cannot be done on the sabbath, is not as puzzling as the lack of securing the tomb on the very first night. This latter incongruity tends to help substantiate the position that the entire account of the guards appears to be a literary composition of Matthew. The strongest historical aspect of the guard account is that of a polemic against the Jewish Jesus people by certain other Jewish people who "down to today," that is, in Antioch, were disseminating such an account.

THE PROMISE/FULFILLMENT ASPECT OF THE RISEN JESUS

The final section of Matthew's resurrection material takes place in Galilee, with the eleven going to a mountain to which "Jesus had told them to go." The "when" of this earlier telling is through the women's message, but only in a general way. No mention is made in the message given by Jesus to the women of a precise time; however, the eleven disciples go to the hill in Galilee at a "given time." When Jesus appears at this mountain rendezvous, Matthew mentions that some of the eleven still doubted—that is, they did not believe. Once more, we see that the New Testament indicates that belief in the resurrection of Jesus is not an easy matter, either in the case of the disciples or in the case of the early Jesus communities generally. In this section, Matthew uses a form of the Greek verb *proserchetai,* "Jesus *came up* and spoke to them." Only in one other instance in Matthew's gospel does Jesus "come up" to the disciples, and that instance is at the conclusion of the transfiguration (17:7). On all other occasions it is the disciples who come up to Jesus. A small detail, indeed, but when taken with others, such as the use of *ēgerthē* (he has been raised), the stress on God's or in this instance Jesus' activity—not our human endeavor—is quite evident. Faith is a gift of God, not something that men or women reach by themselves. Faith in the resurrection is likewise a gift of God, not something we reach by "seeing" or "touching" Jesus' body.

Many authors characterize this section as the "great commission." In a sense, this is correct, but there is something more than simply a commission here. In Dn 7:14ff., we find a clear connection to Mt 28:18–20. When one compares the Greek text of these three verses in Matthew with the Greek text of Daniel, more so the Theodotion text than the S. version, it seems that the author, Matthew, had a Greek text of Daniel in front of him and has borrowed words and phrases from it to formulate his own phrasing of Jesus' last earthly words.[26] When one makes this Greek comparison, one notes a specifically Jewish tone about the passage: namely, a tone of promise and fulfillment. What had been foretold and promised in Daniel was now taking place in the Jesus event (cf. Dn 7:14ff.). Jesus, accordingly, is the fulfillment of the Torah, the writings, and the prophets. It is with this emphasis rather than with an emphasis on commissioning that Matthew concludes his account of the Lord. Daniel 7:14 reads:

> I gazed into the visions of the night,
> And I saw, coming on the clouds of heaven,
> one like a son of man.
> He came to the one of great age
> and was led into his presence.
> On him was conferred *(edothē)*

sovereignty *(exousia)*, glory and
kingship, and men of all peoples,
nations and languages became his
servants (B text: every nation of the earth).
His sovereignty is an eternal sovereignty
which shall never pass away
nor will his empire ever be destroyed.

In the comparison of the two Greek texts, Dn 7:14 and Mt 28:18–20, one notices, in a way far clearer than any English translation can show, how many words and phrases Matthew has borrowed from Daniel. A Jewish person at the time of Matthew who had any recollection of the Daniel material would hear not a commissioning but rather a promise/fulfillment: what Daniel prophesied has been fulfilled in the life, death, and resurrection of Jesus.

Daniel speaks about a universal gathering, and one finds a similar call to a universal dominion, that is, beyond the Jewish boundaries, in Is 2:1–5; 45:18–25; Mi 4:1–3. In several New Testament passages one reads that the early followers of Jesus preached first to Israel—that is, to the Jewish people, in the synagogues, in the temple, and in gatherings of Jewish people generally. As the message about Jesus became less and less accepted, the early followers of Jesus moved outward to the gentile world. The procedure was fairly consistent: first to the Jews, then to the gentiles. With many stops and starts, hesitations and arguments, a gentile direction of the Jesus message gradually became standard. The acceptance of a gentile mission, however, was an issue that needed refinement and clarification. The Cornelius story in Acts is Luke's way of validating the gentile mission. It was Peter, not Paul, who first initiated such a mission. The so-called council in Jerusalem raised further issues: the perduring need for circumcision and the rejection of certain foods. The "Judaizers" mentioned in Galatians indicate that Paul was doggedly attacked by certain Jewish people, now part of the Jesus community, who had serious misgivings about the gentile mission.

After 70 C.E., with the destruction of the temple, a gradual parting of the way occurs, and it is in the first half of the second century that one can begin to speak about a "Christian religion" and a "Jewish religion" as distinct entities. In the gospels and in Paul the Jewish people involved in the Jesus community still considered themselves Jewish. In fact, they gradually came to consider themselves as the true Jews. Matthew's statements were written only at the threshold of this parting of the ways. Still, Matthew indicates that the mission to the gentiles was part of God's (Jesus') command, not something that the community by itself decided on. The Daniel passage as well as other Old Testament passages mentioned above indicate that in the Jewish traditions, there was one tradition that clearly envisioned a universal messianic time: a Galilee of the gentiles that was neither Jewish nor gentile.

The Jesus portrayed here, as Benoit notes, "seems to presuppose that Christ is in heaven, that he has taken possession of his throne. He is Christ the King, in the glory of his Father, and his power is universal."[27] Jesus has, it appears, already ascended. It is the exalted Christ who speaks to his disciples. The text of Matthew implies that resurrection and ascension are simply two sides of the same coin. There was no intermediary stage, that is, a time when Jesus was "only" risen but "not yet" ascended. If Jesus rose, he ascended. The two are synonymous.

The use of the "trinitarian formula" in connection with baptism in no way connotes that at this early stage of the Jesus community a doctrine of the Trinity had been developed. In the New Testament one can say that there is a small beginning, a sort of germ cell, regarding the Trinity, but one cannot say much more.[28] Nor can one deduce that the trinitarian baptismal formula found in Matthew's gospel was the more original formula for baptism. It would seem, rather, that a baptism in the name of Jesus alone antedated the more mature and developed "trinitarian formula." In the history of baptism, the next extant record of a trinitarian formula for baptism is found in the *Didache*.[29] Nonetheless, one cannot read into Matthew's account a theology of the Trinity that makes its appearance only gradually in the church and finds its major expression in the four great councils of the early church.[30]

Still, we do see in this last section a certain "churchiness" about the Matthew material. "Churchiness" may not be a well-chosen term, but there is some sort of institutionalized community in evidence. The verses make sense only in the context of an established Jesus community that has been fairly well developed. This communal dimension to the text and context tends to preclude that these are in any way *ipsissima verba* of Jesus. Evans's judgment on this concluding passage in Matthew reads as follows:

> Thus the concluding verses of this gospel provide a confessional statement for the reader of what it means to become a Christian and to be a Christian in the present, and of the apostolic commission which lies at the basis of present Christian faith and existence.[31]

In my view this kind of interpretation has more "eisegesis" in it than I think is allowable. At this juncture of the postresurrection Jesus community, to speak so self-confidently in terms of "Christian identity," "apostolic commission," and "confessional statement" burdens the text and context with data from later centuries. That there is some institutional and communal identity in this section is clear; that it can be spelled out in such a sophisticated "Christian and confessional" way seems unlikely. The communal identity of a Jesus community is seen in the term "teaching them," but this teaching appears to be more ethical than doctrinal, since the emphasis is on "to observe" rather than on "to know intellectually."

Besides baptism, the followers of Jesus are to "make disciples" and to "preach." Fuller indicates that Matthew sees in Jesus not only a new Moses but one that is greater than Moses, and sees that in Jesus a new Torah, or law, has been given. To preach Jesus is to preach the true Torah;[32] however, the idea of a "new" Torah is foreign to Matthew's theology. Matthew states that Jesus fulfills the already given Torah. What Yahweh had promised in the Torah, the writings, and the prophets is now being fulfilled in Jesus, so that the message of Jesus includes an abiding presence: "I am with you always; yes, to the end of time." This resembles the abiding presence of *shekinah,* but not a new *shekinah.*[33]

Biblical scholars see three distinct elements in this final passage of Matthew: (1) Jesus' declaration of authority; (2) his command to make disciples and preach; (3) his abiding presence in the community to the end of time. Were these three distinct elements part of an earlier tradition? Were they already combined in a unity at some date earlier than Matthew? In what way has Matthew altered them and combined them? A satisfactory answer to these questions has yet to be reached. It is clear, however, that in a descriptive resurrection narrative an author can include faith statements or theological statements both through the dialogue and through the symbolic actions.

In summary, Matthew presents us with an approach to the resurrection of Jesus in which the theme of resurrection with a relationship to exaltation is established; in which an empty tomb is, to some degree, maintained by both the believer in Jesus and the Jewish nonbeliever alike; in which women are associated with the earliest strata of the resurrection/exaltation accounts; in which Galilee is related to the earliest strata of these same accounts; in which belief in the resurrection of

Jesus is not something easy; and in which Jesus as Lord is seen as the fulfillment of the Torah, the writings, and the prophets.

5. LUKE: THE GOSPEL

There is resurrection material both in the gospel of Luke and in the Acts of the Apostles. The gospel, however, is of singular importance, since more space is dedicated to the resurrection. We will consider the gospel of Luke first and then Acts.

Text

Καὶ τὸ μὲν σάββατον ἡσύχασαν κατὰ τὴν ἐντολήν, **24** τῇ δὲ μιᾷ τῶν σαββάτων ὄρθρου βαθέως ἐπὶ τὸ μνῆμα ἦλθον φέρουσαι ἃ ἡτοίμασαν ἀρώματα. 2 εὗρον δὲ τὸν λίθον ἀποκεκυλισμένον ἀπὸ τοῦ μνημείου, 3 εἰσελθοῦσαι δὲ οὐχ εὗρον τὸ σῶμα τοῦ [κυρίου] Ἰησοῦ. 4 καὶ ἐγένετο ἐν τῷ ἀπορεῖσθαι αὐτὰς περὶ τούτου καὶ ἰδοὺ ἄνδρες δύο ἐπέστησαν αὐταῖς ἐν ἐσθῆτι ἀστραπτούσῃ. 5 ἐμφόβων δὲ γενομένων αὐτῶν καὶ κλινουσῶν τὰ πρόσωπα εἰς τὴν γῆν εἶπαν πρὸς αὐτάς, Τί ζητεῖτε τὸν ζῶντα μετὰ τῶν νεκρῶν; 6 οὐκ ἔστιν ὧδε, ἀλλὰ ἠγέρθη. μνήσθητε ὡς ἐλάλησεν ὑμῖν ἔτι ὢν ἐν τῇ Γαλιλαίᾳ, 7 λέγων τὸν υἱὸν τοῦ ἀνθρώπου ὅτι δεῖ παραδοθῆναι εἰς χεῖρας ἀνθρώπων ἁμαρτωλῶν καὶ σταυρωθῆναι καὶ τῇ τρίτῃ ἡμέρᾳ ἀναστῆναι. 8 καὶ ἐμνήσθησαν τῶν ῥημάτων αὐτοῦ, 9 καὶ ὑποστρέψασαι ἀπὸ τοῦ μνημείου ἀπήγγειλαν ταῦτα πάντα τοῖς ἕνδεκα καὶ πᾶσιν τοῖς λοιποῖς. 10 ἦσαν δὲ ἡ Μαγδαληνὴ Μαρία καὶ Ἰωάννα καὶ Μαρία ἡ Ἰακώβου· καὶ αἱ λοιπαὶ σὺν αὐταῖς ἔλεγον πρὸς τοὺς ἀποστόλους ταῦτα. 11 καὶ

24 Very early on Sunday morning the women went to the grave carrying the spices they had prepared. [2]They found the stone rolled away from the entrance to the grave, [3]so they went in; but they did not find the body of the Lord Jesus. [4]They stood there puzzled about this, when suddenly two men in bright shining clothes stood by them. [5]Full of fear, the women bowed down to the ground, as the men said to them, "Why are you looking among the dead for one who is alive? [6]He is not here; he has been raised. Remember what he said to you while he was in Galilee: [7]'The Son of Man must be handed over to sinful men, be nailed to the cross, and rise to life on the third day.'"

[8]Then the women remembered his words, [9]returned from the grave, and told all these things to the eleven disciples and all the rest. [10]The women were Mary Magdalene, Joanna, and Mary the mother of James; they and the other women with them told these things to the apostles. [11]But the apostles thought that what the women said was nonsense, and did

ἐφάνησαν ἐνώπιον αὐτῶν ὡσεὶ λῆρος τὰ ῥήματα ταῦτα, καὶ ἠπί-στουν αὐταῖς. 12 Ὁ δὲ Πέτρος ἀ-ναστὰς ἔδραμεν ἐπὶ τὸ μνημεῖον, καὶ παρακύψας βλέπει τὰ ὀθόνια μόνα· καὶ ἀπῆλθεν πρὸς ἑαυτὸν θαυμάζων τὸ γεγονός.

The Walk to Emmaus
(Mk 16:12–13)

13 Καὶ ἰδοὺ δύο ἐξ αὐτῶν ἐν αὐτῇ τῇ ἡμέρᾳ ἦσαν πορευόμενοι εἰς κώμην ἀπέχουσαν σταδίους ἑξ-ήκοντα ἀπὸ Ἰερουσαλήμ, ᾗ ὄνομα Ἐμμαοῦς, 14 καὶ αὐτοὶ ὡμίλουν πρὸς ἀλλήλους περὶ πάντων τῶν συμβεβηκότων τούτων. 15 καὶ ἐγένετο ἐν τῷ ὁμιλεῖν αὐτοὺς καὶ συζητεῖν καὶ αὐτὸς Ἰησοῦς ἐγ-γίσας συνεπορεύετο αὐτοῖς, 16 οἱ δὲ ὀφθαλμοὶ αὐτῶν ἐκρατοῦντο τοῦ μὴ ἐπιγνῶναι αὐτόν. 17 εἶπιν δὲ πρὸς αὐτούς, Τίνες οἱ λόγοι οὗτοι οὓς ἀντιβάλλετε πρὸς ἀλλήλους περιπατοῦντες; καὶ ἐστάθησαν σκυθρωποί. 18 ἀποκριθεὶς δὲ εἷς ὀνόματι Κλεοπᾶς εἶπεν πρὸς αὐ-τόν, Σὺ μόνος παροικεῖς Ἰε-ρουσαλὴμ καὶ οὐκ ἔγνως τὰ γενόμενα ἐν αὐτῇ ἐν ταῖς ἡμέραις ταύταις; 19 καὶ εἶπεν αὐτοῖς, Ποῖα; οἱ δὲ εἶπαν αὐτῷ, Τὰ περὶ Ἰησοῦ τοῦ Ναζαρηνοῦ, ὃς ἐγένετο ἀνὴρ προφήτης δυνατὸς ἐν ἔργῳ καὶ λόγῳ ἐναντίον τοῦ θεοῦ καὶ παντὸς τοῦ λαοῦ, 20 ὅπως τε παρέδωκαν αὐτὸν οἱ ἀρχιερεῖς καὶ οἱ ἄρχοντες ἡμῶν εἰς κρίμα θανά-του καὶ ἐσταύρωσαν αὐτόν· 21 ἡμεῖς δὲ ἠλπίζομεν ὅτι αὐτός ἐστιν ὁ μέλλων λυτροῦσθαι τὸν Ἰσραήλ·

not believe them. [12]But Peter got up and ran to the grave; he bent down and saw the grave cloths and nothing else. Then he went back home wondering at what had happened.

The Walk to Emmaus
(Also Mk 16:12–13)

[13]On that same day two of them were going to a village named Emmaus, about seven miles from Jerusalem, [14]and they were talking to each other about all the things that had happened. [15]As they talked and discussed, Jesus himself drew near and walked along with them; [16]they saw him, but somehow did not recognize him. [17]Jesus said to them, "What are you talking about, back and forth, as you walk along?"

They stood till, with sad faces. [18]One of them, named Cleopas, asked him, "Are you the only man living in Jerusalem who does not know what has been happening there these last few days?"

[19]"What things?" he asked.

"The things that happened to Jesus of Nazareth," they answered. "This man was a prophet, and was considered by God and by all the people to be mighty in words and deeds. [20]Our chief priests and rulers handed him over to be sentenced to death, and he was nailed to the cross. [21]And we had hoped that he would be the one who was going to redeem Israel! Besides all that, this is now the third day since it happened.

ἀλλά γε καὶ σὺν πᾶσιν τούτοις τρίτην ταύτην ἡμέραν ἄγει ἀφ᾿ οὗ ταῦτα ἐγένετο. 22 ἀλλὰ καὶ γυναῖκές τινες ἐξ ἡμῶν ἐξέστησαν ἡμᾶς· γενόμεναι ὀρθριναὶ ἐπὶ τὸ μνημεῖον 23 καὶ μὴ εὑροῦσαι τὸ σῶμα αὐτοῦ ἦλθον λέγουσαι καὶ ὀπτασίαν ἀγγέλων ἑωρακέναι, οἳ λέγουσιν αὐτὸν ζῆν. 24 καὶ ἀπῆλθόν τινες τῶν σὺν ἡμῖν ἐπὶ τὸ μνημεῖον, καὶ εὗρον οὕτως καθὼς· καὶ αἱ γυναῖκες εἶπον, αὐτὸν δὲ οὐκ εἶδον. 25 καὶ αὐτὸς εἶπεν πρὸς αὐτούς, ῏Ω ἀνόητοι καὶ βραδεῖς τῇ καρδίᾳ τοῦ πιστεύειν ἐπὶ πᾶσιν οἷς ἐλάλησαν οἱ προφῆται· 26 οὐχὶ ταῦτα ἔδει παθεῖν τὸν Χριστὸν καὶ εἰσελθεῖν εἰς τὴν δόξαν αὐτοῦ; 27 καὶ ἀρξάμενος ἀπὸ Μωϋσέως καὶ ἀπὸ πάντων τῶν προφητῶν διερμήνευσεν αὐτοῖς ἐν πάσαις ταῖς γραφαῖς τὰ περὶ ἑαυτοῦ.

28 Καὶ ἤγγισαν εἰς τὴν κώμην οὗ ἐπορεύοντο, καὶ αὐτὸς προσεποιήσατο πορρώτερον πορεύεσθαι. 29 καὶ παρεβιάσαντο αὐτὸν λέγοντες, Μεῖνον μεθ᾿ ἡμῶν, ὅτι πρὸς ἑσπέραν ἐστὶν καὶ κέκλικεν ἤδη ἡ ἡμέρα. καὶ εἰσῆλθεν τοῦ μεῖναι σὺν αὐτοῖς. 30 καὶ ἐγένετο ἐν τῷ κατακλιθῆναι αὐτὸν μετ᾿ αὐτῶν λαβὼν τὸν ἄρτον εὐλόγησεν καὶ κλάσας ἐπεδίδου αὐτοῖς· 31 αὐτῶν δὲ διηνοίχθησαν οἱ ὀφθαλμοὶ καὶ ἐπέγνωσαν αὐτόν· καὶ αὐτὸς ἄφαντος ἐγένετο ἀπ᾿ αὐτῶν. 32 καὶ εἶπαν πρὸς ἀλλήλους, Οὐχὶ ἡ καρδία ἡμῶν καιομένη ἦν [ἐν ἡμῖν] ὡς ἐλάλει ἡμῖν ἐν τῇ ὁδῷ, ὡς διήνοιγεν ἡμῖν τὰς γραφάς; 33 καὶ ἀναστάντες αὐτῇ τῇ ὥρᾳ

22Some of the women of our group surprised us; they went at dawn to the grave, 23but could not find his body. They came back saying they had seen a vision of angels who told them that he is alive. 24Some of our group went to the grave and found it exactly as the women had said; but they did not see him."

25Then Jesus said to them, "How foolish you are, how slow you are to believe everything the prophets said! 26Was it not necessary for the Messiah to suffer these things and enter his glory?" 27And Jesus explained to them what was said about him in all the Scriptures, beginning with the books of Moses and the writings of all the prophets.

28They came near the village to which they were going, and Jesus acted as if he were going farther; 29but they held him back, saying, "Stay with us; the day is almost over and it is getting dark." So he went in to stay with them. 30He sat at table with them, took the bread, and said the blessing; then he broke the bread and gave it to them. 31Their eyes were opened and they recognized him; but he disappeared from their sight. 32They said to each other, "Wasn't it like a fire burning in us when he talked to us on the road and explained the Scriptures to us?"

33They got up at once and went back to Jerusalem, where they found the eleven disciples gathered together with the others 34and saying, "The Lord is risen indeed! He has appeared to Simon!"

ὑπέστρεψαν εἰς Ἱερουσαλήμ, καὶ
εὗρον ἠθροισμένους τοὺς ἕνδεκα
καὶ τοὺς σὺν αὐτοῖς, 34 λέγοντας
ὅτι ὄντως ἠγέρθη ὁ κύριος καὶ
ὤφθη Σίμωνι. 35 καὶ αὐτοὶ ἐξη-
γοῦντο τὰ ἐν τῇ ὁδῷ καὶ ὡς
ἐγνώσθη αὐτοῖς ἐν τῇ κλάσει τοῦ
ἄρτου.

The Appearance to the Disciples
(Mt 28:16–20; Mk 16:14–18;
Jn 20:19–23; Acts 1:6–8)

36 Ταῦτα δὲ αὐτῶν λαλούντων
αὐτὸς ἔστη ἐν μέσῳ αὐτῶν καὶ λέγει αὐτοῖς, Εἰρήνη ὑμῖν. 37 πτο-
ηθέντες δὲ καὶ ἔμφοβοι γενόμενοι
ἐδόκουν πνεῦμα θεωρεῖν. 38 καὶ
εἶπεν αὐτοῖς, Τί τεταραγμένοι
ἐστέ, καὶ διὰ τί διαλογισμοὶ ἀνα-
βαίνουσιν ἐν τῇ καρδίᾳ ὑμῶν; 39
ἴδετε τὰς χεῖράς μου καὶ τοὺς
πόδας μου ὅτι ἐγώ εἰμι αὐτός· ψη-
λαφήσατέ με καὶ ἴδετε, ὅτι πνεῦμα
σάρκα καὶ ὀστέα οὐκ ἔχει καθὼς
ἐμὲ θεωρεῖτε ἔχοντα. 40 καὶ
τοῦτο εἰπὼν ἔδειξεν αὐτοῖς τὰς
χεῖρας καὶ τοὺς πόδας. 41 ἔτι δὲ
ἀπιστούντων αὐτῶν ἀπὸ τῆς χαρᾶς
καὶ θαυμαζόντων εἶπεν αὐτοῖς,
Ἔχετέ τι βρώσιμον ἐνθάδε; 42 οἱ
δὲ ἐπέδωκαν αὐτῷ ἰχθύος ὀπτοῦ
μέρος· 43 καὶ λαβὼν ἐνώπιον αὐτῶν ἔφαγεν.

44 Εἶπεν δὲ πρὸς αὐτούς, Οὗτοι
οἱ λόγοι μου οὓς ἐλάλησα πρὸς
ὑμᾶς ἔτι ὢν σὺν ὑμῖν, ὅτι δεῖ
πληρωθῆναι πάντα τὰ γεγραμμένα
ἐν τῷ νόμῳ Μωϋσέως καὶ τοῖς
προφήταις καὶ ψαλμοῖς περὶ ἐμοῦ.
45 τότε διήνοιξεν αὐτῶν τὸν νοῦν
τοῦ συνιέναι τὰς γραφάς. 46 καὶ

[35]The two then explained to them
what had happened on the road, and
how they had recognized the Lord
when he broke the bread.

Jesus Appears to His Disciples
(Also Mt 28:16–20; Mk 16:14–18;
Jn 20:19–23; Acts 1:6–8)

[36]While they were telling them this,
suddenly the Lord himself stood
among them and said to them,
"Peace be with you."
[37]Full of fear and terror, they
thought that they were seeing a
ghost. [38]But he said to them, "Why
are you troubled? Why are these
doubts coming up in your minds?
[39]Look at my hands and my feet and
see that it is I, myself. Feel me, and
you will see, because a ghost doesn't
have flesh and bones, as you can see
I have."
[40]He said this and showed them his
hands and his feet. [41]They still could
not believe, they were so full of joy
and wonder; so he asked them, "Do
you have anything to eat here?"
[42]They gave him a piece of cooked
fish, [43]which he took and ate before
them.
[44]Then he said to them, "These are
the very things I told you while I was
still with you: everything written
about me in the Law of Moses, the
writings of the prophets, and the
Psalms had to come true."

εἶπεν αὐτοῖς ὅτι Οὕτως γέγραπται παθεῖν τὸν Χριστὸν καὶ ἀναστῆναι ἐκ νεκρῶν τῇ τρίτῃ ἡμέρᾳ, 47 καὶ κηρυχθῆναι ἐπὶ τῷ ὀνόματι αὐτοῦ μετάνοιαν καὶ ἄφεσιν ἁμαρτιῶν εἰς πάντα τὰ ἔθνη—ἀρξάμενοι ἀπὸ Ἰερουσαλήμ· 48 ὑμεῖς μάρτυρες τούτων. 49 καὶ [ἰδοὺ] ἐγὼ ἀποστέλλω τὴν ἐπαγγελίαν τοῦ πατρός μου ἐφ᾽ ὑμᾶς· ὑμεῖς δὲ καθίσατε ἐν τῇ πόλει ἕως οὗ ἐνδύσησθε ἐξ ὕψους δύναμιν.

[45] Then he opened their minds to understand the Scriptures, [46] and said to them, "This is what is written: that the Messiah must suffer, and rise from death, on the third day, [47] and that in his name the message about repentance and the forgiveness of sins must be preached to all nations, beginning in Jerusalem. [48] You are witnesses of these things. [49] And I myself will send upon you what my Father has promised. But you must wait in the city until the power from above comes down upon you."

The Ascension of Jesus
(Mk 16:19–20; Acts 1:9–11)

50 Ἐξήγαγεν δὲ αὐτοὺς [ἔξω] ἕως πρὸς Βηθανίαν, καὶ ἐπάρας τὰς χεῖρας αὐτοῦ εὐλόγησεν αὐτούς. 51 καὶ ἐγένετο ἐν τῷ εὐλογεῖν αὐτὸν αὐτοὺς διέστη ἀπ᾽ αὐτῶν καὶ ἀνεφέρετο εἰς τὸν οὐρανόν. 52 καὶ αὐτοὶ προσκυνήσαντες αὐτὸν ὑπέστρεψαν εἰς Ἰερουσαλὴμ μετὰ χαρᾶς μεγάλης, 53 καὶ ἦσαν διὰ παντὸς ἐν τῷ ἱερῷ εὐλογοῦντες τὸν θεόν.

Jesus Is Taken up to Heaven
(Also Mk 16:19–20; Acts 1:9–11)

[50] Then he led them out of the city as far as Bethany, where he raised his hands and blessed them. [51] As he was blessing them, he departed from them and was taken up into heaven. [52] They worshiped him and went back into Jerusalem, filled with great joy, [53] and spent all their time in the temple giving thanks to God.

Comment

Although Luke apparently had the gospel of Mark before him as he was writing his own gospel, and therefore had as well the passage from Mark I on the resurrection of Jesus, Luke, even more so than Matthew, goes his own way as regards the resurrection of Jesus. For the goals of this present study, four issues are important for some detailed consideration: (1) Luke's central message on the resurrection; (2) the role of the women in the resurrection account; (3) the Emmaus narrative; and (4) the final words of the risen Jesus.

LUKE'S CENTRAL MESSAGE ON THE RESURRECTION

In a manner similar to Mark I and Matthew, Luke stresses that the resurrection of Jesus is the work of God. Luke begins with the women going to the tomb.[34] They find the stone already rolled back from the mouth of the tomb; they enter the tomb and find it empty. Suddenly two men appear to them. Luke uses neither the term *neaniskos* (a young man) nor the term *aggelos* (an angel), but the Greek term for two adult males, *andres*. The inference of a heavenly messenger, however, remains clear. These two men have been sent by God with a message from God.[35] In the description of these two men, Luke may be making some deliberate literary allusion to the transfiguration account, for their clothing is described in similar terms. Both the transfiguration narrative and this resurrection narrative either from a literary or a religious standpoint need to be seen within the Jewish framework of a theophany. It is Yahweh who is speaking in the transfiguration and in the resurrection narrative, and Yahweh does this in the same way that Yahweh spoke to Abraham, to Moses, to Jacob, to Eli, and so on. These two men state that Jesus has been raised *(ēgerthē);* the same Greek word is found in both Mark I and Matthew. The two men make no reference at all to the emptiness of the tomb.

In all of this Luke's message on the resurrection is clear: God has acted in Jesus. Basically, the resurrection is not a Jesus-event but a Yahweh-event. Luke's allusion to Jesus is indirect. The message of these two heaven-sent men indicates that it is the same Jesus who had once spoken about Galilee, who had also been handed over to sinful men, and who had been crucified. The Jesus of history is none other than the risen Lord. Luke refers to Jesus specifically as the Son of Man, whose suffering and death had to take place *(dei).* This necessity is repeated again by Luke in the Emmaus account. Fuller, following Grundmann, indicates that this word, "necessary" *(dei),* involves Luke's entire theological view: "There are two major periods in this salvation history: the age of promise and the age of fulfillment. And it is the Christ event which has decisively inaugurated the age of fulfillment. In this sense, Christ is the mid-point of history."[36]

There is in history an ineluctable force that moves from promise to fulfillment. There is something "necessary" *(dei)* in the way Luke presents the history of salvation. There is something necessary in the slow but unavoidable exodus *(exodos)* of Jesus himself from Galilee to Jerusalem.[37] There is something necessary in the way that the messiah died. But, one might ask, who has determined that all of this is necessary? Luke's answer is abundantly clear: It is Yahweh who has so determined. Salvation history at each stage of its progression takes place because God has so ordained. *Dei*—it is necessary: God's has willed it. It is this consistent approach of Luke throughout the gospel and Acts that allows one to say that the resurrection event is fundamentally and most profoundly an action of God. There is no necessity either by creation itself or by any creaturely thing that brings about the resurrection of Jesus. God's free and gracious will is the only source of its necessity. A free necessity? Indeed! This is what "grace" is all about: God's free gift to a creature, necessitated only because of God's absolute freedom, God's justice, and God's holy love.

Again, it should be stressed that any seeing, touching, or hearing of the risen Jesus—even in the Emmaus narrative—is a secondary issue. The material presented by Luke on the resurrection of Jesus drives us to a much deeper level than any of these sense-perceptible items.

THE ROLE OF WOMEN IN THE RESURRECTION ACCOUNT

The presence of women in the resurrection material of Luke must be considered against two distinct backgrounds. First, there is the background of the traditional material that all four gospels seem to have utilized, namely, a source in which women are clearly presented as an essential part of the resurrection tradition. Second, there is the background of the role of women which one finds specifically throughout the Lucan material. In comparison with all the other gospels, even including that of John, it is Luke's gospel that most includes women within the mission of Jesus.

In Luke, the women are not the same as those in either Mark or Matthew: Mary Magdalene remains the same; Mary the mother of James (the younger) is the same; but we now hear of a Joanna (already mentioned in Luke 8:3), and in the very next part of the same sentence even "other women" *(hai loipai)* are enumerated.[38] Because of the many women involved here, Luke's account appears to intensify the relationship of women both to the resurrection event itself and to its preached tradition. Luke would not have mentioned so many women by name and then deliberately added a reference to other women as well, unless he intended to emphasize something for his own primary readership, namely, his own community. The numerous references to women throughout the Lucan gospel and Acts have a deliberate message for the Jesus community to which the evangelist belonged—namely, that Jesus' entire mission is an inclusive one as he seeks out the lost and sinners and restores them to union with God; Jesus' kingdom is for men and women and shatters the boundaries of clean and unclean.[39]

When the women returned and told what they had experienced, the apostles did not believe. Once again we find an emphasizing of disbelief. The apostles considered the women's account to be delirious raving, *lēros,* but Peter—once again a singling out of Peter—got up and ran to the tomb. He saw only the cloths, nothing else, and returned, wondering what had happened. In this account, slightly different from that in John's gospel, Peter alone goes to the tomb, but only after he had heard the women's message. Even though he finds an empty tomb, Peter does not conclude that Jesus has risen; rather, he remains perplexed. Peter sees an empty tomb, but seeing empty tombs does not cause faith. One does not believe because one has "seen" an empty tomb; one believes in the resurrection because of God's gift of grace. Textually, Luke and John differ so much that one could not say that John depended on Luke. There seems to be some sort of substrate, from which the two accountings are then derived.[40] No matter what the substrate and textual determination might eventually be, this small verse is another indication that faith in the resurrection is a gift of God, not the result of human endeavor.

The reference to Galilee is dramatically altered by Luke. Galilee becomes a matter of mere recollection: "What he said to you while he was in Galilee." Apparently, the women recall that this is indeed what the Lord had once said. In his own way, but similar to Mark I, Luke is using geography theologically, since the centrality of Jerusalem is key to the entire theological picture of Luke-Acts. In Luke all the key events of salvation take place in Jerusalem. For Luke, Galilee could never be the center for the Easter appearances. Jerusalem, the center of the old Israel, is transformed into the center of the renewed Israel.

THE EMMAUS NARRATIVE

In the Lucan account, the lengthy narrative of 24:13–35 recounts the Emmaus journey. This account constitutes twenty-three verses of Luke's entire resurrection section; the remainder is twenty-nine verses. Thus, almost half of what Luke wants to say about the resurrection of Jesus is in this narrative. We will return to this emphasis later, but an author as superb as Luke would not haphazardly devote so much of his text to a particular narrative unless he felt it clearly expressed what he wanted to say about the resurrection of Jesus. In other words, one cannot understand the Lucan view of resurrection without letting the Emmaus narrative serve as a commanding, even perhaps a controlling, statement.

Two disciples, Cleopas and the other, an unnamed person, serve as the main figures, besides Jesus. On their way to Emmaus the disciples encounter an individual whom they do not recognize. (In John's account Mary Magdalene also sees a bodily individual whom she does not recognize.) This detail of nonrecognition, found in both Luke and John, plays a role in the way one interprets the "bodily" resurrection of Jesus, as we shall see below in chapter 3.

These two disciples knew Jesus during his earthly life. For them, he was a prophet and a wonder-worker. He is not confessed as "Son of God." There is no indication at all that prior to the resurrection belief in the divinity of Jesus was a part of discipleship. The two men are Jewish—*our* chief priests and rulers—and from their Jewish background they had hoped that Jesus would be a messiah, although the name itself, *messiah,* is not used, but rather, "the one who was going to free Israel." Nonetheless, the Greek wording hardly deviates from Jewish messianic expectations. In fact the two men refer to Jesus as a prophet (v. 19) and as the one who would save Israel (v. 21).

These two men knew of the women's connection with the empty tomb and a vision of angels; they also speak of "some" who went to the tomb and found it exactly as the women had said—empty. There is some divergence between Peter mentioned earlier as the sole person who went to the tomb and this new description of "some" *(tines).* Neither a living Jesus nor his dead body, however, had been seen by either the women or the "some." No matter how many disciples in all of the gospels had gone to the tomb for whatever reasons and found it empty, not one of them believed. In John's gospel the disciple who accompanied Peter looked into the tomb and "believed," but in what did he believe? The Johannine context provides no clues.

The response of Jesus is central to this narrative, since Luke clearly emphasizes the necessity *(dei)* of such suffering of the messiah. One of the difficulties that the early Jesus communities had to confront was the ignominious death of Jesus. Nowhere in the Old Testament do we find the portrayal of a messiah who should suffer. In the Isaian text the suffering servant is not presented as a messiah. But Jesus begins with Moses and goes through all the prophets, showing how the Jewish

scriptures portrayed a suffering messiah. Later on, this aspect of belief—namely that such suffering and death had been predetermined by
God's revelation—will appear in the early creeds: "was crucified under
Pontius Pilate, and suffered and was buried, and rose again on the third
day *according to the Scriptures.*" Luke, in this section of his gospel,
makes a clear statement reflecting the belief of his community that the
Old Testament was (a) both God's revelation and (b) a revelation that
finds its fulfillment in the life, death, and resurrection of Jesus.

Besides Jesus' ignominious death, the early Jesus communities
had to deal with the delay of the parousia. Luke in the gospel and even
more so in Acts gives his own answer to both of these problematic
issues. The first issue is addressed by pointing out the necessity of the
suffering and dying messiah according to the scriptures, that is, "Moses
and all the prophets." The very Word of God, which the Jews of Luke's
time held to be sacrosanct, had spoken. If Moses and all the prophets
had said that the messiah had to suffer and die, then there could be no
denial of Jesus, even a crucified Jesus, as the messiah. Moses and all the
prophets were for the pious Jews of that time "infallible." Luke accepts
this premise of Jewish belief and interprets Moses and the prophets in a
way that sustains belief in the messiahship of the crucified Jesus. Moses
(the *Torah*), the prophets (the *nebi' im*), and the writings (the *ketubim*)—
that is, the entire Jewish scripture—attest to Jesus. This is Luke's argument, and it is very Jewish. This kind of interpretation is presented as
the only valid way to understand the Torah, the prophets, and the writings as well as the meaning of Jewish religious history. For Luke, the
Jewish Jesus is the center, meaning, and key to all that Judaism stood
for and stands for. The author of this gospel has such a remarkable understanding of this Jewish manner of hermeneutics, that it is only with
difficulty that one might call him a "gentile." The way Jesus appropri-
ates the Jewish scriptures in Luke's account is fundamentally Jewish.[41]

The second issue, the delay of the parousia, is addressed by Luke
particularly in Acts with his theology of the Jesus community, the
ekklēsia. Since there is a delay of the parousia, the community of *qahal,*
the called-by-Yahweh community, the *ekklēsia,* remains and develops
even in a sort of institutional way until it pleases Yahweh to bring about
the fullness of the call, the *qahal,* the *ekklēsia.*[42]

At the end of the Emmaus journey is the meal stop, with its proba-
ble connection to the eucharist. There is also perhaps a strong pastoral
note in this section: in the 70s and early 80s in the community in which

Luke lived there were, of course, no appearances of the risen Lord, but in the communal celebration of the eucharist, in the breaking of the bread, the members of this community could find the risen Lord. A connection between the eucharist and the risen Lord appears to be part of the eucharistic theology of that time and place. These few lines, then, provide us with a small window into the early eucharist at least in the community to which Luke belonged, particularly into its connection with the resurrection and exaltation. In the eucharist Jesus is really present, but this Jesus is the risen and exalted Lord. In other words, the risen and exalted Lord is present in the communal breaking of the bread.[43]

After the blessing of the bread, Jesus disappears and the two disciples return to the eleven, whom they found professing their belief in the risen Lord. The eleven tell the two that Jesus has already appeared to Peter—again a singling out of Peter. The appearance of Jesus to Cleophas and his companion, then, is not presented as the first appearance, nor is it greeted with the same enthusiasm with which the eleven have greeted the appearance to Peter.

Such is the narrative. What key issues does Luke stress by this lengthy account? Clearly, a major emphasis lies in the way in which the Jesus-event interprets the Torah, the prophets, and the writings. For a Jewish audience, what is primarily at stake in this interpretation is the validity and credibility of God's revelation. Once again, the action of Yahweh in the Torah, in the prophets, in the writings, and now in the life, death, and resurrection of Jesus is primary. A Jewish audience could hear this account only as an interpretation of the sacred books of Israel, which are God's word to the chosen people. Some Jewish people did indeed accept this interpretation, and these people became the nuclei of the various, postresurrectional Jesus communities. Luke perhaps is one of such. Other Jewish people, however, rejected this interpretation of the Torah, the prophets, and the writings and continued in the form of Jewish religious life to which they were accustomed.[44]

Nowhere in any of the gospels, in Acts, or in Paul does one find the position that required a person who believed in Jesus to give up Jewish identity. Indeed, the first Jesus communities had a strong Jewish identity. The followers of Jesus at this early stage did not convert from Judaism to Christianity. In the gospels, in Acts, and in Paul such a conversion is nowhere to be found. If "conversion" is meant to be an operative word in this regard, it can only be used as a conversion from one Jewish interpretation of Torah, prophets, and writings to another. Indeed, the early Jesus communities saw themselves as the true Israel. This is clearly the way Luke is presenting the material in the Emmaus narrative. He is saying also that this Jesus-interpretation of Torah, prophets, and the writings is the proper interpretation of the sacred books of Judaism.

The two disciples come to some understanding of what the Jewish scriptures mean, as opened to them by this stranger on the road, namely, a meaning that included the death of Jesus, and which, so they came to believe, had been explained to them by this same Jesus now risen. Their subsequent association with the risen Jesus community means that (1) the Jewish scriptures are presented in a way in which a messiah who dies, even ignominiously, is seen as the true interpretation of Torah, prophets, and writings (Lk 24:25–27); (2) the risen Jesus is seen as the core of their community (24:34–35); and (3) all of this is consonant with the underlying belief in one God, Yahweh, who has chosen this people as his own (24:25–27 coupled with 24:35).

It is God's action, once again, that is paramount—an action of Yahweh that impinged on the two disciples' lives through the sacred Jewish writings and through the events of Jesus' life, now newly interpreted to them, and the presence of Jesus in the breaking of the bread. Luke makes Jesus, in the Emmaus narrative, an interpreter of Yahweh and also the long-awaited messiah.

THE FINAL WORDS OF THE RISEN JESUS

All the events in Luke's final chapter take place on Easter day itself. On this same day but toward evening Jesus appears to all of the disciples, including the eleven and the two who had gone to Emmaus. Even though they had just been described as professing belief in the risen Lord (24:35–37), Luke suddenly portrays them as full of fear and terror. They think that the appearance is that of a ghost *(pneuma),* not of Jesus. Jesus himself comments on these doubts, shows them his hands and feet, and asks them to touch him. Jesus even speaks of his flesh and bones. The resurrection of the Lord is emphasized as a bodily resurrection. Even at this, the eleven remain doubtful. Luke clearly utilizes an earlier tradition about the slowness of the disciples to come to faith in the resurrection. There is some lack of integration of this tradition with what Luke had just presented in the Emmaus story. Moreover, there seems to be some pastoral reason in Luke's account for this heightened emphasis on doubt, much as we saw in Mark II. To allay the doubt, Jesus proceeds to eat some broiled fish, which some biblical authors see as a detail from a Hellenistic source rather than a Palestinian source.[45] Belief in a risen Jesus was not, in Luke's view, an easy attainment.

Luke's account ends with a final instruction. In these parting words Jesus takes up anew the Jewish scriptures: the Torah, the prophets, and the psalms, interpreting them, as he had done above in the story of the two disciples. The words of Yahweh had been spoken about Jesus himself. Luke again presents Jesus as the key to and fulfillment of the Jewish scriptures and therefore of Judaism itself. A suffering messiah is pivotal to this interpretation.

Luke connects this "opening of the Jewish scriptures" to the kerygma, which he then describes: repentance for the forgiveness of sin, preached to all nations, a universal mission of reconciliation (24:47). This preaching begins in Jerusalem: to Israel first, and then to the gentiles. The disciples are to be witness of this new age, and they will be filled with the Spirit. Jesus, however, cautions them to wait in Jerusalem until this occurs.

In the gospel of Luke, on the very same day as the resurrection, Jesus goes to Bethany, located about two miles from Jerusalem, and there he blesses his disciples and ascends into heaven. The disciples worship him and return to Jerusalem joyfully, spending their time in prayer and thanksgiving in the temple.[46] Evans notes that in Luke the resurrection is not an end in itself but a point of transition. "It both looks forward to what is to follow from it, the gift of the Spirit and the mission of the Church, . . . and it also looked back upon as the firm historical base for what is to follow."[47]

Luke, throughout his two books, emphasizes Jerusalem. Jerusalem is the center of the Jewish world, and it precisely this centering which Jesus reconstitutes in himself. The reconstitution is legitimated by Luke, inasmuch as the Jewish scriptures themselves legitimate Jesus. The presence of the early disciples in the temple is part of this legitimation, since the disciples are praising Yahweh for Jesus is the temple itself. True Judaism, according to Luke, is found only in Jesus.

LUKE: THE ACTS OF THE APOSTLES

In the Acts, Luke presents a forty-day period of appearances after the resurrection.[48] A major portion of the material in Acts that focuses on the resurrection is found in the so-called conversion of Saul. These passages will be taken up in the section below on the Pauline letters, since they make better sense when compared to Paul's own personal attestations of this "conversion event."

Text

1 Τὸν μὲν πρῶτον λόγον ἐποιησάμην περὶ πάντων, ὦ Θεόφιλε, ὧν ἤρξατο ὁ Ἰησοῦς ποιεῖν τε καὶ διδάσκειν 2 ἄχρι ἧς ἡμέρας ἐντειλάμενος τοῖς ἀποστόλοις διὰ πνεύματος ἁγίου οὓς ἐξελέξατο ἀνελήμφθη· 3 οἷς καὶ παρέστησεν ἑαυτὸν ζῶντα μετὰ τὸ παθεῖν αὐτὸν ἐν πολλοῖς τεκμηρίοις, δι' ἡμερῶν τεσσαράκοντα ὀπτανόμενος αὐτοῖς καὶ λέγων τὰ περὶ τῆς βασιλείας τοῦ θεοῦ. 4 καὶ συναλιζόμενος παρήγγειλεν αὐτοῖς ἀπὸ Ἱεροσολύμων μὴ χωρίζεσθαι, ἀλλὰ περιμένειν τὴν ἐπαγγελίαν τοῦ πατρὸς ἣν ἠκούσατε μου· 5 ὅτι Ἰωάννης μὲν ἐβάπτισεν ὕδατι, ὑμεῖς δὲ ἐν πνεύματι βαπτισθήσεσθε ἁγίῳ οὐ μετὰ πολλὰς ταύτας ἡμέρας.

1 Dear Theophilus:

In my first book I wrote about all the things that Jesus did and taught, from the time he began his work [2]until the day he was taken up to heaven. Before he was taken up he gave instructions by the power of the Holy Spirit to the men he had chosen as his apostles. [3]For forty days after his death he showed himself to them many times, in ways that proved beyond doubt that he was alive; he was seen by them, and talked with them about the Kingdom of God. [4]And when they came together, he gave them this order, "Do not leave Jerusalem, but wait for the gift my Father promised, that I told you about. [5]John baptized with water, but in a few days you will be baptized with the Holy Spirit."

The Ascension of Jesus

Jesus Is Taken up to Heaven

6 Οἱ μὲν οὖν συνελθόντες ἠρώτων αὐτὸν λέγοντες, Κύριε, εἰ ἐν τῷ χρόνῳ τούτῳ ἀποκαθιστάνεις τὴν βασιλείαν τῷ Ἰσραήλ; 7 εἶπεν δὲ πρὸς αὐτούς, Οὐχ ὑμῶν ἐστιν γνῶναι χρόνους ἢ καιροὺς οὓς ὁ πατὴρ ἔθετο ἐν τῇ ἰδίᾳ ἐξουσίᾳ· 8 ἀλλὰ λήμψεσθε δύναμιν ἐπελθόντος τοῦ ἁγίου πνεύματος ἐφ' ὑμᾶς, καὶ ἔσεσθέ μου μάρτυρες ἔν τε Ἱερουσαλὴμ καὶ ἐν πάσῃ τῇ Ἰουδαίᾳ καὶ Σαμαρείᾳ καὶ ἕως ἐσ-

[6]When the apostles met together with Jesus they asked him, "Lord, will you at this time give the Kingdom back to Israel?"

[7]Jesus said to them, "The times and occasions are set by my Father's own authority, and it is not for you to know when they will be. [8]But you will be filled with power when the Holy Spirit comes on you, and you will be witnesses for me in Jerusalem, in all of Judea and

χάτου τῆς γῆς. 9 καὶ ταῦτα εἰπὼν βλεπόντων αὐτῶν ἐπήρθη, καὶ νεφέλη ὑπέλαβεν αὐτὸν ἀπὸ τῶν ὀφθαλμῶν αὐτῶν. 10 καὶ ὡς ἀτενίζοντες ἦσαν εἰς τὸν οὐρανὸν πορευομένου αὐτοῦ, καὶ ἰδοὺ ἄνδρες δύο παρειστήκεισαν αὐτοῖς ἐν ἐσθήσεσι λευκαῖς, 11 οἳ καὶ εἶπαν, Ἄνδρες Γαλιλαῖοι, τί ἑστήκατε βλέποντες εἰς τὸν οὐρανόν; οὗτος ὁ Ἰησοῦς ὁ ἀναλημφθεὶς ἀφ᾽ ὑμῶν εἰς τὸν οὐρανὸν οὕτως ἐλεύσεται ὃν τρόπον ἐθεάσασθε αὐτὸν πορευόμενον εἰς τὸν οὐρανόν.

Samaria, and to the ends of the earth." [9]After saying this, he was taken up to heaven as they watched him; and a cloud hid him from their sight.

[10]They still had their eyes fixed on the sky as he went away, when two men dressed in white suddenly stood beside them. [11]"Men of Galilee," they said, "why do you stand there looking up at the sky? This Jesus, who was taken up from you into heaven, will come back in the same way that you saw him go to heaven."

Comment

In Acts, Luke utilizes the forty days as a time in which Jesus instructed his apostles. Throughout Acts, these apostles are an exclusive group of twelve. Jesus is portrayed as appearing to them many times, proving by many demonstrations *(en pollois tekmēriois)* that even though he had suffered, he was now alive. The central theme of Jesus' risen message is the kingdom of God which is exactly the same as the central theme of Jesus' preaching during his earthly life.

The forty days are reminiscent of the forty days of Moses on Sinai or the time of Jesus' own desert experience. There is as well a rabbinical use of forty days, which is the time it takes to learn a master's teaching. One can say that in Acts the forty days are more symbolic than historical, but *of what* they are symbolic is not quite clear. The forty days in Acts have a connection with John the Baptist. Just as John the Baptist is the linchpin between the time of Yahweh's formation of the Jewish people and the earthly life of Jesus, so too the forty days form the linchpin between the earthly life of Jesus and the life of the *qahal,* the *ekklēsia,* the Jesus community.

On the final occasion when the apostles meet with Jesus, they ask about the restoration of the kingdom to Israel, a very strong Jewish hope. Jesus does not directly answer their questioning, but advises them not to leave Jerusalem, a detail also mentioned in 1:4, so that they can receive the Spirit. Once that occurs, they will be witnesses *(martyres)* throughout Judea and Samaria, and to the ends of the earth. Acts, as we

know, ends with the preaching of this same kerygma in Rome, considered at that time to be the center of the entire world, whereas Jerusalem was the center only of the Jewish world. Jesus and the Jesus kerygma is clearly presented as the key, center, and focal meaning not only of Judaism but of all creation.

Jesus is then taken from their sight (an ascension or exaltation). As the disciples remain looking up to heaven, two men appear and say: "Men of Galilee." The emphasis on Galilee in the Lucan material returns. This exaltation event marks the end of Jesus' earthly and quasi-earthly life. The Jesus community as described in Acts begins to move forward. This Jesus community, not yet called a "church" in our sense of the term, will not see Jesus in bodily form again until the final parousia, when he will come back in the same way they saw him leave (1:11).

Compared to Mark I and Matthew, Luke has presented many new and diverse elements. One sees, however, that some of these elements of Luke's writings are presented one way in the gospel and another way in Acts, and that there can really be no smooth harmonization process. How these sundry and diverse ideas on the resurrection might be brought together in a unified way will be taken up in chapter 3. Likewise, the material on Paul and his encounter with the risen Jesus will be addressed in the section on Paul's writings later in this present chapter.

6. JOHN I

In the Johannine material there are two voices that are highly significant for an understanding of the resurrection of Jesus: the first, referred to in this study as John I, is the author of the gospel itself. John II, the author of chap. 21, is another person altogether. John II might also be the person who modified the gospel of John. There is as well the possibility of a Johannine school which might have authored the gospel. Let us consider John I and his account of the resurrection.

Text

20 Τῇ δὲ μιᾷ τῶν σαββάτων Μαρία ἡ Μαγδαληνὴ ἔρχεται πρωῒ σκοτίας ἔτι οὔσης εἰς τὸ μνημεῖον, καὶ βλέπει τὸν λίθον ἠρμένον ἐκ τοῦ μνημείου. 2 τρέχει οὖν καὶ ἐπέρχεται πρὸς Σίμωνα Πέτρον καὶ πρὸς τὸν ἄλλον μαθητὴν ὃν ἐ-

20 Early on Sunday morning, while it was still dark, Mary Magdalene went to the tomb and saw that the stone had been taken away from the entrance. ²She ran and went to Simon Peter and the other disciple, whom Jesus loved, and told them,

φίλει ὁ Ἰησοῦς, καὶ λέγει αὐτοῖς, 7Ἦραν τὸν κύριον ἐκ τοῦ μνημείου, καὶ οὐκ οἴδαμεν ποῦ ἔθηκαν αὐτόν. 3 Ἐξῆλθεν οὖν ὁ Πέτρος καὶ ὁ ἄλλος μαθητής, καὶ ἤρχοντο εἰς τὸ μνημεῖον. 4 ἔτρεχον δὲ οἱ δύο ὁμοῦ· καὶ ὁ ἄλλος μαθητὴς προέδραμεν τάχιον τοῦ Πέτρου καὶ ἦλθεν πρῶτος εἰς τὸ μνημεῖον, 5 καὶ παρακύψας βλέπει κείμενα τὰ ὀθόνια, οὐ μέντοι εἰσῆλθεν. 6 ἔρχεται οὖν καὶ Σίμων Πέτρος ἀκολουθῶν αὐτῷ, καὶ εἰσῆλθεν εἰς τὸ μνημεῖον· καὶ θεωρεῖ τὰ ὀθόνια κείμενα, 7 καὶ τὸ σουδάριον, ὃ ἦν ἐπὶ τῆς κεφαλῆς αὐτοῦ, οὐ μετὰ τῶν ὀθονίων κείμενον ἀλλὰ χωρὶς ἐντετυλιγμένον εἰς ἕνα τόπον. 8 τότε οὖν εἰσῆλθεν καὶ ὁ ἄλλος μαθητὴς ὁ ἐλθὼν πρῶτως εἰς τὸ μνημεῖον, καὶ εἶδεν καὶ ἐπίστευσεν· 9 οὐδέπω γὰρ ᾔδεισαν τὴν γραφὴν ὅτι δεῖ αὐτὸν ἐκ νεκρῶν ἀναστῆναι. 10 ἀπῆλθον οὖν πάλιν πρὸς αὐτοὺς οἱ μαθηταί.

"They have taken the Lord from the tomb and we don't know where they have put him!"

3Then Peter and the other disciple left and went to the tomb. 4The two of them were running, but the other disciple ran faster than Peter and reached the tomb first. 5He bent over and saw the linen cloths, but he did not go in. 6Behind him came Simon Peter, and he went straight into the tomb. He saw the linen cloths lying there 7and the cloth which had been around Jesus' head. It was not lying with the linen cloths but was rolled up by itself. 8Then the other disciple, who had reached the tomb first, also went in; he saw and believed. 9(They still did not understand the scripture which said that he must rise from death.) 10Then the disciples went back home.

The Appearance of Jesus to Mary Magdalene
(Mk 16:9–11)

Jesus Appears to Mary Magdalene
(Also Mt 28:9–10; Mk 16:9–11)

11 Μαρία δὲ εἱστήκει πρὸς τῷ μνημείῳ ἔξω κλαίουσα. ὡς οὖν ἔκλαιεν παρέκυψεν εἰς τὸ μνημεῖον, 12 καὶ θεωρεῖ δύο ἀγγέλους ἐν λευκοῖς καθεζομένους, ἕνα πρὸς τῇ κεφαλῇ καὶ ἕνα πρὸς τοῖς ποσίν, ὅπου ἔκειτο τὸ σῶμα τοῦ Ἰησοῦ. 13 καὶ λέγουσιν αὐτῇ ἐκεῖνοι, Γύναι, τί κλαίεις; λέγει αὐτοῖς ὅτι Ἦραν τὸν κύριόν μου, καὶ οὐκ οἶδα ποῦ ἔθηκαν αὐτόν. 14 ταῦτα εἰποῦσα ἐστράφη εἰς τὰ ὀπίσω, καὶ θεωρεῖ τὸν Ἰη-

11Mary stood crying outside the tomb. Still crying, she bent over and looked in the tomb, 12and saw two angels there, dressed in white, sitting where the body of Jesus had been, one at the head, the other at the feet. 13"Woman, why are you crying?" they asked her.

She answered, "They have taken my Lord away, and I do not know where they have put him!"

14When she had said this, she turned around and saw Jesus

σοῦν ἑστῶτα, καὶ οὐκ ᾔδει ὅτι
Ἰησοῦς ἐστιν. 15 λέγει αὐτῇ
Ἰησοῦς, Γύναι, τί κλαίεις; τίνα
ζητεῖς; ἐκείνη δοκοῦσα ὅτι ὁ κη-
πουρός ἐστιν λέγει αὐτῷ, Κύριε, εἰ
σὺ ἐβάστασας αὐτόν, εἰπέ μοι ποῦ
ἔθηκας αὐτόν, κἀγὼ αὐτὸν ἀρῶ.
16 λέγει αὐτῇ Ἰησοῦς, Μαρία.
Στραφεῖσα ἐκείνη λέγει αὐτῷ
Ἑβραϊστί, Ραββουνι (ὃ λέγεται Δι-
δάσκαλε). 17 λέγει αὐτῇ Ἰησοῦς,
Μή μου ἅπτου, οὔπω γὰρ ἀνα-
βέβηκα πρὸς τὸν πατέρα· πορεύου
δὲ πρὸς τοὺς ἀδελφούς μου καὶ
εἰπὲ αὐτοῖς, Ἀναβαίνω πρὸς τὸν
πατέρα μου καὶ πατέρα ὑμῶν καὶ
θεόν μου καὶ θεὸν ὑμῶν. 18 ἔρχεται Μαρία ἡ Μαγδαληνὴ ἀγγέλ-
λουσα τοῖς μαθηταῖς ὅτι Ἑώρακα
τὸν κύριον, καὶ ταῦτα εἶπεν αὐτῇ.

standing there; but she did not know
that it was Jesus. [15]"Woman, why are
you crying?" Jesus asked her. "Who
is it that you are looking for?"

She thought he was the gardener,
so she said to him, "If you took him
away, sir, tell me where you have put
him, and I will go and get him."

[16]Jesus said to her, "Mary!"

She turned toward him and said in
Hebrew, "Rabboni!" (This means
"Teacher.")

[17]"Do not hold on to me," Jesus
told her, "because I have not yet gone
back up to the Father. But go to my
brothers and tell them for me, 'I go
back up to him who is my Father and
your Father, my God and your God.'"

[18]So Mary Magdalene went and
told the disciples that she had seen
the Lord, and that he had told her
this.

The Appearance of Jesus
to the Disciples (Mt 28:16–20;
Mk 16:14–18; Lk 24:36–49)

Jesus Appears to His Disciples
(Also Mt 28:16–20;
Mk 16:14–18; Lk 24:36–49)

19 Οὔσης οὖν ὀψίας τῇ ἡμέρᾳ
ἐκείνῃ τῇ μιᾷ σαββάτων, καὶ τῶν
θυρῶν κεκλεισμένων ὅπου ἦσαν οἱ
μαθηταὶ διὰ τὸν φόβον τῶν
Ἰουδαίων, ἦλθεν ὁ Ἰησοῦς καὶ
ἔστη εἰς τὸ μέσον καὶ λέγει αὐτοῖς,
Εἰρήνη ὑμῖν. 20 καὶ τοῦτο εἰπὼν
ἔδειξεν τὰς χεῖρας καὶ τὴν
πλευρὰν αὐτοῖς. ἐχάρησαν οὖν οἱ
μαθηταὶ ἰδόντες τὸν κύριον. 21
εἶπεν οὖν αὐτοῖς πάλιν, Εἰρήνη
ὑμῖν· καθὼς ἀπέσταλκέν με ὁ
πατήρ, κἀγὼ πέμπω ὑμᾶς. 22 καὶ
τοῦτο εἰπὼν ἐνεφύσησεν καὶ λέγει
αὐτοῖς, Λάβετε πνεῦμα ἅγιον· 23

[19]It was late that Sunday evening,
and the disciples were gathered together behind locked doors, because
they were afraid of the Jewish authorities. Then Jesus came and stood
among them. "Peace be with you,"
he said. [20]After saying this, he
showed them his hands and his side.
The disciples were filled with joy at
seeing the Lord. [21]Then Jesus said to
them again, "Peace be with you. As
the Father sent me, so I send you."
[22]He said this, and then he breathed
on them and said, "Receive the Holy
Spirit. [23]If you forgive men's sins,

ἄν τινων ἀφῆτε τὰς ἁμαρτίας ἀφέωνται αὐτοῖς, ἄν τινων κρατῆτε κεκράτηνται.

they are forgiven; if you do not forgive them, they are not forgiven."

Jesus and Thomas

24 Θωμᾶς δὲ εἷς ἐκ τῶν δώδεκα, ὁ λεγόμενος Δίδυμος, οὐκ ἦν μετ' αὐτῶν ὅτε ἦλθεν Ἰησοῦς. 25 ἔλεγον οὖν αὐτῷ οἱ ἄλλοι μαθηταί, Ἑωράκαμεν τὸν κύριον. ὁ δὲ εἶπεν αὐτοῖς, Ἐὰν μὴ ἴδω ἐν ταῖς χερσὶν αὐτοῦ τὸν τύπον τῶν ἥλων καὶ βάλω τὸν δάκτυλόν μου εἰς τὸν τύπον τῶν ἥλων καὶ βάλω μου τὴν χεῖρα εἰς τὴν πλευρὰν αὐτοῦ, οὐ μὴ πιστεύσω. 26 Καὶ μεθ' ἡμέρας ὀκτὼ πάλιν ἦσαν ἔσω οἱ μαθηταὶ αὐτοῦ καὶ Θωμᾶς μετ' αὐτῶν. ἔρχεται ὁ Ἰησοῦς τῶν θυρῶν κεκλεισμένον, καὶ ἔστη εἰς τὸ μέσον καὶ εἶπεν, Εἰρήνη ὑμῖν. 27 εἶτα λέγει τῷ Θωμᾷ, Φέρε τὸν δάκτυλόν σου ὧδε καὶ ἴδε τὰς χεῖράς μου, καὶ φέρε τὴν χεῖρά σου καὶ βάλε εἰς τὴν πλευράν μου, καὶ μὴ γίνου ἄπιστος ἀλλὰ πιστός. 28 ἀπεκρίθη Θωμᾶς καὶ εἶπεν αὐτῷ, Ὁ κύριός μου καὶ ὁ θεός μου. 29 λέγει αὐτῷ ὁ Ἰησοῦς, Ὅτι ἑώρακάς με πεπίστευκας; μακάριοι οἱ μὴ ἰδόντες καὶ πιστεύσαντες.

Jesus and Thomas

24One of the twelve disciples, Thomas (called the Twin), was not with them when Jesus came. 25So the other disciples told him "We saw the Lord!"

Thomas said to them, "If I do not see the scars of the nails in his hands, and put my finger on those scars, and my hand in his side, I will not believe."

26A week later the disciples were together indoors again, and Thomas was with them. The doors were locked, but Jesus came and stood among them and said, "Peace be with you." 27Then he said to Thomas, "Put your finger here, and look at my hands; then stretch out your hand and put it in my side. Stop your doubting, and believe!"

28Thomas answered him, "My Lord and my God!"

29Jesus said to him, "Do you believe because you see me? How happy are those who believe without seeing me!"

The Purpose of the Book

30 Πολλὰ μὲν οὖν ἄλλα σημεῖα ἐποίησεν ὁ Ἰησοῦς ἐνώπιον τῶν μαθητῶν [αὐτοῦ], ἃ οὐκ ἔστιν γεγραμμένα ἐν τῷ βιβλίῳ τούτῳ· 31 ταῦτα δὲ γέγραπται ἵνα πιστεύσητε ὅτι Ἰησοῦς ἐστιν ὁ Χριστὸς ὁ υἱὸς τοῦ θεοῦ, καὶ ἵνα πιστεύοντες ζωὴν ἔχητε ἐν τῷ ὀνόματι αὐτοῦ.

The Purpose of This Book

30Jesus did many other mighty works in his disciples' presence which are not written down in this book. 31These have been written that you may believe that Jesus is the Messiah, the Son of God, and that through this faith you may have life in his name.

Comment

The following themes have been selected because they will help in this present study of the theology of the resurrection of Jesus: (1) the fundamental message of John I regarding the resurrection of Jesus; (2) the role of Mary Magdalene in the Johannine resurrection accounts and her connection to the empty tomb tradition; and (3) the sending of the Spirit and the resurrection of Jesus.

THE FUNDAMENTAL MESSAGE OF JOHN I
REGARDING THE RESURRECTION OF JESUS

Throughout the gospel of John, Jesus is presented as a very imposing, almost heavenly figure. He is the Logos made flesh; he is greater than Abraham and Moses; he is the vine and the good shepherd; he knows the Father and the Father knows him. Scholars have spoken about the "high christology" of the Johannine gospel. This certainly cannot be denied. John's gospel is, indeed, quite different from the synoptic gospels, and the figure of Jesus has a grandeur and a power that are clearly transcendent. This same quality of transcendence appears in chap. 20 of John's gospel. The risen Jesus is imposing, filled with power, filled with transcendent qualities. Still, the language the author uses in this chapter dovetails well with the language used throughout the gospel. Jesus is center stage, but the Father is unmistakably behind him. We read in 20:17: "Go to my brothers and tell them that I am returning to him who is my Father and their Father, my God and their God." In 20:21: "As the Father has sent me, so I send you." For John, the resurrection is a major manifestation of the Father/God. Jesus is intimately one with this Father/God. Indeed, the concluding passage states that this gospel was written so that we "may believe that Jesus is the Messiah, the Son of God," and that through our faith in Jesus, we may have life (20:31). One must keep in mind that at this stage of thought on the relationship of Jesus to the Father, a trinitarian doctrine had not yet been developed. Without the trinitarian development, it is difficult to understand the relationship between the Father and Jesus. The gospel of John describes the intimacy of this relationship but does not offer much beyond the description.

Even with this caveat, it is clear that once again the author sees in the Jesus event the action of the Father, that is, Yahweh. Touching, seeing, hearing a risen Jesus is not fundamentally what resurrection means (cf. 20:29).

THE ROLE OF MARY MAGDALENE IN THE JOHANNINE
RESURRECTION ACCOUNTS AND HER CONNECTION
TO THE EMPTY TOMB TRADITION

In John's account of the resurrection there is only one woman, Mary Magdalene. No reason such as anointing the body is provided by the author for her presence at the tomb. Discovering that the stone had been removed from the entry of the tomb, she runs to tell Peter and the "other disciple whom Jesus loved." She reports to them that the tomb is empty, not because of a resurrection but because an unknown group of people—"they"—have taken the body and "we" do not know where "they" have placed it. Actually, John uses the term "Lord" instead of body. Throughout his gospel, John has not used the term "Lord"; but now that the resurrection has taken place, John begins to use this term.

Peter is singled out, and this echoes a tradition found in the synoptics. The "other disciple," however, has presented scholars with many difficulties: Is this other disciple, whom Jesus loved, a real and definite individual? If so, then, who is he? Or is the "beloved disciple" merely an idealized disciple, a figure used by John to connote what real discipleship is all about? Over the centuries, biblical scholars have debated these questions, but without any final settlement. At any rate, in the Johannine narrative, the two men are portrayed as running to the tomb, with the other disciple arriving before Peter. This other disciple sees the linens but does not enter the tomb. Peter, when he arrives, goes directly into the tomb. Only then does the other disciple enter the tomb. He sees and he believes (20:8), but what he believes is unclear. Neither the text nor context offers any help on this issue.

Brown indicates that the author is combining in this episode three distinct traditions: (1) a tradition involving several women who came to the tomb early on Sunday morning; (2) a tradition involving Peter, perhaps alone, and other male disciples who came to the tomb after they had heard the report of the women; and (3) a tradition involving the appearance of Jesus to Mary Magdalene.

Chapter 20 is the author's combination of these three earlier traditions into a single whole. His attempt to present a unified narrative of these three traditions is, from a literary standpoint, not terribly successful. There are in the text movements from one tradition to another that do not mesh well or that presuppose a clarity of detail that is not really there. Because of this interweaving of three basic earlier traditions, John's account does not flow smoothly at times, both from a literary standpoint and from a logical standpoint.[49]

The two men then return home. The Johannine accounts of Mary Magdalene and the two disciples indicate and presume an empty tomb. The readers of the gospel, of course, as the author presupposes, already believe that Jesus has risen. The author is not writing a "proof text," and therefore he can presume a faith-stance on the part of his readership. Nonetheless, the readers see, in the way that John recounts these traditions, that belief in Jesus' resurrection is not an easy accomplishment for even such heroes of the faith as Peter, the "other disciple," and Mary Magdalene. The Johannine author also indicates that an empty tomb, by itself, in no way causes faith.

Mary Magdalene returns to the tomb area where she finds two angels *(aggeloi)* sitting on the tomb. They are described in typical Jewish apocalyptic imagery, which indicates that the author is using some traditional material about women at the tomb and of the appearance of an angel. Even with an angelophany, Mary remains rather dense. She states simply that "they" have taken the Lord away and "I do not know where they have put him" (20:13). Not even the presence of angels at the empty tomb prompts Mary to believe that Jesus has risen. Just then she turns and sees someone whom she believes to be the gardener. She asks whether he has taken him *(auton)* away and, if so, where he has put him *(auton)*. Mary is still not presented as a person who believes in the resurrection. Only when the "gardener" answers does she recognize him. This dramatic though small detail is important for an understanding of the meaning of the "bodily" resurrection of Jesus. Mary is presented as seeing a human person, a gardener; she does not recognize who this bodily person is. The question arises as it did in the Emmaus narrative: What kind of body did Jesus now have that he was not even recognized? Brown notes that the risen Jesus had undergone a change from the Jesus of the ministry.[50] In John as in the other New Testament accounts, the risen Jesus has been transformed; his bodiliness is different.[51] Although Mary Magdalene had said *"Rabbouni"* (my dear Rabbi) when she recognized Jesus, she later tells the disciples: "I have seen the Lord!" In this latter episode, Mary Magdalene has come, through the appearance of the risen Jesus, not merely to accept Jesus as a great teacher (rabbi), but more importantly as the Lord, Yahweh-Jesus.

John I clearly indicates that Mary Magdalene was the first to see the risen Lord. This dovetails well with the tradition of the women in Matthew. As mentioned above, the appearance of the risen Jesus to women, which is the first appearance in this tradition, gradually is edged to one side by the emphasis of the early community on the appearance of Jesus to the apostles, the eleven.

John's focus on one woman rather than a group of women also corresponds to his treatment of women throughout the gospel, for example, Martha in the Lazarus narrative; Mary in the Mary-Martha narrative. In the Johannine account, women are deliberately inserted at pivotal moments. In the theology of this author, position, rank, and prestige are not the requisite factors for the meaning of discipleship. Rather, faith and love are. Whereas Peter makes the great confession in Matthew (16:16ff.), it is Martha who does this in John (11:27). At the resurrection, it is Mary Magdalene, not Peter, who is the first to see and to believe in the risen Lord.

The risen Jesus, in his response to Mary Magdalene, indicates that he has not yet ascended: "Do not touch me, for I have not yet ascended to the Father" (20:17). Some scholars believe that exaltation, not resurrection, was the earliest way of understanding the Easter event, and this Johannine mention of "ascension" is rooted in primitive material that stresses the exaltation approach. Be this as it may, the fact that Jesus does not want Mary to touch him has presented scholars with many exegetical difficulties. The scholars' interpretation of this has varied, and many suggestions are only flights of fancy, for example, that Jesus' wounds were still sore, or that Mary Magdalene wanted to receive Holy Communion. The Johannine author uses the narrative involving Mary Magdalene to indicate that resurrection from a tomb is by itself not the meaning of resurrection; ascension—that is, glorification and exaltation—is equally essential. To see the Easter Jesus merely as one who has come out from a tomb is not what the resurrection/ascension/exaltation/sending of the Spirit is all about. Consequently, Jesus instructs Mary to go to his brothers and tell them that he is going back to his Father—exaltation—and not only to his Father and God, but to "your Father" and "your God" as well. The disciples of Jesus are also part of the very meaning of the Easter. Jesus' resurrection/ascension/exaltation is not a private issue, personal to Jesus alone; there is also a communal or social dimension to the resurrection/ascension/exaltation. Mary obeys this instruction of the risen Lord. Mary herself is presented as an apostle, a messenger of good news to the disciples (20:18).

Is the presentation of Mary Magdalene in this section of John's gospel historically accurate? Did it really happen in the way John describes it? That there are many strands of theological overlay in this Johannine presentation cannot be denied, and the Johannine theological material cautions us not to stress the "historicity" as though historical accuracy were the main issue. In the material about Mary Magdalene, belief is far more important. What happened deep within the spiritual depths of this woman Mary is the significant issue. Mary finally accepts Jesus, in spite of his death and burial, as Lord—"I have seen the Lord"—and she announces—*(aggelousa)*—this good news to the disciples. It is the faith-dimension of Mary that we should be concerned about, not merely whether in fact she did this or that. Mary is presented by the author as an example of resurrection faith, a faith that rested not on an empty tomb but on a spiritual and personal encounter with the risen Lord.

THE SENDING OF THE SPIRIT
AND THE RESURRECTION OF JESUS

On the evening of that very same day, the disciples (the author does not say the "Twelve" nor the "apostles") were in a locked room, somewhere in Jerusalem, afraid of Jewish authorities. Jesus suddenly appears to them. The author presents us with a solemn occasion, and all the details, such as the greeting "Peace be with you!" contribute to the solemnity of the event. The author is describing in a narrative fashion a moment of profound religious import. The showing of his hands and side indicates theologically that there is no distinction between the Jesus of history and the Christ of faith, and more pointedly for the period of time when this gospel was written—the last decade of the first century—there can be no docetism. Jesus is not merely an appearance of a man; the risen Jesus is the same Jesus who lived and was crucified. The disciples rejoice; at this moment the author presents no description of unbelief.

Jesus then breathes on them and gives them the Spirit. These details add to the solemnity of the occasion. In yet another part of John's gospel (16:7) Jesus had said that he could not send the Spirit until he had "gone to the Father," that is, until after an ascension or exaltation.

Therefore, at this juncture in the Johannine account, the ascension has already taken place; that is, an ascension/exaltation occurred on the very day of the resurrection. The Johannine author does not record an ascension some forty days later or even later on in the evening of the same day. Jesus' exaltation took place between the appearance to Mary Magdalene and the appearance to the disciples.

The issue of the imparting of the Spirit and the forgiveness of sins is too involved for this present study;[52] however, neither the text nor the context allows for an interpretation that a "sacrament" of penance was instituted at this time. Indeed, the import of the forgiveness of sins is, textually and contextually, far broader than any sacramental ritual. In the Johannine account there is a clear connection between resurrection/ascension and forgiveness of sins or redemption. John is telling us that we are saved not only by the death of Jesus but also by his resurrection. Salvation in the Christian meaning of this term is an Easter event, not simply a Good Friday event, and salvation can only be interpreted within the context of the resurrection/ascension of Jesus. That Jesus offered "satisfaction" for sin on the cross is not a Johannine approach to "salvation." Even the use of the term "Peace!" is already a message of reconciliation. Any Christian theology of reconciliation that does not include the resurrection/ascension as an essential component would seem to be defective. In the following chapter, we will consider this issue further. Here we note that in the Johannine presentation the resurrection and the sending of the Spirit are interconnected.

When the disciples mentioned this appearance of Jesus to Thomas, who had been absent, he refused to believe. John I brings in the earlier tradition of unbelief. The entire episode involving Thomas might very well be a literary creation of John I himself, basing his text on the earlier accounts of the unbelief of the disciples. John I presents Thomas as unbending in his refusal to believe, a person wanting almost certain proof. The proof that Thomas seems to demand involves the very reality of Jesus as the one who had lived in Palestine. It is equally part of the context that Thomas might also be faulted for not believing his fellow disciples, although this does not seem to be strongly important to John I.

Seven days later Jesus appears to the disciples again, when Thomas—specifically mentioned here by John I as one of the "Twelve"—was with them. John I is using in this pericope an earlier tradition of "apostolic disbelief." The doors are again locked, presumably for the same reasons previously presented by the author. Jesus appears and speaks pointedly to Thomas. When Thomas hears the Lord and evidently sees his hands and side, with the scars of his ordeal, he says: "My Lord and my God!" In the Greek we have *kyrios* and *theos*. In so much of the New Testament the use of the word *kyrios* for Jesus shows that calling Jesus *kyrios* was a way that the early Jesus community expressed its belief that Jesus was God. However, clear statements that Jesus is God are not found with any frequency prior to the resurrection in the New Testament writings, and pre-resurrection episodes in which such a belief is stated in the gospels are generally interpreted by biblical scholars as retrojections of Easter faith into the lifetime of Jesus, for example, the transfiguration.[53] Without the resurrection, belief that Jesus is God is unthinkable. In other words, had there been no resurrection, there would have been no Jesus community and consequently no church.

Brown characterizes this statement of Thomas as "the supreme christological pronouncement of the Fourth Gospel." "It is Thomas who makes clear that one may address Jesus in the same language in which Israel addressed Yahweh."[54] Thomas believes in Yahweh-Jesus. This statement of Thomas is, in John I, a "confession" of faith; it is not a logical conclusion to a scientifically verified situation. This confession, likewise, has liturgical overtones, a sort of doxology. The author ends his gospel with a pastoral note, evidently with his own Jesus community in mind: "Blessed are those who have not seen and yet have believed!" (20:29). In Luke, the author reminds his community of the presence of the risen Lord in the eucharist; in John I the author reminds his community of the presence of the risen Lord in their confession of faith. He places these words in the mouth of Jesus, for it is Jesus himself who remains in the community. "I am with you all days."

With these few narratives on the resurrection of Jesus, John I brings his volume to an end (20:30–31). What has been written has had but one purpose: to bring the readers, that is, his own community, to believe that the earthly Jesus is the messiah, the Son of God. Such belief brings life. Acceptance of Jesus is the heart of the Johannine message, because accepting Jesus is accepting the true meaning of the Father, Yahweh. Accepting Jesus is the true meaning of the Torah, the prophets, and the writings. Accepting Jesus is what Judaism over the past centuries was all about.

7. JOHN II

Chapter 21 in John's gospel is an addition by an unknown author whom we will call John II. It is made up of three parts: (1) the risen Jesus' appearance to some disciples at the sea of Tiberias; (2) the risen Jesus' speaking to Peter; and (3) the [second] conclusion of the gospel.

Text

21 Μετὰ ταῦτα ἐφανέρωσεν ἑαυτὸν πάλιν ὁ Ἰησοῦς τοῖς μαθηταῖς ἐπὶ τῆς θαλάσσης τῆς Τιβεριάδος· ἐφανέρωσεν δὲ οὕτως. 2 ἦσαν ὁμοῦ Σίμων Πέτρος καὶ Θωμᾶς ὁ λεγόμενος Δίδυμος καὶ Ναθαναὴλ ὁ ἀπὸ Κανὰ τῆς Γαλιλαίας καὶ οἱ τοῦ Ζεβεδαίου καὶ ἄλλοι ἐκ τῶν μαθητῶν αὐτοῦ δύο. 3 λέγει αὐτοῖς Σίμων Πέτρος, Ὑπάγω ἁλιεύειν. λέγουσιν αὐτῷ, Ἐρχόμεθα καὶ ἡμεῖς σὺν σοί. ἐξῆλθον καὶ ἐνέβησαν εἰς τὸ πλοῖον, καὶ ἐν ἐκείνῃ τῇ νυκτὶ ἐπίασαν οὐδέν. 4 πρωΐας δὲ ἤδη γενομένης ἔστη Ἰησοῦς εἰς τὸν αἰγιαλόν· οὐ μέντοι ᾔδεισαν οἱ μαθηταὶ ὅτι Ἰησοῦς ἐστιν. 5 λέγει οὖν αὐτοῖς [ὁ] Ἰησοῦς, Παιδία, μή τι προσφάγιον ἔχετε; ἀπεκρίθησαν αὐτῷ, Οὔ. 6 ὁ δὲ εἶπεν αὐτοῖς, Βάλετε εἰς τὰ δεξιὰ μέρη τοῦ πλοίου τὸ δίκτυον, καὶ εὑρήσετε. ἔβαλον οὖν, καὶ οὐκέτι αὐτὸ ἑλκύσαι ἀπὸ τοῦ πλήθους τῶν ἰχθύων. 7 λέγει οὖν ὁ μαθητὴς ἐκεῖνος ὃν ἠγάπα ὁ Ἰησοῦς τῷ Πέτρῳ, Ὁ κύριός ἐστιν. Σίμων οὖν Πέτρος, ἀκούσας ὅτι ὁ κύριός ἐστιν, τὸν ἐπενδύτην διεζώσατο, ἦν γὰρ γυμνός, καὶ ἔβαλεν ἑαυτὸν εἰς τὴν θάλασσαν· 8 οἱ δὲ ἄλλοι μαθηταὶ τῷ πλοιαρίῳ ἦλθον, οὐ γὰρ ἦσαν μακρὰν ἀπὸ τῆς γῆς ἀλλὰ ὡς ἀπὸ

21 After this, Jesus showed himself once more to his disciples at Lake Tiberias. This is how he did it. ²Simon Peter, Thomas (called the Twin), Nathanael (the one from Cana in Galilee), the sons of Zebedee, and two other disciples of Jesus were all together. ³Simon Peter said to the others, "I am going fishing."

"We will come with you," they told him. So they went and got into the boat; but all that night they did not catch a thing. ⁴As the sun was rising, Jesus stood at the water's edge, but the disciples did not know that it was Jesus. ⁵Then he said to them, "Young men, haven't you caught anything?"

"Not a thing," they answered.

⁶He said to them, "Throw your net out on the right side of the boat, and you will find some." So they threw the net out, and could not pull it back in, because they had caught so many fish.

⁷The disciple whom Jesus loved said to Peter, "It is the Lord!" When Simon Peter heard that it was the Lord, he wrapped his outer garment around him (for he had taken his clothes off) and jumped into the water. ⁸The other disciples came to shore in the boat, pulling the net full

πηχῶν διακοσίων, σύροντες τὸ δίκτυον τῶν ἰχθύων. 9 ὡς οὖν ἀπέβη-
σαν εἰς τὴν γῆν βλέπουσιν
ἀνθρακιὰν κειμένην καὶ ὀψάριον
ἐπικείμενον καὶ ἄρτον. 10 λέγει
αὐτοῖς ὁ Ἰησοῦς, Ἐνέγκατε ἀπὸ
τῶν ὀψαρίων ὧν ἐπιάσατε νῦν. 11
ἀνέβη οὖν Σίμων Πέτρος καὶ
εἵλκυσεν τὸ δίκτυον εἰς τὴν γῆν
μεστὸν ἰχθύων μεγάλων ἑκατὸν
πεντήκοντα τριῶν· καὶ τοσούτων
ὄντων οὐκ ἐσχίσθη τὸ δίκτυον. 12
λέγει αὐτοῖς ὁ Ἰησοῦς, Δεῦτε
ἀριστήσατε. οὐδεὶς δὲ ἐτόλμα τῶν
μαθητῶν ἐξετάσαι αὐτόν, Σὺ τίς εἶ;
εἰδότες ὅτι ὁ κύριός ἐστιν. 13
ἔρχεται Ἰησοῦς καὶ λαμβάνει τὸν
ἄρτον καὶ δίδωσιν αὐτοῖς, καὶ τὸ
ὀψάριον ὁμοίως. 14 τοῦτο ἤδη
τρίτον ἐφανερώθη Ἰησοῦς τοῖς
μαθηταῖς ἐγερθεὶς ἐκ νεκρῶν.

Jesus and Peter

15 Ὅτε οὖν ἠρίστησαν λέγει τῷ
Σίμωνι Πέτρῳ ὁ Ἰησοῦς, Σίμων
Ἰωάννου, ἀγαπᾷς με πλέον τούτων;
λέγει αὐτῷ, Ναί, κύριε, σὺ οἶδας
ὅτι φιλῶ σε. λέγει αὐτῷ, Βόσκε τὰ
ἀρνία μου. 16 λέγει αὐτῷ πάλιν
δεύτερον, Σίμων Ἰωάννου, ἀγαπᾷς
με; λέγει αὐτῷ, Ναί, κύριε, σὺ
οἶδας ὅτι φιλῶ σε. λέγει αὐτῷ, Ποί-
μαινε τὰ πρόβατά μου. 17 λέγει
αὐτῷ τὸ τρίτον, Σίμων Ἰωάννου,
φιλεῖς με; ἐλυπήθη ὁ Πέτρος ὅτι
εἶπεν αὐτῷ τὸ τρίτον, Φιλεῖς με;
καὶ λέγει αὐτῷ, Κύριε, πάντα σὺ
οἶδας, σὺ γινώσκεις ὅτι φιλῶ σε.
λέγει αὐτῷ, Βόσκε τὰ πρόβατά
μου. 18 ἀμὴν ἀμὴν λέγω σοι, ὅτε
ἦς νεώτερος, ἐζώννυες σεαυτὸν

of fish. They were not very far from land, about a hundred yards away. [9]When they stepped ashore they saw a charcoal fire there with fish on it, and some bread. [10]Then Jesus said to them, "Bring some of the fish you have just caught."

[11]Simon Peter went aboard and dragged the net ashore, full of big fish, a hundred and fifty-three in all; even though there were so many, still the net did not tear. [12]Jesus said to them, "Come and eat." None of the disciples dared ask him, "Who are you?" because they knew it was the Lord. [13]So Jesus went over, took the bread, and gave it to them; he did the same with the fish.

[14]This, then, was the third time Jesus showed himself to the disciples after he was raised from death.

Jesus and Peter

[15]After they had eaten, Jesus said to Simon Peter, "Simon, son of John, do you love me more than these?"

"Yes, Lord," he answered, "you know that I love you."

Jesus said to him, "Take care of my lambs." [16]A second time Jesus said to him, "Simon, son of John, do you love me?"

"Yes, Lord," he answered, "you know that I love you."

Jesus said to him, "Take care of my sheep." [17]A third time Jesus said, "Simon, son of John, do you love me?"

Peter became sad because Jesus asked him the third time, "Do you love me?" and said to him, "Lord,

καὶ περιεπάτεις ὅπου ἤθελες· ὅταν δὲ γηράσῃς, ἐκτενεῖς τὰς χεῖράς σου, καὶ ἄλλος σε ζώσει καὶ οἴσει ὅπου οὐ θέλεις. 19 τοῦτο δὲ εἶπεν σημαίνων ποίῳ θανάτῳ δοξάσει τὸν θεόν. καὶ τοῦτο εἰπὼν λέγει αὐτῷ Ἀκολούθει μοι.

you know everything; you know that I love you!"

Jesus said to him, "Take care of my sheep. [18]I tell you the truth: when you were young you used to fasten your belt and go anywhere you wanted to; but when you are old you will stretch out your hands and someone else will tie them and take you where you don't want to go." [19](In saying this Jesus was indicating the way in which Peter would die and bring glory to God.) Then Jesus said to him, "Follow me!"

Jesus and the Beloved Disciple

20 Ἐπιστραφεὶς ὁ Πέτρος βλέπει τὸν μαθητὴν ὃν ἠγάπα ὁ Ἰησοῦς ἀκολουθοῦντα, ὃς καὶ ἀνέπεσεν ἐν τῷ δείπνῳ ἐπὶ τὸ στῆθος αὐτοῦ καὶ εἶπεν, Κύριε, τίς ἐστιν ὁ παραδιδούς σε; 21 τοῦτον οὖν ἰδὼν ὁ Πέτρος λέγει τῷ Ἰησοῦ, Κύριε, οὗτος δὲ τί; 22 λέγει αὐτῷ ὁ Ἰησοῦς, Ἐὰν αὐτὸν θέλω μένειν ἕως ἔρχομαι, τί πρὸς σέ; σύ μοι ἀκολούθει. 23 ἐξῆλθεν οὖν οὗτος ὁ λόγος εἰς τοὺς ἀδελφοὺς ὅτι ὁ μαθητὴς ἐκεῖνος οὐκ ἀποθνήσκει. οὐκ εἶπεν δὲ αὐτῷ ὁ Ἰησοῦς ὅτι οὐκ ἀποθνήσκει, ἀλλ᾽, Ἐὰν αὐτὸν θέλω μένειν ἕως ἔρχομαι [, τί πρὸς σέ];
24 Οὗτός ἐστιν ὁ μαθητὴς ὁ μαρτυρῶν περὶ τούτων καὶ γράψας ταῦτα, καὶ οἴδαμεν ὅτι ἀληθὴς αὐτοῦ ἡ μαρτυρία ἐστίν.

Jesus and the Other Disciple

[20]Peter turned around and saw behind him that other disciple, whom Jesus loved—the one who had leaned close to Jesus at the meal and asked, "Lord, who is going to betray you?" [21]When Peter saw him, he said to Jesus, "Lord, what about this man?"
[22]Jesus answered him, "If I want him to live until I come, what is that to you? Follow me!"
[23]So a report spread among the followers of Jesus that this disciple would not die. But Jesus did not say that he would not die; he said, "If I want him to live until I come, what is that to you?"
[24]He is the disciple who spoke of these things, the one who also wrote them down; and we know that what he said is true.

Conclusion

25 Ἔστιν δὲ καὶ ἄλλα πολλὰ ἃ ἐποίησεν ὁ Ἰησοῦς, ἅτινα ἐὰν

[25]Now, there are many other things that Jesus did. If they were all

γράφηται καθ᾽ ἕν, οὐδ᾽ αὐτὸν οἶμαι   written down one by one, I suppose
τὸν κόσμον χωρῆσαι τὰ γραφόμενα   that the whole world could not hold
βιβλία.   the books that would be written.

Comment

This chapter of the Johannine gospel has antiquity on its side. P66 and Tertullian attest to this. Scholars will undoubtedly continue to research its origin and its connection to the gospel itself. Internal to this final chapter or epilogue is the question of the relationship between vv. 1–14 (section 1 above) and vv. 15–23 (section 2 above). Even section 1 may be composed of several previous strands of data, or at least a tradition of an episode with a catch of fish and an episode with a meal.

In the New Testament (Paul, Luke, Mark II, and also the non-canonical *Gospel of Peter*), there is an indication of an appearance of the risen Lord to Peter, even, perhaps, a first appearance. Vv. 1–14 may be a Johannine version of this Petrine tradition. In this version of John II, the Beloved Disciple makes the confession: "It is the Lord!" Peter then jumps overboard and comes to shore. There are definite relationships between this account and that of Lk 5:1–11. It is quite possible that both Luke and John II are using the same earlier material, each in his own way. It may be easier to consider the episode in Luke as more natural, since the disciples were still in the fishing business. After the resurrection, they did not seem to continue in the fishing business. However, if the male disciples, and Peter in particular, had returned to Galilee after the death of Jesus, discouraged and dismayed because of the brutal ending of Jesus, then a return to fishing could be seen as a possibility.

The key to this section of John II is the phrase "Jesus revealed himself" *(ephanerōsen)*. God takes the initiative, and this manifestation of Jesus, of God's glory, is a theme that runs through the entire Johannine gospel. In the Johannine theology there is a revelatory aspect to Jesus' life, death, and resurrection. This is not a revelation simply for the sake of revelation; rather, it is a revelation made to a group who subsequently preached the good news of this revelation. In other words, the revelation made by God in the Jesus-event is not a personal, private matter; it has a communal dimension. John II is telling his readers something about their own community as well as a narrative about some of the disciples including Peter.

In the meal part of this episode, we have again a connection with other resurrection episodes, involving a meal (Luke, Acts, Mark II). Besides using this meal motif, John II also has a Petrine commission. The threefold question, "Simon, Son of John, do you love me?" leads up to the commission itself. Peter professes his love, a profession made much more poignant since he has denied Jesus, also in a threefold way. With each of Peter's professions, Jesus makes a response: "Feed my lambs; tend my sheep; feed my little sheep." This "commissioning" squares well with the "catching of fish," which has the connotation of making disciples.

Could one also see a eucharistic symbolism in this meal of John II? Biblical scholars are not in agreement on this matter. There are some reasons in favor of such a symbolic connection, but there are other factors that militate against such eucharistic overtones.

Since this volume is concerned with the resurrection narratives, this is not the place to discuss the position of Peter in the early church structure, and therefore the papal structure of later years. That Peter is commissioned fits in well with most of the resurrection appearances, in which there is also some charge of mission. In John II, Peter is clearly called on for an "apostolic mission" or "apostolic discipleship," and also for some sort of authoritative commission. To find in this commissioning an explicit statement that Peter is above all other members of the Twelve seems to go far beyond either the text or the context of John II.

The fate of Peter is also referred to in John II. Biblical scholars have at times argued that the text itself has been somewhat reshuffled. Are vv. 18–23 an addition to the original text, as Bultmann suggested?[55] Or are vv. 20–23 perhaps an added section? No doubt the discussion will continue on the relationships and interrelationships of various verses in this section, either among themselves or with the entire chapter. It seems more than likely that Peter had already died when this part of the gospel was written, and that he had even died as a martyr. There is a pastoral question that appears in this section of John II, which some of the community to which John II belonged posed with insistence: If the end-time has already started, and if the resurrection has already begun, why would there be hostility to those who preach the good news, and why would discipleship end in ignominious death? It is not insignificant, then, that the risen Lord and God in John II says to the still earth-bound Peter, "Follow me!" right after he had mentioned that Peter was going to die at someone else's hands. Discipleship of the risen Lord and God does not mean that risen life, with its lack of pain, death, and sin, has fully commenced. Risen life is indeed "already," but it is also "not yet," and the negativity of the "not yet" can involve a disciple in a fate similar to the crucified Lord. Peter is no exception.

John II adds still another voice to the many who speak about the risen Lord. In his testimony we find themes supported by other sources as well: the appearances are effected by Jesus [God] not by any human effort; Peter is singled out in a special way; an appearance includes a mission and a commission; risen life, which has already begun, does not preclude death and hostility here on earth; belief in the risen Jesus involves a price that a disciple of the Lord must be willing to pay. In all of this there are surely many pastoral overtones, which indicate that the author was not simply completing the gospel text with additional information about Jesus but that he wanted to say something rather specific to the community out of which and for which he was writing this chapter of the Johannine gospel. Although it is an appended chapter, it remains part of the canonical New Testament, and as such it too must be considered the revealed Word of God.

8. PAUL

Of all the writers of the New Testament, Paul is the only one who personally witnessed the risen Lord and has, consequently, written about this encounter from the standpoint of his own experience. Nonetheless, it is necessary to keep in mind certain characteristics of this man, Paul, as he speaks to us in his letters about the experience of the risen Lord.

First, Paul was a Jew of the pharisaic tradition (2 Cor 11:22; Phil 3:5–6; Gal 1:14), which believed in the resurrection from the dead. Before his conversion he was called Saul, and he did not need an experience of a risen Jesus to bring him to belief in the resurrection, which was a hallmark of true pharisaical teaching. Belief in the resurrection from the dead—and, for a Jewish scholar, belief therefore in bodily resurrection—was a given. Paul had no need to be convinced of a bodily resurrection; it was already part of his belief-system, and not simply a part but a central aspect of his belief system.

For Paul, then, Jesus' resurrection was not a "proof." Paul had not been looking for some sort of external proof, so that his own faith in the bodily resurrection from the dead might be substantiated. This aspect of

Paul's own belief should caution us, as we read through his letters, for we cannot read his comments on the resurrection as a sort of "proof." We cannot read his comments with our own presuppositions. Rather, we must strive to see what were Paul's own presuppositions on this matter of resurrection.

As a well-educated and pious pharisaical Jew, Paul believed that the bodily resurrection from the dead was not an individual event. Evans notes that "resurrection is certainly not something which could have been arrived at by reflection on the Old Testament."[56] Evans notes that apocrypha and apocalyptic literature are needed for such a belief; he cites such works as 2 Esdras, 2 Maccabees, the Wisdom of Solomon, *1* and *2 Enoch, 2 Baruch, Jubilees,* the *Assumption of Moses,* the *Psalms of Solomon,* 4 Maccabees, and (if pre-Christian in origin) the *Testaments of the Twelve Patriarchs.* In Jewish thought, the belief that there might be life after death begins to emerge only from about the time of Daniel (ca. 165 B.C.E.) and develops slowly down to the end of the first century C.E.

At the time of Paul, there were many variations in the way some Jews, but not all, came to consider life after death, or the bodily resurrection from the dead. D. S. Russell and P. Hoffmann trace the many variations, the most important of which seem to be the following: (1) There would be a resurrection of good Jews only *(Psalms of Solomon, 1 Enoch).* (2) There would be a resurrection of all Jews, good and evil, with a general judgment, in which the good would be rewarded with the kingdom, and the evil would be punished by a "second death" or by Gehenna. In this approach, bodily resurrection by itself would not necessarily be something salutary, since evil Jews would also be raised from death in bodily form, but would not be "saved." Salvation is something distinct from bodily resurrection (Daniel, *1 Enoch, 2 Baruch*). (3) There would be a resurrection of all men and women, Jews and gentiles alike, and for judgment as in (2) above (*Sibylline Oracles,* 2 Esdras, *Testament of the Twelve Patriarchs*).

Besides these variations of the resurrection, the literature also attests to variants regarding place, time, and form. It would be difficult to discover exactly the way in which Saul, prior to his "conversion" to Jesus, understood the resurrection. However, in all of these variants, the resurrection is seen in a collective form. Jesus' resurrection, from this Jewish background, cannot be understood as an isolated, personal, individual, unique situation. If Jesus did rise bodily from the dead, then his resurrection is at the same time related to the bodily resurrection of others (good Jews only, or all Jews, or Jews and gentiles); and the opposite is true as well—the resurrection of others is related to the resurrection of Jesus.

Of key importance, however, is the fact that Paul is the only New Testament author who out of his own personal experience records a description of an appearance of the risen Lord, and he does this, as we shall see, with a great deal of reticence. Keeping in mind these items in Paul's own theological background, let us consider Paul's presentation of the resurrection.

The Appearance to Paul
According to His Own Writings

In his letter to the Galatians, Paul writes:

> The fact is, brothers, and I want you to realize this, the Good News I preached is not a human message that I was given by men; it is something I learned only through a revelation of Jesus Christ. (1:11–12)

In this section, Paul uses the word "reveal," which he repeats once more in v. 16: "to reveal his Son in me." Paul considered the appearance of Jesus to him, then, as a revelation. Revelations have, as we know, ordinarily been called "religious experiences." Prior to this experience of the risen Lord, Paul was not an irreligious man; he was, rather, a deeply committed religious person, and in this respect he resembled all the other disciples of Jesus. Paul was not "converted" from being ungodly to God-fearing, from being irreligious to religious. Even Paul's antipathy to the Jesus community, which Luke in Acts tends to exaggerate and embellish, stems from his religious beliefs. Paul indicates this when he presents elements of his own autobiography:

> Take any man who thinks he can rely on what is physical; I am even better qualified. I was born of the race of Israel, and of the tribe of Benjamin, a Hebrew born of Hebrew parents, and I was circumcised when I was eight days old. As for the Law, I was a Pharisee; as for working for religion, I was a persecutor of the Church; as far as the Law can make you perfect, I was faultless. (Phil 3:4–6)

Paul's words are very clear; he was a religious man and even his stance against the Jesus group was founded on religious reasons. Paul's religious base was already an intrinsic part of his character, when Jesus appeared to him in this "revelation." We might describe Paul's religious situation as follows: after this revelation of the risen Jesus, Paul came to believe no longer simply in Yahweh but in Yahweh-Jesus.

This revelation is not seen by Paul as a private apparition, for in the letter to the Galatians Paul clearly places this revelation within the context of his own prophetic vocation. Biblical scholars, for example, X. Léon-Dufour and L. Cerfaux, connect this passage to the verse that follows—Paul's mention of his revelation: "The God who had specially chosen me while I was still in my mother's womb called me through his grace and chose to reveal his Son in me, so that I might preach the Good News about him to the pagans" (Gal 1:15–16), with Is 49:1: "Yahweh called me before I was born. From my mother's womb he pronounced my name." This connection with Isaiah makes explicit the "mission" aspect of Paul's encounter with the risen Jesus. Isaiah had been called to a mission by Yahweh, long before he even knew about it—"before I was born," and "from my mother's womb."

In Galatians, Paul indicates also that it was the Lord himself who revealed himself to Paul, and that this revelation involved a mission. It was the Lord himself, no other person, who commissioned Paul. In manifesting himself to him, Christ conferred on Paul his own mission.[57] In all of this Paul clearly states that it was God who took the initiative; Paul is the object of a divine action. This action of God included the "vocation" of Paul, a mission that involved his own life and the lives of others. Paul simply uses the term "revelation" *(apocalypsis)* and "to reveal" *(apocalypsai)*. It does not seem that Paul, at this time in his life, had been in Jerusalem: "It should come as no surprise that there is no mention in his epistles of Paul having been anywhere in or near Jerusalem prior to his conversion. Indeed, there is strong reason to suspect the contrary."[58] Acts overstates the matter when it says that Paul had been brought up in Jerusalem and had sat at the feet of Gamaliel (22:3), or that he had taken part in the killing of Stephen (8:1; 7:58; 22:20). Nor had Paul brought anyone from Damascus to Jerusalem (9:2). All of these seem to be Lucan embellishments. Rather, it appears that at this juncture of his life Paul was not personally known either in Jerusalem or in Judea. Moreover, after the revelation of Jesus, Paul did not go to Jerusalem. In fact, we do not know anything about his life for the next "three years" (Gal 1:17–18). If he withdrew into some area of Arabia, more than likely an urban area, he was trying to reassemble his life. After all, he had pursued biblical studies from an early age; he had done fairly well within the Jewish religious structure; and his future seemed bright. The revelation of the risen Lord altered his life plans and life goals. Undoubtedly, he needed time to come to grips with the changes this "conversion" to Yahweh-Jesus involved. He writes in Philippians: "Because of Christ I have come to consider all these advantages that I had as disadvantages" (3:7). Long before Nietzsche, we see here a case of the "reevaluation of all values." Only after this lengthy, rather hidden period of his life, did Paul go to Jerusalem to see Cephas.

In Philippians 3:8, Paul sees that there is a "supreme advantage of knowing Christ Jesus, my Lord." This is not a customary way of speaking for Paul. Generally, he speaks about being "known by God" not "knowing God." If we do know God it is only in a partial way, through a mirror, darkly. In the revelation that God made to Paul, there is some sort of knowledge on Paul's part: a profound knowledge that transformed his entire life and his entire being. Beyond that, Paul is quite reserved in what he says.

Paul also speaks about being captured: "Not that I have become perfect yet: I have not yet won, but I am still running, trying to capture the prize for which Christ Jesus captured me" (Phil 3:12). A. Deissmann saw this being captured as a Hellenistic type of conversion.[59] J. Lebreton described it as a violent seizure by God.[60] Cerfaux describes it as being touched by the resurrection, in the sense that Christ makes Paul a part of risen life.[61] Perhaps no satisfactory resolution of the matter will ever be established, but the "being captured" already indicates that the initiative is with God and the capturing was for a purpose. Paul is still running, that is, in his efforts to bring the good news to the world. The entire tenor of this section also indicates that the "capturing" is not a physical or bodily experience, but rather a deep, spiritual experience. Paul is evidently alluding to his own religious experience in his encounter with the risen Christ.

In 1 Corinthians we have another reference to Paul's religious experience. In defending his position to the Corinthian community, he says: "Have I not seen Jesus, our Lord?" Later, in this same letter he says: "and last of all he appeared to me too" (15:3–8). In contrast to the letter to the Philippians, in which he speaks of "my Lord," Paul, in the letter to the Corinthians, says "our Lord." Once again, Paul is referring to the origin of his own vocation and apostolate, for this is the very reason he is claiming acceptance and credibility in the Corinthian community. "Our" Lord appeared to Paul, not for himself alone, since the Lord is already shared (our), and since the appearance of the Lord to Paul makes him as acceptable as all other apostles. Paul clearly indicates that his "seeing" the Lord was the same as Peter's "seeing" the Lord.

In his conclusion to a section on the resurrection appearance to Paul, Léon-Dufour first of all says:

> The former persecutor has now become a witness of the grace of God. Thus God's unmerited initiative is emphasized. . . . The persecutor becomes an adherent of the faith, the runner is overtaken in his race, he who did not know Christ "knows" him.[62]

Paul is a transformed individual, and this transformation is described in a variety of terms: a revelation, being seized by Christ, knowing Christ, seeing Christ, an appearance. In all of this, God is presented as the initiator, and through the event Paul is given a mission. The more one reflects on this aspect of Paul's life, the more clearly one sees that this experience of the risen Lord, no matter how it might be described, was fundamentally a religious experience in the life of this man, Paul. This means that Paul, who is the only person among all the New Testament authors who has written from a personal and experiential standpoint about the appearance of the risen Lord, describes this occurrence in religious-experience terms. All the others—Mark I, Mark II, Matthew, Luke, John I, John II—did not write from their own personal experience of a revelation or of an appearance of the risen Lord. They all talk about someone else's experience. Paul, however, talks about his own experience, and he talks about it as a religious experience. Beyond that, Paul equates his experience of the risen Lord with the appearances to Peter, to James, to the apostles, to the five hundred, which means that we, for our part, should interpret these same appearances to Peter, James, the apostles, and so on, in religious-experience terms as well. Paul's accounting provides us with one of the major hermeneutical keys for an understanding of what the "apparitions" of the risen Lord were all about.

The Appearance to Paul Found in Acts

When we consider Paul's "conversion" as recorded in the Acts of the Apostles (9:1–19; 22:6–16; and 26:12–18), we find ourselves closer to the style of the gospel accounts of the resurrection appearances than to the style of Paul's own personal considerations of Jesus' appearance to him. The picture of Paul that is presented to us in Acts does not coincide well with the portrait of Paul that we find in Paul's own letters. Indeed, scholars like M. Dibelius and E. Haenchen, to mention only two, have raised serious doubts that the author of Acts even knew Paul.[63]

In Acts, a narrative style has taken over, which means, usually, that some point is being made by storytelling. The "conversion" of Paul is narrated on three distinct occasions in Acts, and each version is a little different. The three accounts, however, seem to agree on the following points: (1) Saul is en route to persecute the Jewish Jesus believers; (2) he is met by Jesus himself; (3) he is brought to the ground; (4) Saul recognizes and believes in the risen Lord; and (5) the mission to the non-Jews is entrusted to him. The remaining details of the three accounts are quite varied. This is evident when they are viewed in a synoptic way.

VERSION 1 (ACTS 9:1–9)	VERSION 2 (ACTS 22:6–16)	VERSION 3 (ACTS 26:12–18)
Meanwhile Saul was still breathing threats to slaughter the Lord's disciples. He had gone to the high priest and asked for letters addressed to the synagogues in Damascus that would authorize him to arrest any followers of the Way, men or women that he could find.		
Suddenly, while he was traveling to Damascus and just before I reached the city, there came a light from heaven all around him.	I was on that journey and nearly at Damascus when about midday a bright light from heaven suddenly shone around me.	And at midday, as I was on my way, Majesty, I saw a light brighter than the sun come down from heaven. It shone brilliantly around me and my fellow-travelers.

He fell to the ground and then he heard a voice saying: "Saul, Saul, why are you persecuting me?" "Who are you, Lord?" he asked, and the voice answered: "I am Jesus, and you are persecuting me. Get up now, and go into the city, and you will be told what you have to do."

I fell to the ground and . . . and heard a voice saying "Saul, Saul, why are you persecuting me?" and . . . he said to me, "I am . . . Jesus, the Nazarene, and you are persecuting me." The people with me saw the light but did not hear his voice as he spoke to me. I said: "What am I to do Lord?" The Lord answered: "Stand up and go into Damascus and there you will be told what you have been appointed to do."

We all fell to the ground, and I heard a voice saying to me in Hebrew, "Saul, Saul, why are you persecuting me? It is hard for you, kicking like this against the goad." Then I said: Who are you, Lord?" And the Lord answered, "I am Jesus, and you are persecuting me. But get up and and stand on your feet, for I have appeared to you for this reason to appoint you as my servant and as witness of this vision in which you have seen me, and of others in which I shall appear to you. I shall deliver you from the people and from the pagans, to whom I am sending you to open their eyes, so that they may turn from darkness to light, from the dominion of Satan to God, and receive, through faith in me, forgiveness of their sins and a share in the inheritance of the sanctified.

The men traveling
with Saul stood
there speechless,
for though they
heard the voice
they could see
no one.

Saul got up from the
ground, but even with
his eyes wide open, he
could see nothing at
all, and they had to
lead him into Damas-
cus by the hand.
For three days he was
without his sight, took
neither food nor drink.

The light had been so
dazzling that I was blind
and my companions had
to take me by the hand;
so I came to Damascus.

A disciple called Ana-
nias, who lived in
Damascus, had
a vision in which he
heard the Lord say
to him: "Ananias!"
When he replied,
"Here I am Lord," the
Lord said: "You must
go to the Straight Street,
and ask at the house
of Judas for someone
called Saul, who comes
from Tarsus."

Someone called Ananias,
a devout follower of the
Law and highly thought
of by all Jews living
there, came to see me
and said: "Brother Saul,
receive your sight."
Instantly my sight came
back and I was able to
see him.

The texts from chapters 9 and 22 continue the story of the meeting of Ananias and Saul. Haenchen, following Dibelius, considers these accounts to be popular traditions regarding Paul's conversion.[64] However, larger issues must be taken into account before one concentrates on these three accounts of Paul's "conversion." What is the relationship between Luke and Paul? Did Luke actually know Paul? Did he travel with

Paul, as much of the latter part of Acts might indicate? Why is there such a divergence between Paul's approach to Jesus and Luke's? Why is the picture of Paul in Acts markedly different from that in Paul's own writings? These and many others are the kinds of questions that need to be considered before one undertakes any analysis of the three versions of Paul's "conversion" described in Acts.

It would be far beyond this present volume to enter into these questions in any detail. Dibelius, in contemporary times, has moved these kinds of questions to the foreground. His analysis of the speeches in Acts has indicated that Acts cannot be seen as a "historical" narrative in the modern sense of the word "historical." Remarkably, at about the same time in which the authors of the gospels were writing their compositions, Tacitus was writing the *Annals of Rome*. In these *Annals* (11.24) Tacitus presents us with a speech by the emperor Claudius in which he describes the right of honors to the Gauls. This speech was delivered before the Roman senate. The Latin has a certain elegance about it, and the emperor's speech, in Tacitus's account, sounds worthy of the occasion. However, in our own century scholars have discovered another version of this speech, which is quite different from the Latin form of Tacitus. Tacitus the historian surely knew what Claudius had said, but the emperor's speech did not have the elegance and polish an imperial oration ought to have. Tacitus, therefore, rewrote the speech, providing it with imperial grandeur. His historical work, *The Annals of Rome,* was meant to edify the younger generations of the Roman aristocratic world. Claudius's speech, as delivered, would only horrify them; its Latin forms were poorly constructed; it needed to be recast in regal form. As a historian, Tacitus felt no hesitation in doing this.[65] History, in the first century C.E., did not demand the facticity of the twentieth century. What Tacitus did without compunction—changing history to meet certain standards of morality and formality—the biblical writers also did.

Flavius Josephus was no different. He too was a historian, living at almost the same period. His *Antiquities* presents the books of Moses as true history.[66] Nonetheless, Josephus interprets the Mosaic books in a most free and allegorical way. For instance, Josephus describes the situation of Abraham and Isaac, when they were on their way to offer a sacrifice. Presumably, they spoke to each other for the last time as they were walking up the hill. But after Abraham had taken up the knife to kill Isaac, yet before the angel came to stop him, Abraham, in

Josephus's account, delivers a lengthy speech to his terrified son. This speech is Josephus's creation, which he presents as history—but not in the twentieth-century understanding of history. Von Ranke's approach to history, so dominant in our own century, was not the approach of the first-century writers.

Today we have many "historical" novels, but we realize that the primary genre is novel or story. History is simply background. The authors of these "historical novels" create dialogue, narrative incidents, etc., and the more they do this, the better the novel becomes, but often the worse the history becomes. For writers in the first few centuries C.E., speeches and narrative accounts clarified and interpreted the major points that were being made. These early authors had no intention of falsifying "history." They were writing history in a moral and uplifting way; their purpose was to present heroes: emperors who acted and spoke as emperors should, even though in real life they hardly measured up to such imperial standards. They were writing religious history in which the most important aspect was to interpret clearly what earlier religious patriarchs had done. If this meant adding dialogue, creating narratives, then such measures were to be expected.

Luke is no different. The speeches in Acts are all written by Luke for a specific purpose as far as his text is concerned. They are not actual transcriptions of Peter's speeches or Paul's speeches or Stephen's speeches. The narrative sections of Acts bear a similar interpretation. Often a speech is broken off by some external situation, which brings out the main point Luke is attempting to underscore, for example, 22:1–21, with the point about the mission to non-Jews; see also 7:53; 23:6; 10:7. Luke creatively presents a speech and just as creatively formulates a narrative.[67]

If this aspect of presentation is frequent throughout Acts, then the three versions of Paul's "conversion" might easily share in this creative and artistic approach of Luke as well. Moreover, the divergences between the understanding of Paul in Acts and the picture of Paul in his own writings is extensive enough to suggest that Luke did not really travel with Paul and was not personally close to Paul. The three versions, then, might in reality be less "historical" and more "literary."

G. Lohfink has summarized the scholarship dealing with the genre of these three accounts, and he cautions us not to take these versions in any literal sense.[68] As regards the form of these accounts, there seems to be an "appearance dialogue" genre in all three versions:

Introductory conversation	. . . speaking to him
Twofold naming	Saul, Saul
Question of Jesus	Why do you persecute me?
Introduction of Paul	. . . but he said
Paul's question	Who are you, Lord?
Introduction of answer	But he said . . .
Self-revelation of Jesus	I am Jesus and you are persecuting me.
Commission	Get up and . . .

There appears to be something contrived or stylistic about this appearance of Jesus to Paul. If one looks through the Old Testament there are similar appearances of God (or an angel of God).

JACOB: FIRST ACCOUNT

In the command to Jacob to return to his home country, the angel of God appears: "In the dream, the angel of God called to me: 'Jacob!' And I answered: 'I am here.' He said, 'Look up and see. . . . I am the God of Bethel'" (Gn 31:11–13).

The call:	Jacob
The answer:	I am here
Self-revelation:	I am the God of Bethel
Commission:	Go back to the land in which you were born

JACOB: SECOND ACCOUNT

In the command of God to Jacob to go to Egypt, we read: "God spoke to Israel in a vision at night: 'Jacob! Jacob!' and I answered: 'I am here.' He replied: 'I am God, the God of your fathers,' he continued: 'Do not be afraid of going down to Egypt . . .'" (Gn 46:2–5).

The call:	Jacob! Jacob!
The answer:	I am here
Self-revelation:	I am God, the God of your fathers
Commission:	Go to Egypt

MOSES

In the appearance of God to Moses in the burning bush: "God called to him from the middle of the bush, 'Moses! Moses!' He said: 'Here I am!' He answered, 'Come no nearer.' He said, 'Take off your shoes, for the place on which you stand is holy ground. I am the God of your fathers, the God of Abraham, the God of Isaac and the God of Jacob'" (Ex 3:2–10).

The call:	Moses! Moses!
The answer:	Here I am
Self-revelation:	I am the God of your fathers
Commission:	I am sending you to Pharaoh

VARIOUS OTHERS

One could also consider Gn 22:1, 11 during the account of the offering of Isaac by Abraham, or 1 Sm 2:4–14 and the first call to the young prophet Samuel. In all of these there is a pattern, a sort of literary genre to describe a revelation or a great religious experience: (1) the calling by name; (2) the answer of the individual; (3) the self-revelation of God; and (4) a commission by God.

In Acts, Luke continues to use this Jewish genre to indicate a revelation from God to a person. For instance, in the call of God to Ananias (9:10ff.), we find a pattern that is almost the same as that in Genesis 22, in which God calls Abraham. There seem to be four elements involved in these appearance narratives: (1) the double name calling (Jacob, Jacob! Saul, Saul!); (2) the answer or questioning by the one involved (Who are you? or: I am here); (3) the self-revelation of God (I am the God of your fathers); (4) the commissioning to do something (Go and do . . .).

Apparently, this was a Semitic stylistic form or literary genre that expressed an appearance of God to someone. This form was not be taken literally in the sense that this is precisely the "historical" way it happened. Rather, by using this stereotyped form, the various biblical authors were alerting their readers that God had intervened in the life of some major religious figure. Luke's use of this genre would say to his readers, particularly the Jewish readers, that if they believed (as they assuredly did) that God had spoken to Abraham, to Jacob, to Samuel, and so on, the same God has now once again spoken or revealed himself to

Saul. In other words, the revelation made to Saul is equated with the accepted revelations made to Abraham, Jacob, Samuel, and the others. Biblical scholars have compared the Greek version of such Old Testament passages with the Greek text of Acts, and they see a clear connection between God's revelation to Abraham in Genesis and God's revelation to Ananias in Acts. Clearly, Luke is using a stylized genre for a definite theological purpose. That Jesus used precisely those words or that Saul asked precisely those questions appears quite unfounded. If the heart or core of these three versions, the actual appearance of Jesus to Saul, is seen ultimately to be a literary composition, used to express a revelatory event, then the more marginal details in these three versions cannot be taken in any literal, fundamentalist or historical way. The three versions are all composed by the artist Luke. Like Tacitus and like Josephus, Luke tells us a story not to deceive his readers but to indicate what is actually happening: Yahweh-Jesus is revealing himself to Saul. Such a revelation is a religious experience.

Thus, whether one considers the letters of Paul himself or the three accounts of Paul's "conversion" in Acts, the commanding and controlling factor remains: a religious experience. How does one present in writing the profundity of a religious experience? How can one transcribe from the depths of one's being the very experience of God's presence to an individual? In the next chapter, we will take up this approach to the resurrection accounts in a deeper way. Nonetheless, at this juncture of our study, it is important to see that both Paul and Luke are struggling to describe a religious experience: the experience of the risen Jesus, confessed as Yahweh-Jesus.

SUMMARY OF CHAPTER 2

Much more could be said regarding these voices on the resurrection of Jesus. Other New Testament authors could also be cited, for example, the author of the book of Revelation, the author of 1 and 2 Peter, the author of the letter to the Hebrews. In all of these writings, there are clear indications of the early Jesus community's belief in the risen Lord. These additional authors, however, do not focus directly on the resurrection; rather, they treat the resurrection tangentially, whereas the authors mentioned in this present chapter focus directly on the resurrection of Jesus and its impact on the first followers of this same Jesus. With this additional material in mind but not under direct scrutiny, we can make the following statements on the New Testament material.

1. The resurrection sections of the New Testament present the reader with a variety of voices. A major issue in these voices is this: in the resurrection of Jesus God has acted. The resurrection is an action of God.

2. These voices, however, do not present us with a systematic and logical account of the resurrection. In many ways, they do not even provide us with a theology of the resurrection. Each author stresses aspects of the resurrection germane to his own purposes.

3. Nonetheless, the resurrection passages of these authors are considered by the Christian community to be "canonical." In these human words Christians hear the Word of God. No Christian theologian nor Christian leader can teach or preach the resurrection of Jesus with this solid canonical New Testament base.

4. Accordingly, all theological and systematized presentations of the resurrection must be based on and flow from this biblical source. Any and every presentation of the resurrection of Jesus must begin from and be founded on these human words in which we hear the very Word of God, even though these human words speak in many differing ways about the resurrection.

3

A Theology of the Resurrection

In the preceding two chapters, we have first surveyed the work of contemporary scholarship on the resurrection of Jesus. We have noticed that this contemporary scholarship leads one into an approach to the resurrection that is rather different from the approach one finds either in the popular and pastoral area of church life or in the traditional pre–Vatican II theological approach to the resurrection.

In the *popular and pastoral approach* the focus on the resurrection of Jesus has remained more or less physical, historical, or even fundamentalist. In this view, people actually saw Jesus after the resurrection, touched him, heard him, watched him eat—all in the way in which ordinarily people see others, touch others, hear others, and watch others eat. This physical approach to the resurrection guarantees that Jesus had truly risen from the dead. There is, of course, a spiritual dimension to this rather physical approach: namely, we too one day will rise and be with Jesus. Death will not be our final end. Life in heaven is what we hope for, and this hope motivates us to lead better Christian lives now, so that we too will rise from the dead, go to heaven, and be with the risen Jesus. The renewed theological scholarship on the resurrection understands the seeing, hearing, and touching of Jesus' risen body to be secondary issues; even the empty tomb is a secondary issue. Because of this difference in approach and this difference in what is primary and what is secondary, there seems to be a widening divergence between the popular and pastoral approach to the resurrection of Jesus and the theological developments of the past eight decades..

In the pre–Vatican II *theological approach,* the resurrection of Jesus, as we noted in chapter 1, played a rather minor role in the area of

105

christology. Roman Catholic scholars of that period who wrote on christology generally devoted only a page or two to Jesus' resurrection. In the area of Roman Catholic apologetics, the resurrection of Jesus fared better. A more lengthy treatment of the resurrection was made, but controlled by the position that the resurrection "proved" the veracity of Jesus' words, promises, and above all his claim to divinity. Many Protestant theologians, during that same pre–Vatican II period, were struggling to counteract the influence of Schleiermacher on Protestant theology. Contemporary Protestant and Roman Catholic research on the resurrection of Jesus in no way makes apologetics the center or controlling factor of its understanding of the resurrection. Indeed, any effort at apologetics is seen as secondary or even tertiary.

In chapter 2 we considered in some depth the data of the New Testament, that is, the many voices that speak to us about the resurrection of Jesus. We found that there was not a single or monolithic approach to the resurrection of Jesus; rather, the New Testament presents us with a variety of voices and a variety of emphases. In that variety of voices, only one voice spoke from the personal experience of an encounter with the risen Jesus, namely, Paul. In this present study, the voice of Paul has a quite significant position.

In this chapter, I will gather together some of the material from the two preceding chapters in what might be described as a systematic theology of the resurrection of Jesus. Nonetheless, an initial caveat is necessary. Since we are dealing with a profound mystery of our Christian faith, it is next to impossible for anyone to arrive at *the* theology of the resurrection. A transcendent mystery by its very nature disallows any presentation of a comprehensive and final statement, that is, *the theology* of such a mystery. In a totally different philosophical and religious background, the *Tao Te Ching* of Lao Tsu begins:

> The Tao that can be told is not the eternal Tao.
> The name that can be named is not the eternal name.[1]

In this verse, Lao Tsu is saying that if there is an eternal mystery such as Tao, one cannot understand it fully nor name it clearly. Whoever claims to understand it or name it cannot be said to have really understood or named the unending mystery. The Christian belief in the resurrection is just such a mystery: it too can never be understood fully nor named clearly. Church leaders, whether ecclesiastical or theological, can only point to the mystery and describe it in an insufficient way. There never was nor will there ever be *the theology* of the resurrection. Rather, there is with each generation a re-reading of the sacred texts and making these texts meaningful in the concrete lives of each generation. This process is called tradition; it is also called renewal, or even spiritual life and interiorization. The names are many, since the mystery is multidimensional, but each name, inadequate though it might be, means an interpretation of the texts within the framework of a particular lived, communal, Christian experience of the gospel.

Consequently, the following material is presented simply as *a theology* of the resurrection, a gathering together of a few issues that in a gathered state might point to aspects of the mystery of resurrection that will help move the discourse a step further.

PRELIMINARY CONSIDERATIONS

I wish to focus the resurrection material on an issue that for the most part is avoided: namely, the issue of "religious experience." As we have seen in chapter 2, biblical scholars have done a masterful task in providing a clearer understanding of both text and context. They have carefully described the genre an author has used; they have provided historical and Semitic nuances which at times were overlooked. They have also stayed away from any systematic approach, stating at times quite openly that they are biblical scholars not systematic theologians. When one turns to the systematic theologians, even in the renewed research on the resurrection by both Protestant and Roman Catholic scholars, the area of "religious experience" has not been moved to center stage. There seems to be a fear that religious experience opens discourse to something "subjective" and something "personal."

I am in full agreement with such hesitation. From Descartes through Kant and Heidegger, Western philosophy has tended to move into the subjective, and not without strong opposition. In Western philosophical thought, existential phenomenology has been a major force toward authenticating the role of the subjective in human phenomena, and the influence of Kant and Heidegger has entered into the theological world particularly through Bultmann and Tillich, Marèchal and Rahner. Schillebeeckx, particularly in his work on the eucharist, has also infused Western theology with phenomenological thought patterns. A purely objective way of thinking appears to be an impossible goal; there is always something subjective in all human activity, even in the area of science, as M. Polanyi has pointed out. Totally objective language also appears to be an impossible goal, in spite of the efforts of many linguistic philosophers.

There is no doubt that my own theological thought has been deeply influenced by my study of Heidegger, Merleau-Ponty, and Ricoeur, and to some degree Whitehead. Through them I have also been influenced by the way they have interpreted Kant, Hegel, Nietzsche, Freud, and Jung. This contemporary philosophical and even philo-psychological positioning has impacted my study of Alexander of Hales and John Duns Scotus. These may seem like strange bedfellows, but there is some connection between the stress on *haecceitas* in the scotistic framework and the analysis of the *Dasein* in Heidegger.[2]

It is hoped that this philosophical-theological background of my thought will be clear. When, as noted above, I have studied authors writing on the resurrection of Jesus, I have found a strong reticence on their part to say anything about what happened to, in, and with the humanity of Jesus. That Jesus was raised from the dead, that he ascended into heaven—the exaltation motif—that he is with Yahweh as *Kyrios,* that is, "sitting at the right hand of the Father," and that he has sent the Spirit of Holiness to his disciples—all these issues are mentioned. But what about the humanity of Jesus in its own identity? What can we say about the resurrection and Jesus' own experience as a human being? These kinds of questions are not generally addressed. *That* Jesus' human nature was transformed in some way is a major part of the resurrection event; *what* this transformation might be is more often than not described in quite general and abstract terms. This is not meant to be a question of psychologically analyzing how Jesus felt. That is not the issue. Being human on this earth is one way of being human; being human in risen life is quite another way of being human. At the resurrection the human nature of Jesus underwent a major transformation. Is there any way to understand, in some degree, what this transformation involved. I believe there is.

Let us begin with the disciples. At the heart of belief in the risen Jesus, the disciples, both men and women, underwent a faith experience. The deepest reaction to the presence of the risen Jesus in these men and women was a response of faith, which, however, involved a radical change in their religious understanding. They continued to have a self-identity as religious Jewish persons. They came, through their faith response, to the belief that all that Jewish history and the sacred texts had promised was now realized in the Jesus-event, which included his earthly life, his death by crucifixion, and his risen life. Whenever one undergoes a major religious transformation, people have called this change a profound religious experience. The disciples of Jesus were no different from others who, through the centuries, have experienced a religious transformation.

Paul's letters provide us with a major clue to this aspect of the resurrection. Paul clearly believed that the risen Jesus had appeared to him. The risen Jesus had commissioned him to be an apostle, so much so that Paul saw himself on equal footing with the Twelve. In his letters, one might ask, how does he describe this appearance of the risen Jesus? As we shall see, much of the terminology he uses reflects the ways in which others have tended to speak of a religious experience. It is my thesis that this reality of a religious experience serves as a major hermeneutical key to understanding what Paul very cautiously attempts to say about his encounter with the risen Jesus. In Acts a quite different genre is used. We shall compare the two approaches: one by Paul, who is speaking from his own experience; the other by Luke, who is relating the account second-hand. Although Luke uses a very different genre, it is quite consistent throughout the Lucan material.

I wish to stress that an analysis of the resurrection texts on the basis of religious experience does not in any way mean that religious experience is the most important reality of the resurrection event. The most important reality in the resurrection event is and remains the grace-filled and free action of God: God raised Jesus from the dead. The mystery of the resurrection is the mystery of God's own self: the mystery of God's absolute freedom, the mystery of God's unconditional grace, the mystery of God's unending justice and compassion. The mysterious center of the resurrection event remains always with God alone. Everything else is secondary, an effect of the uncaused love of God. This secondary status applies to the human nature of Jesus as well. From a human standpoint, Jesus did not raise himself from the dead; God did. From a human standpoint, Jesus did not merit the resurrection; the absolute free God is not bound by any human work, including the human works of the human Jesus.

The following considerations on the role of religious experience, then, must be seen against this background of God's mystery, God's freedom, God's grace in the resurrection event. The religious experience aspect is a response to what God has done; indeed, religious experience remains the only true and profound way a person of faith can and should respond to the inbreaking presence of God in one's life. It is not that we have loved God first; rather, God has first loved us and given us through grace the very possibility to love God in return. At the heart of religious experience, then, is this human return of love to a prior gift from divine love.

The genre for describing religious experience that one finds in the gospels and Acts deals with the use of language for varying aspects of New Testament thought. The gospels, as is well known, are in a general way divided into three major areas. These can be put into a schematic form:

A	B/1	B/2	C
Preexistence accounts and infancy accounts	The public life of Jesus	The arrest, trial, and death of Jesus	Resurrection accounts: apparitions, empty tomb

Section A. This section uses "beginning language." Here the authors are talking either about the pre-beginning of a human creature— that is, preexistence—or about the pre-birth, that is, from the time of conception onward. In both instances, there was a time when the human nature of Jesus, like all created realities, did not exist. As Tillich said so often: it is an issue of non-being/being. It is an issue of absolute beginning, that is, the coming from non-being into being. Whenever one is asked to talk about absolute beginnings, the answers, if there are any, are highly imaginative. For instance, were one to ask you to describe your conception and birth, you would have no first-hand recollections of this. You could relate what your parents or others might have told you, but this is second-hand. You might say, to borrow from Sartre, that your birth was the greatest event in history, or it was the worst event. In talking about absolute beginnings one does not have to be consistent. On a given occasion, one could say that one's birth was of immense value; on another occasion, the same person might say that his or her birth was of little value. When one attempts to describe one's birthing, there is but one kind of language possible, namely, the language of imagination. Is it not in keeping with this that in the infancy narratives of Matthew and Luke we find poetry, midrash, a fairly contrived Moses-Jesus motif, or a rather contrived John the Baptist-Jesus sequencing. In other words, the poetic aspects of the infancy narratives raise the issue: What is the linguistic genre at work in these verses? Imagination, poetry, midrash, contrived parallelisms, and other such genres are found in all the epic poetry of human culture, from Homer's *Iliad* to the works of Dante, to the plays of Shakespeare, to the poems of T. S. Eliot. The use of imagination in no way necessarily implies falsehood and deceit. Rather, some of the most profound truths have been expressed through imaginative language. Many mystics of all religions have expressed their profound religious experiences through the medium of poetry and imaginative writing.

Section B/1 . . . B/2. In this section we find the public ministry of Jesus and his arrest, trial, and death. I call this "middle language," since it describes events that take place in the middle area of one's life, that is, between the two extremes of conception/birth on the one hand and death on the other. Middle language expresses events and experiences that are common to all men and women: that we talk, that we eat, that we sleep, that we cry, that we walk, that we experience our human life in a thousand ways each day. When we share these middle experiences with others, we do not need to speak in poetry, in imaginative prose, in story, in the artistic symbols of the fine arts. Through our language we generally convey both the thought and the mood in which we find ourselves. It is clear that we still use symbols to communicate: the symbolism of language and facial expression, the symbols of gesture and nonverbal expression, but the linguistic communication is, in and through these symbols, readily understood. One can follow the preaching-teaching-healing career of Jesus in a fairly clear way. Then Jesus went to the sea of Galilee or to Nazareth or to Jerusalem—all these details are fairly self-evident when communicated. We are in the middle of our own lives talking with someone or hearing about someone who is also in the middle of his or her life. Middle language evidences this middle-of-life framework.

Section C. In this section we find existence after death. We even find death itself. This is "ending language." Just as beginning language needed, to a high degree, the use of imagination, so too does ending language. Were one asked to speak about his or her death, the same problems begin to arise that we noted in speaking about one's conception and birth. Even Jesus, whom we believe was raised from the dead, never described what the dying process actually was. No one truly knows how the final stages of the death process are experienced.

That there is imagination at work in the resurrection accounts is clear. Matthew's imagination has given to us the earthquake and the sleeping soldiers together with their awakening and their meeting with the chief priests. He has also given us an account of the exaltation, the ascension, of Jesus. Luke in particular has used ending language in a major way. As we noted above, almost one-half of his chapter on the resurrection event is dedicated to the two disciples and their trip to Emmaus. In this story Luke is expressing to his readers what the presence of the risen Jesus in one's life is all about. In Acts, there is the imaginative use of the forty days, and the apocalyptic and imaginative use of exaltation/ascension material. However, it is in Paul that we see ending language—that is, imaginative language—at work. He uses the term *ōphthē*, which has connections with the theophanies in the Hebrew writings. Paul is saying that Yahweh has "appeared" to him in the same way that Yahweh appeared to Abraham, Moses, Jacob, Samuel, and so on. Luke's threefold account of Paul's conversion also indicates a contrived apparition genre, highly reminiscent of theophanies in the Hebrew writings.

Once more, one might ask: Does not the use of imaginative language in the resurrection narratives compromise their "truth" value? If these accounts really did not happen, what value do they have? When we were children, we heard stories that began: "Once upon a time . . ." Were these stories of no value? Indeed, did we not learn what is and what is not of value precisely from such stories. Later we understood that Hansel and Gretel were not actual historical figures. We learned that Santa Claus was really our mother and father. Although we learned that they did not have that "historical" truth of our family and neighbors, still, through such stories, we learned profound values that have affected our lives. Classical literature of Greece and Rome abounds in such writings. Classical literature in China, Korea, Japan, and Vietnam also employs imaginative literature to speak about profound human truths and values.

Western mystics and Eastern mystics as well have consistently used imaginative language and poetry, painting, and music to convey their deepest religious experiences. It should be of no surprise, given all of this, that both the preexistence and infancy narratives, as well as the resurrection narratives of the New Testament also use poetry and imag-

ination to convey the foundational religious experiences of the Christian community.

CHURCH TEACHING AND
A THEOLOGY OF THE RESURRECTION

Christian theology is not merely the theology of the twentieth century, nor is it simply the theology of the high scholastic period, nor the
theology of the reformation period. Christian theology is never the theology of a single person. Christian theology arises from the church
community, and this church community begins with Jesus and his disciples and moves down the centuries as generation after generation of
Christian communities strive to make the good news of the Jesus-event
central to their own lives. For any given aspect of our Christian faith, the
entire history of Christian theology must be considered, and no one area
merits a preferred, even less an exclusive, stance.[3] There never has been
nor will there ever be a "golden age" of theological thought, which becomes the measure for all other theological endeavors. Clearly, the biblical data serve as canonical texts, but each generation and each
community of Christians has been asked to interpret and reinterpret
these texts in the circumstances of their own lives. Text and interpretation can never be separated. This is why our sacred texts have over the
centuries served the Christian communities so well. Again and again
past interpretations of these sacred texts have had to be reclaimed and
personalized by each succeeding Christian community.

On rare occasions does the leadership of the churches come together and issue solemn statements on matters of the Christian faith. Of
all such meetings of church leadership, the first four councils of the
church have a special place of honor.[4] In slightly differing ways, mainstream Christian churches have accepted the solemn statements of the
first four councils of the church. Other church councils and meetings,
whether under the aegis of the Orthodox churches, the Roman church,
or the Anglican or Protestant churches, have produced solemn statements, but one cannot say that such statements are given the same respect by the church catholic as the statements of these first four
councils.

For Roman Catholics, it is important to note again that apart from
a brief mention of the mystery of the resurrection of Jesus in various official Christian creeds, there has been no solemn or official statement of
the church regarding the resurrection.[5] A Roman Catholic can certainly

say that belief in the resurrection of Jesus is catholic and divine faith, *de fide catholica et divina.* Indeed, belief in the resurrection of Jesus is central to Christian faith. Further specification of this resurrection has never been the subject matter of any solemn and official statement of the Church. The same cannot be said about Jesus as truly human and truly divine. There have been solemn and official statements on the hypostatic union, and these have been made primarily in the first four councils of the church. From conciliar statements and from the early creeds of the church, we find only a repetition of New Testament passages: Jesus died, was buried, and on the third day rose again according to the scriptures.

From the standpoint of biblical scholarship, J. Fitzmyer has proposed that the *praeconium paschale,* the essential Easter message found in the gospels, reads as follows:

Mk 16:6:	Do not be alarmed. You are looking for Jesus the Nazarene, the one crucified. He has been raised. He is not here.
Mt 28:5:	Do not fear, for I know that you are looking for Jesus, the one crucified. He is not here; for he has been raised as he said.
Lk 24:5–6:	Why do you look for the living among the dead? He is not here but has been raised.[6]

Such New Testament citations are indeed clearly central to resurrection faith and to its interpretation, but one should pause and reflect on these statements. What is the core message in these New Testament passages? What is so important about them? What is it that ultimately we are asked to believe? A mere recital of these New Testament passages does not clearly present us with the *praeconium paschale.*

One answer might be: It is the risen Jesus. But this answer is in many ways ambiguous. The "risen Jesus" might have as its focus the human Jesus, now risen, the creaturely Jesus now risen, the finite Jesus now risen. In other words, the focus might be on that part of the Chalcedonian statement which stated that Jesus was truly human, perfect in his humanity, consubstantial with us, born in time of Mary. The bishops at Chalcedon clearly stated as a matter of our faith, that Jesus was truly human. The bishops stressed the full humanity of Jesus: his creatureliness and his finiteness. Christian faith, however, is not ultimately creature-oriented or human-oriented. Christian faith, in its most profound reality, is oriented to the transcendent God. That is why a serious reading of the three verses mentioned above should lead one to consider more deeply the phrase "he has been raised," which occurs in all three synoptic gospels. Jesus has been raised but by whom? The answer, of course, is God. Ultimately, the resurrection of Jesus is much more a *theo*logical mystery, that is, a mystery centered on *Yahweh,* than it is a *christo*logical mystery, that is, a mystery centered on the Word *incarnate.* The profundity of the mystery of the resurrection centers on the gracious and free act of God, raising the dead Jesus to risen life. It centers on what God is doing, not what Jesus is doing nor what we are doing. It centers on the action of God, not on the action of any human, including the human nature of Jesus.

All other questions and issues, such as What kind of body did he have? Could he be touched? What were the appearances? are important in their own right and in their own place. None of these issues, however, lies at the very heart of the resurrection mystery.

I do not wish to imply that a theology of the resurrection is a point of departure, an *Ausgangspunkt,* for all of christology, much less *the* point of departure. Indeed, one enters into a theology of the resurrection with much antecedent material. Long before one begins to speak of the resurrection of Jesus, the Christian has already moved from an earlier point of departure. Philosophical anthropology is needed for this entry into resurrection theology. Christology in its widest meaning is also needed. So too ecclesiology or a theology of Christian community is requisite. Of very high significance is the need to bring to a theology of resurrection a theology of grace as well as a theology of the Holy Spirit. The mid-twentieth-century European approach to christology with its point of departure in the resurrection of Jesus has been studied but has not been found convincing. J. Sobrino, for instance, mentions this hesitation to make the resurrection of Jesus a "starting point" for christology:

> The resurrection of Christ as the starting point for christology has the New Testament apparently in its favour. Chronologically, both faith and christology occur, in the strict sense, after and as a result of it. Nevertheless, the resurrection of Christ presents a serious methodological difficulty if we are to convert it into a starting point, analogous to that posed by the dogmatic and New Testament formulas. . . .

It is not a useful starting point, since until we are clear about who was raised (Jesus of Nazareth), why he was raised (so that God's justice might be made manifest against a world of injustice), how we gain access to the risen one (in the end, through discipleship of Jesus), the resurrection does not necessarily lead to the true Church.[7]

In the final chapter of this book, I will again address the issue of the resurrection within the framework of a total christology, and indicate in a more comprehensive way why the resurrection of Jesus cannot be the point of departure for christology. My effort at this juncture is simply to present, as best I can, an attempt at a theological analysis and synthesis of the data that we have considered in the preceding chapters.

RELIGIOUS EXPERIENCE: THE EARLY DISCIPLES

The men and women whom Jesus attracted to his circle of disciples and who remained close to him down to his arrest, trial, and death were basically religiously oriented people. They were, prior to their meeting with Jesus, already good Jewish people: prayerful and seriously intent on their spiritual life. In none of these disciples, with the exceptions, possibly, of the apostle Matthew and of Mary Magdalene, do we find any great conversion from a nonreligious way of life to a religious way of life. In fact, all of the specifically named disciples, men and women, seem to be presented by the gospel authors as God-fearing Jewish people in search of a deeper way to develop their spiritual goals. Even when there seems to be a critical breakdown in Jesus' ministry, the so-called *Galilean crisis,* for example, these disciples continue to stay with Jesus. Although they did not see him as the "Son of God," an understanding to which they came only after the resurrection, they nonetheless saw him as their spiritual leader, one sent by God—perhaps a prophet, perhaps even the messiah. With the arrest and trial of Jesus, and especially with his death, there is reason to believe that the male disciples left Jerusalem and retreated to their well-known and therefore more secure environs in Galilee. These male disciples had no premonition that Jesus would rise; for all they knew, the entire "Jesus-event" had ended in disgrace and disappointment. The women who remained in Jerusalem did not have any premonition of a resurrection either. They came to the tomb, perhaps to anoint the corpse. The death of Jesus had brought their belief in him to a disappointing end as well.

The New Testament gives us abundant evidence to show that the next stage was caused by God's action: "God raised Jesus from the dead" is a frequent way of expressing New Testament resurrection faith. Divine intervention, not human activity, lies at the very heart of the resurrection event, and therefore we can say that God intervened in the lives of these God-fearing, spiritually minded but devastated men and women. In the resurrection event, God acts; men and women respond. This response of the disciples was not primarily that they could "see" Jesus; that they could "hear" Jesus; that they could "touch" Jesus; that they could "see him eat"; or any other physical, sensate response. The major response of these men and women was a response of faith. This cannot be stressed enough. Too often, in answer to the question, What happened on that first Easter day? the emphasis moves almost immediately to physical issues such as seeing, touching, hearing, and the like. The faith aspect, however, must clearly be kept in the center, for it is indeed the controlling issue as far as the disciples are concerned. Moreover, this faith factor determines the way the appearances are described in the New Testament, not the other way around. In other words, the seeing, touching, and hearing do not determine faith; faith is first, and this is then described in the narratives of seeing, touching, hearing, and so on. The faith element provides the fundamental motif that governs the way in which the apparitions are described in the New Testament and the fundamental way these narratives are to be interpreted. For the men and women disciples who eventually believed, this faith element was *a religious experience*. Here is the hermeneutical principle for understanding the disciples' response to the act of God in their lives: an act of God that in its totality we call the resurrection event.

One might too easily say, however, that these men and women in and through the resurrection event came to believe that Jesus was the Lord or even that he was the Son of God without really unpacking what this faith implied, particularly for a Jewish person of that period of history. What did faith really mean to a Jew in the first century C.E.? In our Christian and often scholastic approach, faith is understood as an "assent of the mind to truths revealed by God, not because of their intrinsic evidence, but because of the authority of God who reveals them." The *Catechism of Trent,* Leo XIII, Vatican I, and the *Baltimore Catechism* have all impressed this understanding of faith on the rank and file of Roman Catholic believers. Doubts of faith are, as a result, intellectual doubts. A doubt of faith means that one does not give intellectual assent. True faith means that truths are intellectually accepted on the basis of the authority of God, speaking through the church.[8]

Such an intellectual approach to faith is not very biblical. For the Jew at the time of Jesus, faith was a commitment of the whole person to God. One of the biblical terms for faith is the word *amen*. *Amen* derives from the root *MN*. Originally, this root word and its derivatives focused on the action of "picking up something."[9] In the course of time, as the usage of this term developed, words derived from *MN* meant the "picking up" of an infant and from this action went on to include the entire process of forming a child into an adult. Parental and familial training has as its goal the development in the young person of a sense of self-reliance. A mature individual is one who is no longer emotionally, physically, psychologically overly dependent on a mother or a father. A mature individual is one who has a basic amount of self-confidence. Moreover, when the infant is picked up by the mother or father, the parent too feels confident, since the child is safe. The infant as well feels confident, since he or she can trust the sheltering arms of the parent. As the child grows, the parent's task is to build up a sense of self-reliance, so that as a mature individual the son or daughter can eventually cope with the world's ups and downs. Parents are remiss in their task if, as the child begins to reach a mature age, he or she has little, if any, self-reliance, so that the child now becoming chronologically an adult still clings to parental supports, fearing to leave home and live on one's own. Only after this mundane history of the Hebrew word *MN* and its cognate words did the term take on, in the course of Jewish history, a religious use, but the underlying notion of trust remained evident even in this religious overlay of meaning.

In a deeply religious and theological sense, the Jewish person one finds described in the Torah, the prophets, and the writings can say that Yahweh is faithful. Such a description of Yahweh rings like a refrain throughout the psalms. The meaning is clear: Yahweh is reliable, is trustworthy, is faithful. Indeed, one can place one's entire life, one's existence, in the hands of Yahweh; one can rest one's whole weight on Yahweh, and Yahweh will not fail. In the Jewish framework, Yahweh is indeed trustworthy. This notion of a God in whom we can trust implicitly and totally lies at the heart of the Jewish understanding of faith.

In the scholastic understanding of faith, mentioned above, one cannot say that God is faithful. God does not give "assent of the mind to truths revealed by himself, not because of their evidence, but because of the authority of himself who revealed them." Faith, given this scholastic definition, has no place in one's discourse about God.

Not only is Yahweh faithful, but the goal of the Israelite's spiritual life is to be a man or woman of profound faith, that is, one who allows Yahweh to trust him or her. The book of Job is a masterful description of God placing his trust in a human person. In spite of all that happens to him, Job remains faithful. His entire being trusts in Yahweh and remains so trusting. Job is a man of faith. It is, however, in Deutero-Isaiah that the ideal of Jewish faith is described in its strongest way. Faith, in this Old Testament writing, is conceived of as meaning, the meaning of existence itself. Human life has meaning only when Yahweh enters the picture and is accepted as my Yahweh, or better *our* Yahweh. When Yahweh comes into view, then all those characteristics that make Yahweh the ultimate concern of one's life come into play: his might, his power to work miracles, his purpose in choosing his people, his disposition to love, the constancy and fidelity of his conduct, the realization of his word and his plan, his demands, his justice. This is faith in Yahweh: this is what allows one to say that Yahweh is full of faith, faithful. Our faith-response is taking this Yahweh with complete seriousness. Our faith-response is to live within the meaning framework of this faithful Yahweh. It is as complete a trust in Yahweh as possible.

The prophet Jeremiah lashes out at the lack of faith in the Jewish leaders of his day: his castigation of "idolatry" among the people and the leaders of Judah focused on their lack of reliance on Yahweh. His dispute with the king, Jehoiakim, centers on the reliance on false Gods and on the Egyptians, rather than a reliance on Yahweh. Zedekiah fares no better. Ezekiel, during the exile, eloquently expresses the same view. Deutero-Isaiah portrays a God whose word is full of power. What Yahweh says is infallibly done. The messianic glory, the kingdom of Yahweh, is at hand and about to be not only restored but established in a superabundant way. Not only Jews but all peoples will see the greatness of God. If the suffering servant songs are genuinely part of Deutero-Isaiah, then they represent a powerful reliance of Israel on Yahweh in spite of suffering.

Stress must be placed on this Jewish approach to religious faith, namely, that it is always a response to an initiative of a faithful God. God acts first; then, and then only, does a man or woman respond or react. Second, the response is deeply religious: it is a total entrusting of one's person and one's life to God. It is not simply an intellectual assent; it is a deep and comprehensive personal commitment.

Only on this Jewish basis do the words of Thomas: "My Lord and my God!" or the words of Peter: "I do believe" have their full meaning. No longer did these men and women place their total trust in Yahweh; they now placed their total trust in Yahweh-Jesus. This is what is meant by their belief in the "divinity" of Jesus. The faith, the trust, which they as pious Jews had in Yahweh, now extends to the presence of God in the human Jesus. They may not have done this immediately after the Easter morning, since the accounts do mention, and often at great length, the difficulties of unbelief. Nonetheless, as they moved from hesitant unbelief to an ever-deepening belief, this total entrusting of their persons, their lives, their futures was given over to Yahweh-in-Jesus. For them there was no longer any way to Yahweh except in and through Jesus, not because he was some sort of mediator or intercessory channel but because he was Lord, messiah, even eventually Son of God. This is precisely what is meant by their resurrection faith; and it is precisely what is meant by any Christian community's resurrection faith. Jesus is both human and divine. Christians place their trust in the divine presence which they experience in and through the primordial sacrament, the humanness of Jesus.

It might be difficult to consider this entrusting of their lives to Jesus as a "conversion"; after all, they were already God-fearing believers. What really is at stake here is their faith-response to the action of God in Jesus, which involved the totality of their lives. Such a response to God's action can only be called a profound "religious experience," a profound and life-changing religious experience. It is an experience, since something actually occurred in their lives; it is religious, since it involved in a most central way Yahweh. This coming to belief in Yahweh-Jesus radically changed the lives of these disciples. With this faith in the risen Lord, Yahweh-Jesus, they became believers. With and in such faith the disciples saw themselves as the fulfillment of Jewish religious and theological aspirations.

When this radical, spiritual, and religious understanding of resurrection faith is taken seriously, then such other details as what the disciples heard, saw, touched, and so on become far less important. It was not because they saw, heard, and touched that they believed; it was because God himself acted within the depths of their persons that they believed. The narratives on the apparitions are, consequently, ways of expressing this deep religious experience.

In this view, as the reader undoubtedly has perceived, *religious experience* is presented as the controlling factor for the theological interpretation of the resurrection event as it affected the disciples. In order to substantiate such a position, let us return to the New Testament data, not so much in an exegetical fashion, as was done in chapter 2, but in a theologically analytical way.

THE NEW TESTAMENT DATA: PERSONS

As far as the gospels are concerned, one should recall that there are not really that many appearances of Jesus to the disciples. If we list the appearances as they appear in each of the New Testament authors, we find the following:

Mark I	None
Mark II	Mary Magdalene
	Two men in the country
	The eleven
Mark III	Disciples (possibly)
Matthew	The women
	The eleven
Luke	Two men on the road to Emmaus
	Peter
	The eleven
John I	Mary Magdalene
	The eleven (without Thomas)
	The eleven (with Thomas)
John II	Seven disciples

The list could be established in another way according to persons:

Peter	Luke in passing only
Mary Magdalene alone	John I
	Mark II
The women	Matthew
	Mark I
	Luke
Two men	Luke
	Mark II

The eleven	Matthew
	Mark II
	Luke
	John I
	Acts
The seven	John II

All told, the gospel accounts indicate approximately sixteen named people: the eleven (including Peter and the seven), the two disciples on the way to Emmaus, Mary Magdalene, and at least two other women. Paul mentions the following: Peter, James, the Twelve, all the apostles, five hundred, and Paul himself. Of these, Peter and the Twelve are mentioned in the gospels. The others are found only in Paul's letter to the Corinthians. Acts refers generically to many apparitions to the apostles during the forty days.

Leaving to one side, for the moment, Paul's inclusion of the five hundred, we could add to the sixteen people mentioned in the gospels two more—Paul himself and James, thus raising the total number to eighteen. When we consider this list, we notice that in the New Testament there remains only one on this list who speaks from personal experience, namely, Paul. For this reason, his own description of the appearance should be considered with great care. All the other writers are giving second-hand accounts, that is, about someone else who experienced an apparition of the risen Lord.

NEW TESTAMENT DATA: THE ISSUE OF MISSION

Let us consider the New Testament data once more but from the aspect of a mission or a commission. Remarkably, an analysis of the various apparition texts indicates that for the majority of instances, but not in all instances, the apparition of Jesus to an individual disciple or to a group of disciples included a mission, or a commissioning to go and do something. We note:

Mary Magdalene in John I	Go and find the brothers and tell them . . .
The women in Matthew	Go and tell my brothers that . . .
The two in Luke	(There is no explicit command to "do something," but the two felt constrained to return to Jerusalem immediately and tell the others.)

The eleven in Mark II	Go out to the whole world and proclaim . . .
The eleven in Matthew	Go, therefore, and make disciples of all nations, baptize them . . .
The eleven in Luke	You are witnesses to this (i.e., what Jesus had just explained as regards the scriptures)—and a witness is always a witness *of* someone/something *to* someone)
The eleven in John I	As the Father sent me, so I am sending you . . .
The eleven in Acts	You will receive power when the Holy Spirit comes to you and then you will be my witnesses not only in Jerusalem but to all
The seven in John II	To Simon Peter Jesus says: Feed my lambs. Look after my sheep . . .
Paul in Acts and in Paul's own letters	Go and . . .

Connected to these statements of the risen Lord to go and do something, we also have the words of the angel:

Mark I	Go and tell his disciples and Peter . . .
Matthew	Come and see the place where he lay, then go quickly and tell his disciples . . .

It is difficult to find in all the material an appearance narrative that in some way or another is not also connected with a mission. None of the appearances is meant to be a private matter; they all have a social or communal dimension, which is an integral part of the resurrection kerygma.

The Christian church is a resurrection church, which springs from the act of Yahweh in the life, death, and resurrection of Jesus as well as from the appearances of the risen Lord to the disciples, who not only changed their own faith lives in a radical way, accepting Jesus as the Lord of their lives, but who also went out to the wider world and shared this good news of the Lord. If the dominant or controlling theme for an understanding of these resurrection accounts is that of a religious experience, then this nonprivatized aspect must be taken into account. No true religious experience of the risen Lord occurs without the persons involved sensing the urge to "go" and "do" something. Faith in the risen Lord is not simply a personal moment in one's spiritual journey. This social and communal dimension is as valid for Christians today as it was for the disciples to whom Jesus appeared. In a genuine sense, through our Christian faith Jesus "appears" also to us, and we in turn are commissioned and missioned to go and do something.[10]

The church is a community of believers that moves outward; a community that has a message which it shares. The church is not first constituted and then given a mission. The very constitution of church involves a mission. Had the early disciples been touched by the risen Lord and then done nothing socially or communally about their religious experience, there would be no church today. This is the reason why the church is an Easter church. At the center of the church is the risen Lord, but the risen Lord who has appeared to the disciples and told them to go and spread the good news.

The birth of the church is a process that includes the resurrection-ascension-sending of the Spirit. The birth of the church is the constituting of a missionary church. This is the ecclesiological dimension of the resurrection event.

In saying this, however, I do not want to say that the early disciples, in and through the apparitions to them, had any self-identity as "church," in the sense that we understand it today. *Ekklēsia,* the Greek word in the New Testament that is usually translated as "church," reflects at this early stage not a "church" distinct from Judaism but rather the *qahal,* those whom God has called. The New Testament authors all wrote in Greek, although most of these writers were Jewish. Moreover, they were writing, for the most part, to communities that were mostly Jewish. What would these Jewish people have understood when they heard, in the various writings of the New Testament, the Greek word *ekklēsia?* The answer is clear. As Jews, they would have immediately connected this to the Hebrew *qahal,* a term used often in the Torah, the prophets, and the writings to indicate Yahweh's calling them out to be Yahweh's people.

In the apparitions and their faith-event, the early disciples, who were all Jewish, were called out by Yahweh-Jesus to be the true Israel. How easy it would have been for them to make the connection between *ekklēsia* and *qahal*. If, at first, all they believed was that Jesus was the messiah, then this acceptance of the messiah Jesus indicated that the true Israel, the final Israel, had begun and that they, the disciples, had been called out by God to form this new Israel. Jesus' own selection of the Twelve further strengthened their self-identity as *ekklēsia* in the sense of *qahal,* not in the sense that they were forming a new religion, a "church," quite distinct from Judaism. This cautions us, then, from giving any "Roman Catholic" or "Christian" interpretation to those New Testament texts that use the Greek term *ekklēsia.*

This constitution-mission aspect, which is an essential part of the appearances of the risen Lord, also indicates an essential dimension to the holiness or spirituality in the church. Spirituality is not a private matter, and belief, whether by the early disciples or by subsequent disciples, involves a mission, a "going" and a "doing." If we today claim that we too believe in the risen Lord, then this same risen Lord is telling us, in our own context, to "go" and "tell" and "do." The church is an Easter church; Christian spirituality is likewise an Easter spirituality. To overlook this Easter dimension in the striving for a holy life is to miss the center of the Christian life: God in the sacrament of the risen human Jesus appears to us and sends us. The religious experience of the first disciples remains a paradigm for all genuine Christian religious experiences of the Lord.

HELLENISTIC AND SEMITIC ANTHROPOLOGY

Biblical scholars, both Jewish and Christian, in the past two centuries have studied the Jewish world and its *Weltanschauung* in a quite thorough way. On the issue of anthropology, that is, on the issue of the way a human person was understood, let me cite one such author, Xavier Léon-Dufour, who speaks for the majority. Léon-Dufour advises us that the Hellenistic view of death and the Jewish view of death are anthropologically quite different:

> At the risk of somewhat simplifying the data, though not the radical opposition of Hellenistic and Semitic thought, we can describe the situation as follows. In Greek thought, man is made up of soul and body. The soul is immortal, while the body is a material entity placed at his disposal temporarily and in which it is held prisoner. At death, the soul is set free from its prison, the body. According to this view of man, resurrection would involve the restoration of the

soul to the body—whether as in Pythagorism, to a new body
through the transmigration of souls, or as in hellenized Christianity,
to one's own body, which had become a corpse.[11]

According to a Hellenistic interpretation of the death and resurrection of Jesus, there was an immortal soul in Jesus that did not die. The
death of Jesus in this view (like the death of every man and woman) is
simply the death of the body, while the soul, being immortal—not able
to die—lives on. The resurrection of Jesus is, consequently, the restoration of the immortal soul to the mortal body. It is this view that in many
ways has dominated Christian theology and has provided the basis for
many of the theological opinions about the resurrection. The Hellenistic
interpretation, however, has never been officially adopted by any of the
Christian churches.

The Semitic way of considering the human structure is different.
To cite Léon-Dufour once more:

> According to Jewish anthropology this cannot be the case. . . . The
> word *soul* becomes increasingly frequent, but it never stands for
> some spiritual or immortal substance as opposed to a body which is
> material and mortal. Death is still referred to in terms of man's
> being "reunited with his fathers"; although, it is occasionally spo-
> ken of as a separation of soul and body, this does not involve the lib-
> eration of the soul, which thus does not become "spiritual" in the
> Greek sense of the word. The souls of the dead, still "corporal" in
> an attenuated way, go, if not to dark Sheol, at any rate into the
> "repositories" where they wait inertly for the last day. So the resur-
> rection consists in the dead man entering into fullness of life, in a
> new kind of existence and form.[12]

It is this Semitic view that dominates the New Testament, not the
Greek view. In the New Testament, consequently, Jesus' death and resurrection are described in the Jewish terms of a "total death," that is, the
body and the "soul." God raised not simply the body from the dead, but
the total human nature of Jesus from the dead. When one interprets the
gospel accounts of the death and resurrection of Jesus from the standpoint of the Hellenistic dualism, an immortal soul and a mortal body,
we have a serious instance of "eisegesis," a reading into the text of an
interpretation totally foreign to the text. According to Semitic thought
patterns, the complete humanness of Jesus died; it was this complete

humanness of Jesus that was then raised from the dead. Jesus' complete human nature, accordingly, experienced death and experienced risen life.[13]

J. McKenzie in his synthesis of Old Testament religious thought, says exactly the same thing: "In spite of the use of such words as flesh, spirit, and soul, the OT conceived of the human being as a unity and not as a composite of different principles." McKenzie cites a "classic remark" of H. Wheeler Robinson about the Greek view of human existence as an "incarnate spirit," while the Jewish view is that of "an animated body." After an overview of the Hebrew term *nefesh*, McKenzie notes: "In none of these instances, taken singly or together, is there anything resembling the 'soul' of Greek and modern thought. This difference has important corollaries in the biblical idea of survival after death."[14]

Authors such as Léon-Dufour and McKenzie are urging scholars today to return to the Semitic way of understanding resurrection, since this is clearly the framework out of which the New Testament writers themselves interpreted death and resurrection generally, and the death and resurrection of Jesus in particular. All the voices we considered above express a Semitic view and understanding of death and resurrection. Unless one is sensitive to this approach, the very meaning of these authors regarding the risen Lord can easily be misunderstood and interpreted in an eisegetical way rather than an exegetical way.

It is also true that the New Testament writers do not attempt to describe this risen life of the human Jesus in any philosophical way. Rather, they use a descriptive method. Jesus in his "new human form" walks with the disciples on their way to Emmaus, but he is not recognized. He is seen by Mary Magdalene, but she does not recognize him. Jesus appears suddenly to the disciples in an upper room and just as suddenly disappears. He enters a room that is locked. He ascends into heaven and out of sight. All of this indicates that the risen Jesus in his human or bodily form differs from the earthly Jesus in his human or bodily form. There is something new about the human way of existing as regards the risen Jesus.

The newness of life that these New Testament authors describe is not confined simply to recognition factors and movement factors, a body with preternatural gifts. In the appearances Jesus is often confronted by the disciples' doubt, but finally he is confronted by the disciples' faith in him as messiah and Lord. The disciples come to believe in the appearance of Jesus just as they as good Jews believed in an appearance of Yahweh himself. Risen life is life in Yahweh and with Yahweh. Risen life is confessed as the very life of Yahweh in, through, and with Jesus. Risen life is eventually associated with the profession of God's presence in Jesus, abstractly called the divinity of Jesus. Jesus' risen human life reveals in a way in which his earthly life did not the very presence of Yahweh in him. Jesus' risen human life reveals in a way in which his earthly life did not what is the depth, the height, the breadth, and the length of the incarnation.

The total humanity of Jesus was raised from the dead, and this was an experience that involved for Jesus' humanity itself a profound religious depth. Some might say: indeed, Jesus, in his humanness, was the one who rose, and this was clearly an experience, even a religious experience, but let us pass on to the "more important" aspects of Jesus' resurrection: namely, What really happened? What kind of a body did he have? Did the disciples actually touch him? Did he retain the scars on his hands and feet? Did he really eat with the disciples? How often has one read a book on the resurrection of Jesus or heard a sermon on the resurrection of Jesus, in which these kinds of questions appeared to be the overriding ones. The issue of religious experience is shunted to one side as an interesting theological discussion, tangential to the main issues at hand. What actually and historically happened at the empty tomb, and what actually and historically happened to the disciples are *the important questions.* Nonetheless, one should more importantly ask: What is the most important faith aspect concerning the resurrection of Jesus? The faith acceptance of Jesus as Lord on the part of the disciples is clearly far more profound than any historicity of the empty tomb material or any historicity of the appearance material. The acceptance of Jesus as Lord was, for each of these disciples, a profound religious experience. Whether one considers Jesus in his humanity or the disciples who "saw" the risen Lord, religious experience seems to be the controlling factor, and this factor should likewise be central and controlling for the way in which one interprets the resurrection of Jesus.

THE RESURRECTION OF JESUS HIMSELF

Quite rightfully, the New Testament authors never attempt to describe the actual resurrection of Jesus. Apocryphal gospels of the second century, however, are not quite so modest. In them we do find rather fantastic descriptions of the actual resurrection of Jesus. I do not want to be less modest, but theologians of the past have touched lightly on the issue of Jesus' own resurrection. Indirectly, by a discussion of what constitutes a "risen body" these theologians have addressed the issue. I would like to move in a different way, but in a measured and cautious way. Although nowhere in the four gospels is the actual resurrection of Jesus portrayed, still, throughout all the narratives on the risen Lord in the canonical gospels, the actual resurrection of Jesus, his body and his spirit, is not absent. It is presupposed. The creedal statements of the early church indicate that Jesus truly died, that he was buried, and that he rose from the dead.

Both the death process and the resurrection process apply only to Jesus' humanity. His divine nature did not die, and his divine nature did not rise from the dead. When we speak of the resurrection of Jesus, we are confronting two distinct aspects: (1) the action of God, and (2) the human response to this action of God.

1. The Action of God. Undoubtedly, the most important aspect of any and all discussion and meditation on the resurrection of Jesus is God's action. God raised Jesus from the dead. Not only is this an action of God, but it is a free, unmerited, grace-filled action of an absolutely free God.[15] In the Council of Chalcedon there is a declaration of faith that states that Jesus was truly human and truly divine. Since death is not applicable to divinity, death can only be applied to his humanity. Since resurrection is a resurrection from the dead, the resurrection of Jesus can only be applied to his humanity. Likewise, the gospels indicate to us that resurrection of Jesus took place in his humanness. The gospels use the term *ēgerthē* (he has been raised). God's action of grace is central.

2. The human response to this action of God. The action of God awaits a human response. Not only is this response found in the faith-response of the disciples, but there is also a response by the human nature of Jesus to this unbelievable gift of risen life. These human responses are not the most profound issue in the resurrection of Jesus, but they are, in a secondary way, at the very heart of the meaning of resurrection. It is in this response area that I wish to discuss the religious experience of Jesus' humanity.

His return to life, however, is more than a mere resuscitation. In the gospels we have the three instances of someone returning to life, three instances of resuscitation: the one of the widow's son at Nain, Jairus's daughter, and Lazarus. In all three instances, death is presumed (even in the case of Jairus's daughter), and the three people are brought back to human life as they had lived it and as they continued to live it until they died once more. This is not what the gospels say about Jesus' return to life; this is not what Christian faith says about Jesus' return to life. Jesus did not simply come back from the dead to the human life to which he had been accustomed. For Jesus the resurrection was a rising to *new* life, more pointedly, a new life *in God*.

What one brings into the discourse on resurrection by way of theological anthropology cannot help but affect the interpretation of Jesus' risen life. In some past Roman Catholic theological thought on Jesus, even within the twentieth century, Jesus has been presented as someone who, from the first moment of his conception, enjoyed the beatific vision. Deep within the humanness of Jesus there was this union in which Jesus' human mind and heart enjoyed the perfection of knowing God face to face. It was called a "perfection" and therefore could hardly be increased since it was "perfect." In such a view, Jesus was already "in heaven," even though he was still walking this earth. Indeed, theologians, following Pius XII, claimed that this beatific vision belonged to Jesus from the first moment of his conception onward in virtue of his person, his task, and his love.

If such were the case, then major difficulties arise: for instance, why did Jesus, as we read in the gospels, go off to pray. If he were enjoying the beatific vision at all times, what need would there be to take time "off" for prayer? Thomas Aquinas offers us the standard answer for this although we find it already proposed by Gregory the Great:

> As God, Christ could accomplish all that he desired, but not as man; because as man he was not omnipotent, as has been said above. Yet even though in his one person he was God as well as man, he wished to offer prayers to the Father. It was not that he, as a person, lacked any power; he did this for our instruction.[16]

Jesus went aside to pray not for any personal need or personal growth but for our instruction and our edification. This response cannot be given to Luke's description of Jesus in the garden of Gethsemane, with its accounting of Jesus' fear and bloody sweat. At this difficult moment, Jesus' prayer is not primarily for our edification. Jesus' prayer truly "implies that the meaning of his life cannot be complete without reference to Someone else, even though Jesus himself is gradually fashioning the meaning of his life."[17] Jesus, in other words, could only say yes to God, and this had taken place long before the scene on the Mount of Olives. The verses that describe his sweat pouring out like blood (Lk 22:43–44) might not even be original to the Lucan text. Whether they are original to the text or not, one might ask: What role did it play in the life of Jesus if he had the beatific vision from the first moment of his conception onward? The details of the Mount of Olives are not primarily for our edification; rather, they indicate Jesus' own human, religious struggle.

The baptism of Jesus is presented as a memorable event in the human life of Jesus. Jesus' own baptism by John, though played down in some of the gospel accounts, was itself a religious moment. But if Jesus enjoyed the beatific vision throughout his life, what spiritual role did this baptism of Jesus by John play in Jesus' own life? Was it again an action that Jesus did for our edification only?

In recent times, theologians, and particularly many Catholic theologians, have addressed themselves to the question of Jesus' human knowledge and have portrayed Jesus as "growing in knowledge" during his lifetime.[18] This is not the place to enter in any great detail into the question of the knowledge of Jesus, but let us presuppose for a moment that Jesus himself actually did grow in knowledge, and therefore did not have from the first moment of his conception onward the beatific vision. If that were the case, then we could easily state that Jesus prayed and that his times for prayer were indeed religious moments in his life, moments in which Jesus, in his humanity, "grew" in his knowledge of God. The prayer at Gethsemane would be interpreted in this way. The baptism would also be seen as a moment of prayer in Jesus' life. These occasions, as well as many others during the earthly life of Jesus, were occasions not for our edification only, but for the spiritual growth of Jesus himself. They were moments of religious experience.

Even were one to shy away from a "growth" in the knowledge of Jesus, one must still ask whether such occasions, attested to by God's revelatory Word, are presented as moments of great religious value in the earthly life of Jesus or not? Can we simply describe them as exemplary actions of Jesus, for our edification but not for his own human religious experience?

It is clear that one does not enter into a discussion of the resurrection of Jesus with empty hands. One brings a philosophical and theological anthropology into the hermeneutics of this discourse. This has been noted above in the differences between Hellenistic philosophical anthropology and Semitic anthropology. It is also seen in a philosophical and theological anthropology that allows for a "beatific vision from the first moment of conception onwards." In recent times, this philosophical and theological anthropology has been at the base of the discussion of the knowledge of Jesus.[19]

The resurrection of Jesus must be seen not simply as life after death. More fundamentally, it is life in God, life with God, life in God's love and peace, after death. It is this "in God" and this "with God" which characterizes the risen life far more than the "after death" aspect. Jairus's daughter, the son of the widow at Nain, and Lazarus all had life "after death." What they did not have was "risen" life, or a distinctive way of human living "with God" and "in God." By saying this, I wish to argue that the human nature of Jesus, which through the hypostatic union was already "united" with God, came to be in a special way even more intimately "united" to God: (a) through moments of prayer, during his earthly life, and (b) through the special event called resurrection.

The resurrection of Jesus, then, though not described by the canonical gospels, was a religious event in the human life of Jesus. Since it was not simply a resuscitation, a coming back from the dead, the religious aspect of this risen life offers us the key to the meaning of resurrection: a new way of human existence "in God" or "with God." Jesus experienced God in a way that he, in his humanity, had never experienced God before. God's activity in the resurrection event was not merely a raising of Jesus from the dead; it was far more profoundly a raising of Jesus' humanity into an intimacy with God's own life which Jesus' humanity, up to that time, had never experienced before.

RELIGIOUS EXPERIENCE

When one speaks of an "experience of the transcendent or of God," one generally calls this a "religious experience," and this is the rubric that best seems to describe what happened to the humanness of Jesus in the resurrection. The resurrection, as far as Jesus' humanity was concerned, was an overwhelming or profound religious experience for him. All the gospels state that Jesus himself was raised from death to life, and therefore they say something indirectly about Jesus' own resurrection. All describe this risen life as a life specially touched by God himself, and so they qualify the kind of life Jesus enjoyed in the risen state. The combination of two terms, *life* and *risen*, provide the basis for describing the resurrection in terms of "religious experience."

Since the motif of religious experience is a controlling factor in my discussion of the resurrection, I want to be quite clear as to what I mean by this term *religious experience.*

1. It is a human experience: as such, nothing is being said about the divinity of Jesus, as though the divinity of Jesus could "experience" anything. This restriction to the human side of Jesus prevents any diminution of his divinity and limits the area of discourse solely to that of Jesus' human nature. Only by a *communicatio idiomatum* does one say, for instance, that God died on the cross. Actually, it was the human dimension of Jesus that underwent death. Death is a human experience. Similarly, it is only by *communicatio idiomatum* that one might say: "The Son of God rose from the dead." Since God could not or cannot die, only the human nature of Jesus could actually rise from the dead. The rising from the dead is, then, a human experience. The resurrection event is an act of God, for God raised Jesus from the dead. In this sense, it is a divine action. However, the object of this divine action is the human nature of Jesus. This human nature, having passed through death, was raised from death. This is the first point that must be kept in mind: religious experience has reference only within the human dimension.

2. "Religious experience" means that there is an experience of the divine; otherwise, one would not call it a "religious" experience. The experience is a human one, in which God is religiously involved. It is the human experience of God's inbreaking into one's life that substantiates the qualification *religious*. One can experience this inbreaking of God into human experience in a multiple way: for example, God as a judging God, as a forgiving God, as a loving God, as a revealing God, and so on. This inbreaking of God into our human experience need not be joyful or pleasant; it can be painful and tragic. In contemplative prayer, there can be the ecstasy of the unitive life, but there can also be the dark night of the senses and the dark night of the soul.

3. The presence of God in one's life brings about some change. A human person is not the same after this inbreaking of God into one's life. In other words, this presence of God, is not something neutral or

something indifferent. Rather, God's presence produces a response: conversion, contrition, thanksgiving, adoration, love, and so on. One's human life has been changed or transformed after a true religious experience.

If these three elements help define a religious experience, then, if applied to Jesus' own resurrection, we can say: (1) Jesus' resurrection was a human experience; (2) Jesus' resurrection was a human experience of God; and (3) Jesus' resurrection changed the humanity of Jesus in some way. Of these three statements, it is the third that might seem to cause the most concern. In traditional scholastic theology, God has been described as unchangeable, since God is the zenith of all being, *Esse Ipsum,* infinite life. The very term "infinite" means that there are no limits *(fines).* The creature, however, is "finite," that is, there are limits *(fines).* There are, then, boundaries that can be crossed, stages that can be surpassed. Only God is infinite, that is, without limits and boundaries; the creature is finite, that is, with limits and boundaries. The crossing of a boundary or limit by a finite creature is often called "growth" or "development."

The humanity of Jesus is finite. To say otherwise would be heresy and completely against the statements of the Council of Chalcedon. The human mind of Jesus is therefore finite, that is, limited. Jesus, in his human nature, was not and could not be omniscient. If one were to say that the human mind of Jesus, because of the hypostatic union, was omniscient, one has made a creature "divine." Whenever one breaks down the division of created/creator some sort of pantheism develops. The human will of Jesus was created and therefore finite. To say that the human will of Jesus was omnipotent leads one into the same pantheism and the same denial as the Council of Chalcedon. The human nature of Jesus in all its specific aspects and its totality is finite, created, limited. It has boundaries that can be surpassed, limits that can be expanded, and structures that can be developed. In other words, the human nature of Jesus can change, and it can change not only physically but also religiously. Even if one were to hold to the theological opinion that Jesus' humanity enjoyed the beatific vision, this beatific vision is created, limited, and therefore able to be surpassed and changed. If one were to hold that Jesus' human knowledge was indeed limited, as ours is, then it is perhaps clearer that Jesus grew in his religious appreciation of the divine life.

A religious experience as far as the human nature of Jesus is concerned involves change: in his moments of prayer, Jesus' human nature grew in his intimacy with God; so too in the resurrection Jesus' human nature grew in its intimacy and oneness with God's own life. Jesus, in his humanness, experienced Yahweh in ways that until the resurrection he had never experienced before. He experienced life with Yahweh, which is what risen life is all about. Risen life is not simply life; it is much more than simply being alive. It is life with God, and it is this "with God" in intimacy, closeness, and union that gives risen life its ultimate meaning.

NEW TESTAMENT DATA: APPARITIONS

In the New Testament we find descriptions of these religious experiences in the apparition passages. Scholars have attempted to classify the various apparition accounts. R. Fuller, for instance, proposes two kinds: (a) church-founding apparitions; and (b) mission-sending apparitions.

> The appearances to Peter and to the Twelve share a common function. In these appearances the Risen One initiates the foundation of the eschatological community: they are "Church-founding appearances." As such they must be distinguished from the later appearances, whose function is the call and sending of apostles to fulfill a mission.

Again: "The appearance to the Twelve in 1 Corinthians 15:5 was a 'Church-founding' appearance, whereas the appearance in Matthew 28:16-20 is a mission-inaugurating one." Fuller, with his understanding of "Church-founding" appearance wants to stress that God in the risen Jesus founded his church, his assembly. The community did not arise from some human need for comfort at a time of bereavement or for any other reasons. The Jesus community took shape because of divine action. In this Fuller is clearly correct. Can such an action be separated from a mission-inaugurating action? It does not seem that this can be the case. There is no church unless there is at the same time a "mission."[20] There is, therefore, no founding of a church distinct from a sending out on a mission. A solid theology of church does not allow one to make an either/or approach—founding or sending.

Léon-Dufour makes a distinction between the "official" and

"private" appearance narratives, but again the distinction cannot be overdrawn. The private appearances are to such individuals as the women (Matthew), Mary Magdalene (John I, Mark II), and the disciples on the road to Emmaus (Luke, Mark II). Léon-Dufour makes this distinction because these private appearances "lack a content which relates to the Church," and even more "they have been adapted to a greater extent."[21]

Léon-Dufour's position seems to be strengthened by the fact that in Paul's letter to the Corinthians no women are mentioned as witnesses of an "appearance." Generally speaking, it is asserted that in the Jewish framework of that period of time, women could not be considered "official witnesses." The appearance of Jesus to women, accordingly, could only be considered a "private" appearance. When one considers the role the women play in the gospels, it is difficult to relegate their "appearance" experiences to the private sphere. This does not seem to be what the authors are saying.

As regards the disciples on the way to Emmaus it would be difficult to understand Luke's description as lacking a content that relates to the church. Given the fact that the narrative accounts for almost one half of Luke's presentation on the risen Lord, it would seem that Luke clearly wants to say something to his community, not only about a past private event but also about the community itself. The presentation by Jesus of Moses and the prophets clearly is meant by Luke to relate Jesus and his death to the self-identity of the "church," the Jesus community. Moreover, the extent of the narrative raises the question as to why such length has been adopted. Luke did not organize this lengthy passage merely to present some past, private narrative; he wanted to say something to his own community about what it means to believe in the crucified and risen Jesus. It is difficult to bypass a community orientation for this Lucan "adaptation." Léon-Dufour's distinction does not seem to be adequate.

C. H. Dodd, from a form-critical study of the appearance narratives, divides them into: (a) concise narratives; (b) circumstantial narratives; (c) mixed narratives. Concise narratives have a fivefold pattern: (1) a description of the disciples, bereft of Jesus; (2) the appearance of Jesus; (3) his greeting; (4) their recognition; and (5) Jesus' word of mission. The appearance of Jesus to the women in Matthew, as well as the final appearance of Jesus to the eleven in Matthew, and the first appearance to the eleven in John I are classified as concise narratives.

Circumstantial narratives are dramatically told incidents in which recognition of Jesus is the main issue. The Emmaus narrative and the Lake Tiberias narrative are classified as circumstantial narratives.

Mixed narratives combine both forms: to the eleven in Mark II, to Thomas in John I, and to the eleven in Luke. From the standpoint of "form" Dodd's division has merit, but to make any judgment beyond the issue of "form" does not seem to be viable.

In all of this, it is evident that any classification of the appearance accounts of the resurrection has a certain arbitrariness about it. The New Testament clearly does not present us with a uniform pattern to the appearances, nor is there a consistency of pattern even within a single author. Prior material has been adapted by various authors, each for his own purpose. In all the accounts, however, God in and through Jesus is portrayed as the main agent and the first agent. Yahweh-Jesus breaks into the life of the disciples. Second, the response is a faith-response, not simply a recognition of a physical sort (seeing, hearing, touching, etc.). One must read beyond the descriptive touching, seeing, and hearing, for only in doing so will one truly encounter the profound meaning of the resurrection: God's primary action and the religious-experience reaction of the humanness of Jesus.

HOW TO DESCRIBE A RELIGIOUS EXPERIENCE

In our long Christian tradition, there have been many holy people, saints, who have enjoyed profound religious experiences and have left us some sort of accounting of these experiences. Names such as Teresa of Avila, John of the Cross, Francis of Assisi come readily to mind. Spiritual writers indicate that there are stages to this unitive process: the first stage is one in which God holds captive our free will; the second stage is one in which God holds all our faculties captive. It is interesting to note that this "being captured" by God is a phrase Paul himself used. The third degree is ecstatic union. According to St. Teresa, God gives a person such awareness of supernatural realities that the person speaks of heavenly secrets, of imaginative visions that cannot be described, of mental visions that one cannot formulate. The final stage is transforming union. St. Teresa gives a detailed description of the ceremony of this mutual engagement between Christ and the soul.

St. Francis of Assisi, after his vision of Jesus on Mount Alverno, writes poetry: the Canticle of the Creatures. On the heels of his death is the volume entitled *Sacrum Commercium,* in which Francis and some of his brothers pursue Lady Poverty to the top of the mountain. St. John of the Cross draws a pictorial map and writes a poem, and only then does he write an interpretation of the poem and an explanation of the map, which we know as the *Ascent of Mount Carmel*. Teresa of Avila's book has the imaginative title *The Interior Castle or Mansions*. In English spirituality there is *The Cloud of Unknowing*. Again and again, these saintly Christians, who have experienced something of God's revelation in their lives, namely, an appearance of God to them in the risen Lord, have resorted to imagery, to poetry, to poetic narrative, and to descriptive pictures. Somehow we accept this as a normal way of describing the profound religious experiences that mystics have of the unitive way. When we pick up the New Testament, which is telling us even more authoritatively about the depth and height, the length and breadth of the spiritual life, we tend to refuse entry to imaginative literature, to poetic forms, to literary genres. The New Testament speaks, so we demand, of facts, and of historical facts at that, as though the rapture of a Teresa, a John of the Cross, a Francis of Assisi is not a "fact" or a part of their personal "history." Heaven is not acres of real estate with castles and mansions. We realize that Teresa is using picture language to discuss religious reality. Heaven is not on the top of a mountain, even a Mount Carmel, and there is no map that we can follow to arrive at it. John of the Cross is using figurative language to make sense of realities that defy description. The creatures are figuratively called "brother" and "sister" in the poem of Francis of Assisi.

In our own lives, pedestrian though they might be as far as the spiritual life is concerned, we too have had a few moments at least of deep prayer. We have had our own religious experiences. Were we to attempt to communicate what we experienced, would we not also resort to images, to poetry, to pictures, to descriptive language? Would we not speak of brilliant light, of sounds no one else heard, of visions no one else saw? How else could we explain the peace deep within us without imaginative language or song or color?

When one asks, what was it like to have experienced the risen Lord, would Luke be far afield if he wrote: Let me tell you how it was? Once upon a time two men were walking along a road, when a stranger came and joined them on their journey. . . . Is this any different than the child saying to his or her parent, tell me a bedtime story, and the parent immediately begins: Once upon a time. . . ? How many teachers have said to their students: "I am going to tell you a story, so pay attention.

Once upon a time. . .'? We grew up perhaps on fairy tales, stories that began "once upon a time." We came to know that they were not "true," that there were no seven dwarfs, no Snow White, no magic prince, but we did know that the values in these stories were "true." In a way adapted to children, ideals of right and wrong, good and evil, love and sacrifice were communicated through such stories, and these ideals were real and true. In many instances, such ideals continue to guide the lives of children-grown-to-adulthood. In this sense, the power of these ideals is indeed real and historical.

Paul did not use such stories, but he tells us in more abstract ways what the risen Lord had done in his life. This action of Yahweh-Jesus was for him real, not imaginative; it happened and therefore God's action historically transformed Paul's life, but when he mentions "capture" he does not mean this in a physical, owner-catches-wayward-slave approach. The capturing was deep in his heart and mind and soul and person. God did not appear with irons and shackles. The image is used by Paul to communicate something of the power of God's presence in his life when the risen Lord transformed him. Paul is not actually running a race; the race is an image. Paul was indeed called by the Lord, but it was not a voice that everyone heard, or that even he heard with his ears. It was a voice deep within him, calling him and commissioning him. The paradigm for understanding the resurrection appearances is Paul's description in his letters, not the narratives in the gospels or the narratives in Acts about Paul's calling and commissioning. The narratives need to be interpreted by Paul's personal accounting, not vice versa.

SUMMARY OF CHAPTER THREE

The main issues in this chapter can be summarized as follows:

1. The most profound reality in the resurrection of Jesus is primarily *theological* and only secondarily *christological:* the grace-filled action of God, raising the full humanness of Jesus to new life with God.

2. This action of God, this inbreaking of God into the humanness of Jesus and the humanness of the disciples evoked a reaction: this interplay of God's primary action and human secondary reaction is what one usually calls a "religious experience."

3. Key to an understanding of the resurrection of Jesus, then, is the issue of religious experience: faith responding to the presence and

action of God. Indeed, the issue of religious experience should be one of the most controlling hermeneutical components of any and every reflection on the resurrection of Jesus.

4. Religious experience throughout human history has been expressed and described by imaginative language. Most people do not find this difficult when dealing with the writings of a mystic. There is, however, resistance when one comes to the most mystical event in the life of Jesus and a major mystical event in the lives of the early disciples. "Apparitions" are often not placed primarily in the same category as religious experience; too often they are placed primarily in the category of a tangible historical event.

5. The thesis, then, of this chapter has been an effort to justify the controlling and major hermeneutical role of religious experience for a solid theological understanding of the resurrection of Jesus.

4

The Resurrection and
a Unified Christology

Until now our focus has been specifically on the resurrection of Jesus, and only in passing on the entire christological enterprise. We have considered the substantial and revolutionizing research on the resurrection that has occurred in this century. We have studied in detail the numerous voices in the New Testament itself which speak to us about the resurrection. We have considered a theology of the resurrection that finds its centering in religious experience, a reality far more important than any so-called historical detail about the resurrection event. In this final chapter, I would like to consider the resurrection of Jesus in its relationship to the other major areas of christology. In doing this, I want to stress that there is need to theologize on the resurrection of Jesus within the context of a unified christology. This phrase, *unified christology,* will be the centering issue in this entire final chapter.

It has been mentioned above that the resurrection of Jesus was considered to be the starting point for much European christological writing, particularly Roman Catholic, from about 1950 to about 1970. Liberation theology has critiqued such a beginning and centers its own christological endeavors in the historical aspects of Jesus' life and message. To some degree the current interest in the Jewishness of Jesus also moves in a direction other than the resurrection of Jesus as the *Ausgangspunkt* for a christological synthesis. It is my own judgment that both of these movements away from any centralizing of the resurrection for christology are quite correct, and this judgment would hold for other similar resurrection-centering endeavors by other biblical scholars and theologians as well. Methodologically and theologically, the resurrection cannot be the point of departure for a unified theology, as I hope to indicate in the following pages. This decentralization of the resurrection, however, does not mean in any way that the mystery of the resurrection of Jesus is consequently of little value. To read any of the twentieth-century authors who depart from the resurrection as the point of departure for christology as though they were belittling the resurrection would be a total misreading of their intentions and efforts. Indeed, on the basis of all the research and writing on the resurrection of Jesus that has taken place during this present century, one can only conclude that such research and writing have truly helped to integrate the resurrection even more intimately into the total christological vision, into a unified christology. As we have seen in the preceding chapters, however, the results of this current research in many ways support neither the popular understanding of the resurrection among Roman Catholics and Protestants, nor some of the liturgical expression of the celebration of the paschal event, nor do what might be called the "standard" theological interpretation of the resurrection, which presents the theology of the resurrection as the major proof for the message of Jesus as well as for the divinity of Jesus. These very dichotomies raise the issue: Where does one find a unified christology?

There is, of course, a thesis or position to this present chapter, which I wish to propose as essential for any study of christology, be it biblical, historical, systematic, or liturgical. Two fundamental issues or aspects of this *single* thesis or position constitute its structure: (1) The first issue can be called *the need for a unified christology.* (2) The second issue can be called *the relationship between a theology of grace and various christological statements.* Let us consider each of these issues separately, even though they are interrelated. Together they present a single thesis or position.

THE NEED FOR A UNIFIED CHRISTOLOGY

Many books on christology, both Protestant and Roman Catholic, do not, in my view, offer a unified christology.[1] Many of these books are indeed well crafted and profoundly insightful, but in the end they do not integrate the basic components of their christology into a unified whole. This seems to be true whether the centralizing emphasis is on the divinity of Jesus, the redemptive act of Jesus, or the mystical nature of Jesus. In order to clarify this criticism, let us once again consider the threefold division of the gospel material on Jesus.

The four gospels, taken as a group, contain material that falls under the following three headings:

A. The Preexistence of Jesus and the Infancy Narratives
        Preexistence: Jn 1:1–18
        Infancy narratives: Mt 1–2
                        Lk 1–2

B. The Public Ministry of Jesus
        Part 1: The message and life-style of Jesus:
                        Mk 1–13
                        Mt 3–25
                        Lk 3–21
                        Jn 1:19–17:26
        Part 2: The arrest, trial, and crucifixion of Jesus:
                        Mk 14–15
                        Mt 26–27
                        Lk 22–23
                        Jn 18–19

C. The Resurrection Narratives of Jesus
                        Mark I 16:1–8
                        Mark II 16:9–20
                        Mark III 16 [added on]
                        Mt 28
                        Lk 24
                        John I 20
                        John II 21

Each of the gospel authors arranges the material in these three sections in his own distinctive manner. Let me cite the views of some authors regarding these distinctive arrangements and constructions.

According to D. Harrington, the outline of Mark's gospel displays a "tight geographical-theological structure" that involves the activity of Jesus in Galilee, the journey from Galilee to Jerusalem, the activity of Jesus in Jerusalem and his arrest and death.[2] J. D. Kingsbury uses a three-part structuring of Matthew's gospel, exclusive of the infancy narratives.[3] C. H. Lohr divides Matthew's material into a series of rings, centering on chapter 13.[4] Luke's gospel moves in a theo-geological way. There is an exodus of Jesus from Galilee to Jerusalem, where he is arrested, is killed, and is raised.[5] In John's gospel we find a prologue, a book of signs, a book of glory, and an epilogue.[6] Even within each of these distinctive outlines or emphases or structures, the material in all four gospels can still be divided content-wise through the threefold division noted above. The fundamental issue, therefore, remains: how to unify: (a) the preexistence/infancy narrative sections with the material on (b) Jesus' public ministry and his arrest, trial, and crucifixion and (c) finally unify all of this material with the various New Testament voices on the resurrection of Jesus.

This endeavor at unifying all of these gospel sections is no easy task. One might possibly say that this is accomplished thematically: that is, the christological unity in each gospel is secured by a central theme particular to the gospel in question. The following summaries offer a few such examples of this endeavor for a unified christology which several scholars of note have developed.

> The focus of Mark's theology is the focus of Jesus' theology—the kingdom of God.[7]

> The gospel [of Matthew] has two focuses, Jesus as the Christ and the near approach of the Kingdom of God which Jesus proclaims. These focuses should not be separated, whereas the entire Gospel could be read with either focus in view.[8]

> Luke demonstrates that God through Jesus was faithful to promises made to Israel, but in an unexpected way to include Gentiles, the unclean, the poor, women, Samaritans, rich toll collectors, and assorted other outcasts as well as elect people who are repentant of their initial rejection of Jesus, God's prophet and Chosen one. This Israel is called reconstituted Israel. In it is found continuity with the old.[9]

> Investigation of Johannine christology is demanded by the focus of the Gospel itself. John 20:31 points to faith in Jesus as "Son of God" as the source of eternal life. . . . The Gospel makes it clear that this faith is the condition of salvation.[10]

Even though a theme unites a given gospel, time and again one finds in theologically developed christologies that it is the second section mentioned above (the public ministry of Jesus) that seems to be the disunifying key—namely, the arrest, trial, and death of Jesus. How do the arrest, trial, and death fit into a message on the kingdom of God? On Jesus as the Christ? On God's fidelity to the promises? On faith in Jesus as the source of salvation? My efforts in this chapter will, it is hoped, indicate ways in which such a unification might take place and in which a doctrine of grace can still be fully maintained.

Another attempt to unify christology might be called the "classical attempt," namely, that Jesus is divine. Jesus' divinity unifies all that he does in the same way that one can say that God unifies all of creation. Nicaea, Ephesus, and Chalcedon are called on as the major bases for such a "classical" christology. The so-called Roman Catholic manual theology by and large presented this kind of "classical" theology. These manuals emphasized the divinity of Jesus. Indeed, most of the material in these manual theology christologies was dedicated to the divinity of Jesus. Two problems appear in almost every presentation of this "classical" christology: the first problem is to maintain, as Chalcedon clearly states, the full humanity of Jesus. In some of these presentations of the classical christology, any emphasis on Jesus' humanity was seen as presenting an enormous threat to the divinity of Jesus.[11] The second problem centers on the arrest, trial, and death of Jesus. In the "classical" christology, too often the Johannine approach to Jesus' death is used almost exclusively. "A little while you will see me and again a little while you will not see me." In other words, Jesus as God, with full divine knowledge, knew that even though he was going to die, he would rise. In such a presentation, death tends to become emasculated. The death of Jesus tends to be presented as a sort of "glitch" that indeed has been foreknown and forewilled, but because of the divinity of Jesus and his knowledge of his own glorious resurrection, it is not the agony of death that is typical of the human condition. Because of the divinity of Jesus and because of his own foreknowledge of the resurrection and all that the resurrection means, Jesus' death is atypical of human death.[12] From a theological standpoint, the death of Jesus is seen as a *remedium peccatorum,* a remedy for sins, particularly the "original sin" of Adam and Eve and the "actual sins" that became a consequence of this "original sin." The view that the cross of Jesus is a remedy for sin and therefore the source of human salvation has become a major part of the "classical" presentation of christology, both in Roman Catholic and in Protestant circles. However, it is quite clear that the central message of Jesus' preaching was not that he was going to die on the cross as a remedy for all sin and therefore as the sacrifice that brings about the salvation of every human person. In the gospels this is never presented as the basic message of Jesus' own preaching. Because Jesus himself never preached that his death was the remedy of sin and the source of all salvation, we see already a serious issue for a unified christology. We will return to this disunity material momentarily.

In each of the gospels, it is the public ministry of Jesus that receives the lion's share of the material. More chapters are devoted to this public ministry of Jesus than to either the pre-existence/infancy section or to the resurrection section. After a lengthy, quiet, and hidden life, about which the gospels say very little, Jesus suddenly moves into the public arena as a religious preacher, a revivalist, similar in many ways not only to John the Baptist but also to other similar Jewish religious preachers of his time. In his chronologically brief public ministry, the message of Jesus has, however, touched the lives of thousands of people over the succeeding centuries. Each gospel author spends page after page recounting in detail the public life of Jesus. Each gospel writer is, in his own distinctive way, a talented writer, and any author who spends most of one's time and effort on one aspect of the theme is clearly indicating to the readers that the very length of this material is vital to the meaning of the entire work.

Let us first of all consider this concentration on a particular theme from a methodological standpoint. Methodologically, one needs first of all a critical text. Our twentieth century has been graced with the development of such a Greek text: the Nestle-Aland edition. From the very beginning of the Jesus movement, no other century has been so graced. Clearly, the Nestle-Aland Greek New Testament still has textual problems, as one sees in the apparatus found on almost every page. When one studies these "textual problems," however, one realizes that they constitute a very small percentage of the textual issues. One might say that this particular Greek edition of the New Testament offers us a critical text that is about 95 percent valid, with only about 5 percent of the textual issues still undecided. I choose 95/5 percent almost at random, but what I wish to state is this: the critical Greek text we have at hand presently is the best our world has ever had and whatever further embellishments and clarifications might be made are minor.

Second, from a methodological standpoint, there is a need to develop an adequate social-political and religious context for the text. A text without context can indeed be meaningful, but without an adequate context the meaning one finds in a given text might not be the meaning of the author nor might it be the meaning of its time. When one disregards the context of a given text and emphasizes simply a "meaning," the danger of ideology becomes alarmingly real.[13] Once again, in our own century, historical studies about the political, social, and religious situation of Palestine at the time of Jesus have been developed in a major way. This has been done to some extent by Christian authors, and therefore with a certain Christian bias. This has also been done to some extent by Jewish authors, and therefore with a certain Jewish bias. When one begins to put the Jewish and the Christian investigations on this "second temple" period together, one truly is enriched with a political, social, and religious view of Palestine that no other generation to date has had.[14]

The textual and contextual methodological considerations are mentioned simply to note that they must be involved. I have no intention of focusing on these methods; however, on the basis of the critical text and the adequate contextual understanding, I do want to consider, third, the internal methodological issue: namely, the unification of the three sections about Jesus, mentioned many times above, in any and every presentation of the "gospel message."

It is a commonplace today to say that in the message and example of Jesus the kingdom of God is centralizing, centralizing to his message and to his living example. He preached the kingdom of God and he lived the kingdom of God. In the last one hundred or so years the theme of the kingdom of God in Jesus' preaching has sparked considerable discussion among biblical scholars. Early on in this time frame, J. Weiss in opposition to Ritschl argued that the kingdom of God in Jesus' preaching was not simply a matter of interior spirituality but a far more objective reality. Moreover, comparisons of the kingdom to a territory or a land or a treasure did not do justice to the meaning of Jesus.[15] For his part, Weiss could not understand how a cosmic destruction of this present world could be maintained in today's scientific and technological understanding of our environment. Ultimately, Weiss saw the objective kingdom on the other side of history.

C. H. Dodd stressed that the kingdom preached by Jesus was a now-but-not-yet reality.[16] Scholars have called Dodd's position a realized eschatology; however, his emphasis on the realized aspect of the kingdom appeared to some scholars as missing or to some degree underestimating the not-yet aspect.

J. Jeremias stated that the kingdom was in process of realization, thus maintaining a now approach and a not-yet approach as well.[17] Jeremias, however, clearly indicated that there is a complexity in this "kingdom" preached by Jesus. He divided his material into four themes, but they are all interrelated: (1) The kingdom is God is at hand. (2) The kingdom of Satan is coming to an end. (3) The quenched Spirit has returned. (4) The poor have the good news preached to them.

All such divisions have both strong points and clear limitations, and Jeremias's fourfold description is no exception. However, it is clear that the starting point for Jeremias, as for so many other biblical scholars, is the kingdom of God as the central issue in the message and life of Jesus. God's kingdom or presence is already at work in creation, but since God is supreme holiness and love, the more that God's presence is found in our lives the less evil will be in our lives. "Satan is overcome" is, therefore, the flip side of the kingdom of God is at hand. Part of the good news is clearly this: evil is not the final answer; God alone will be and is the final answer.

When Jeremias speaks of the return of the quenched Spirit, he is picking up on a folk-religious belief at the time of Jesus. With the death of Haggai, Zechariah, and Malachi (roughly in the sixth century B.C.E.),[18] prophecy ended or was "quenched." The common folk belief was this: when the Spirit of God returned, the messianic time would begin. This return of the Spirit, the messianic time, was itself the activation of God's kingdom, presence, and power in our lives.[19] Again, in Jeremias's thought there is a connection between the meaning of "kingdom" and the return of the quenched Spirit. In other words, in Jeremias this latter emphasis on the Spirit fills out part of the very meaning of the New Testament term *kingdom*.

In his last theme, namely, the poor have the good news preached to them, Jeremias indicates that the kingdom of God far surpassed many of the then-current interpretations of the Torah and of the prophets as well. The manner in which some of the Jewish leadership of Jesus' time determined what is clean and what is unclean is not the way God judges, nor was it, as Jesus mentioned, the meaning of God's Torah itself. The poor are central to an understanding of God's kingdom.

All four issues that Jeremias describes hover around the central theme: kingdom of God. All four issues help to give some additional light to this mystery of God's presence and power in our lives. In other words, if I am reading Jeremias correctly, there are not four different themes to the message of Jesus, but rather a central theme that is refracted in the fourfold prism described above.

In today's christological literature there has been no little criticism of the term *kingdom*,[20] and with good reason, since in English at least there is a masculine overtone to the word, which one does not necessarily find in other languages such as German, French, or Spanish. In other words, part of the criticism about the use of the term *kingdom* must be seen within a linguistic framework. Often this linguistic aspect of the issue is overlooked or the entire issue is presented only from an "English" framework. Nonetheless, even a linguistic framework can give rise to an ideological framework, and this is where the greatest criticism of the term *kingdom* lies. An almost exclusive masculinity is seen within the ideological meaning of "kingdom." An overbearing "paternalism" is likewise seen within the ideological meaning of "kingdom." Today, many women rightfully question these ideological implications, but so also do many men.[21]

Although the word *kingdom* has had a long history in our English theological material, it carries with it not only a male and paternalistic overtone but also overtones of enormous positive value. A major dilemma has developed: to change the term might avoid any male and paternalistic overtone, but the substitute term might also be disengaged from the profound spiritual and theological overtones that the term *kingdom* has developed over the centuries. Therefore care must be taken when one exchanges a key word for a substitute word.

There is a complexity to the central message of Jesus, and even the word *kingdom* by itself does not clarify this total complexity. In English, two other terms have appeared with some frequency: *reign* and *realm.* These two terms remove an overt paternalism, but they both continue an emphasis or sense of power and spatiality. The terms *kingdom,* or *realm,* or *reign* cannot be seen simply as words that encapsulate perfectly the central message of Jesus. One word alone, even though that word is used by the gospel writers themselves, cannot be held up in any fundamentalist way as "the teaching" of Jesus.[22]

The term *kingdom* is symbolic, and, as N. Perrin notes, it is a "tensive symbol."[23] If this is true, it is most helpful to keep in mind all that Tillich has written on the issue of religious symbol.[24] A symbol tends toward a multiple interpretation. Once the word "kingdom" is seen as a symbol, then other ideas can be used to help decipher the symbol or, better, to point more sharply toward the multivalent reality to which the symbol refers. Thus, instead of "kingdom of God," substitutes could be used. I would like to offer the following list but with no intention of giving any priority to the various themes:

Presence of God	Justice of God
Love of God	Holiness of God
Compassion of God	Goodness of God
Mercy of God	Creativeness of God
Power of God	Grace of God
Forgiveness of God	Relatedness of God

When these aspects of God are highlighted, it is clear that the symbol *kingdom of God* does what all symbols do. They reveal and they camouflage. To some extent the symbol *kingdom of God* does reveal something of the power and presence of God, but when one says the compassion or mercy of God, one points to a reality that the symbol *kingdom* does not reveal in any immediate or direct way. Thus, there is both a revealing and a camouflaging aspect to the very term *kingdom of God,* and this is even more evident when it is seen specifically as a tensive symbol.

Clearly, each of the above substitute terms has a similar fate. Each, as a symbol, has its own positive value and its own limitation. Many other terms could easily be added to the list above; my list is not meant to be exhaustive. Along with so many other contemporary theologians, I am struggling to find a term that maintains the holiness and justice of God, on the one hand, and the widest inclusivity of creatures, on the other hand. It is with this openness and inclusiveness that I hope you, as readers, will interpret my thoughts and words in the following pages. I realize that at times my words will trip me up and my thoughts will not be as clear as I might wish, but I hope my intention is clear and my direction is inclusive. It is also true that I will continue to use the term *kingdom of God,* even with all the above hesitations, but I do so since I do not believe any substitute term maintains the positive overtones that this particular term has. Having developed this brief *apologia pro verbis meis,* let us continue our search for a unified christology.

This complexity about the kingdom has been highlighted by the excellent work of L. Boff, *Jesus Christ Liberator,* and especially of J. Sobrino in his latest volume, *Jesus the Liberator.* Both of these authors stress that the kingdom of God must involve a diminishment of evil, particularly evil social structures, which are found both in the social-political arena and in the ecclesiastical arena. A kingdom-of-God theology and spirituality that are not evident in social-political struggle are hardly consistent with Jesus' teaching. A kingdom-of-God theology and spirituality that are not evident in a Christian ecclesiastical struggle are even less tolerable.

Second, the poor in the works of these and other liberation theologians are a very special *locus theologicus*. These theologians argue that one cannot begin to understand the meaning of the kingdom of God unless one listens to the poor. God speaks the message of this kingdom preferentially through them. In these writers we see more clearly than in Jeremias that the issue "the poor have the good news preached to them" is an essential part of the very meaning of kingdom.

> Jesus, too, understands final reality as a dual unity, a God who gives himself to history or a history that comes to be according to God. This dual unity, which is final reality, is what is formally meant by the expression "Kingdom of God" and is what Jesus preached.[25]

Sobrino goes on to describe how liberation theology understands the kingdom of God and how this understanding distinguishes it from other present-day theologies of the kingdom.[26] He mentions:

> *1. The Kingdom of God in the presence of and against the anti-Kingdom.* One cannot understand the Kingdom of God apart from the anti-kingdom's presence in our daily life, both socially and ecclesiastically. Anti-kingdom is not simply a "not-yet" component; it is a present destructive power against all that the Kingdom of God stands for.

> *2. The Kingdom belongs to the poor.* The poor are not simply poor in spirit, but the concrete groupings of poor and marginated that populate our concrete lives. These are the poor to whom the good news of the Kingdom is addressed. These are themselves the good news. These are a major *locus theologicus* in which one finds the very meaning of the New Testament message.

> *3. The historical dimension of the Kingdom.* Oppression and slavery at every level must be confronted by the Kingdom of God. Any theology and spirituality which assuages these realities of the anti-kingdom with promises of a heavenly Kingdom indicate that such a

theology and spirituality have not yet understood the very meaning of the kingdom of God.

4. The popular dimension of the Kingdom. God's primary election is not the Church, but the people, especially the poor people. Only if and when the Church champions the people whom God has primarily addressed and chosen can the Church itself be seen as "people of God."

In these ideas of Sobrino, there is much that calls into question the standard theological approach of many Roman Catholic theologies, many Eastern church theologies, and many Protestant theologies. Because of the circumstances of Central America in which Sobrino has done his major work, the materially poor, the politically and socially marginalized are brought to center stage. Were one to look more globally at the meaning of the poor and the marginalized, many other groups would certainly need to be seen at this center stage, this *locus theologicus,* including the following:

Women.   By this one should not merely mean Christian women and their ranking within the ecclesiastical structure; nor should one overfocus on the Roman Catholic issue of the ordination of women. Rather, the issue should include women throughout the world. Is there equality, dignity, and freedom for every individual or not?[27] Not only are baptized, Christian women a major part of this *locus theologicus,* but women throughout the world, regardless of their religious affiliation. Until women globally are respected for their equality, dignity, and freedom, the gospel message makes no sense. Unless those who are the leaders, both ecclesiastical and theological, of the various Christian churches cry out against women's lack of equality, dignity, and freedom, such leadership can be judged as misconceiving the call of the gospel.

Racial and Cultural Minorities.   Christianity has been and remains basically a Euro-Anglo-American entity. Fundamentally, the theology, the liturgy, the symbol system, the spirituality, the institutional structures are Euro-Anglo-American. Centuries of colonialization linked with church mission have engraved this into almost every area of our world. Roman Catholic, Protestant, and Eastern churches are racially and culturally churches to which "others" are at times invited to be members. Too often, such people are, either because of race or because of culture, seen as second-class members. The more such racially diverse and culturally diverse members take on the elements of the centralizing church, the more "included" they become.

In theological history it is fascinating to see how a strongly Jewish group of Jesus-people gradually but with much struggle became a Greco-Roman people. This was the first instance of inculturation by the Christian community. It is equally fascinating to see how this community only a few centuries later experienced a second inculturation—at least in the West—vis-à-vis the so-called Germanic tribes. The early Byzantine Christian empire became, in the West, the Holy Roman Empire. With the American and French revolutions and the cultural changes these involved, most of the Western Protestant and Roman Catholic churches struggled against any new, secular inculturation. This process is still going on with many fits and starts.

It is equally fascinating to see that in the globalization of our world from the late Middle Ages onward, the very idea of inculturation, at least as understood by the Christian churches, rarely meant a mutual process of inculturation. The Euro-Anglo-American power position almost always dominated the evangelizing efforts of both Protestant and Roman Catholic missions.

Why are these issues fascinating? For me, they are fascinating because they raise the issues of racism and monoculturalism in churches, which on the basis of christology should have no tolerance at all of any racism or monoculturalism. This kind of fascination is not a happy fascination; rather, it is a fascination that unfortunately evil, too, can bring about.

Sexual Minorities. Roman Catholic and many Protestant churches alike have been uneasy over the current rethinking of sexuality. Some of this uneasiness appears in the stance toward women generally. Some appears in the stance toward those who are married and divorced. In certain cultures it appears in the stance toward culturally accepted polygamy. It appears in the stance toward same-sex sexuality. There are no quick theological answers for any of these issues as far as the sexual aspect is concerned. There appears to be a marked hesitation to rethink human sexuality generally. Christian positions on sexuality that have been held for centuries do not easily lend themselves to fundamental rethinking. Still such theological rethinking of human sexuality is going on today, whether church leadership approves or not.[28] On the practical level, Christian people who are not in ecclesiastical or theological leadership positions are following their own consciences, in spite of leadership statements. For such people, being a Christian and following one's conscience on sexual issues has ceased being a defining matter. Once again, the message of Jesus was and remains an inclusive message. This is the basic thrust of the "kingdom of God." Humanly speaking, we generally as existential groups of Christians need at times to put up barriers, but whenever we do, the message of Jesus asks of us a basic question: Why? We need to justify every barrier.

Members of Other Religions. Evangelization is an "in word" in contemporary Western theology, but evangelization involves an encounter with other major and minor religions that include the majority of this world's population. Does a christology imply that only those who believe in Jesus will be saved? Or does a christology, with its focus on the kingdom of God, not the church of Jesus, imply that salvation is an inclusive, not an exclusive, issue? From fundamentalist Christian groups to all the mainline Christian churches, these questions are present and in various ways the churches are attempting to answer them. More often than not, the very answers the churches develop complicate the issue of a unified christology.

Certainly others will think of groups beyond the ones mentioned above and ask that they be included as well. Again, I do not wish to offer a final listing, but only say that the "marginalized," which liberation theologians of Central and South America tend to emphasize, need to be seen in a more globalized way. There is a very inclusive center of poor or marginalized that must be seen, heard, and followed as one of the gospel's major *loci theologici*. Only when this begins to take place will we make major steps toward a unified christology.

More recently still, J. Meier has in a rather exhaustive way drawn together the antecedent Jewish roots for this preaching of the kingdom by Jesus.[29] The term is found sparsely in the Torah, the prophets, and the writings. It is found more frequently in the inter-testamental writings. Meier constructs an artificial summary of the meaning of the kingdom:

> It would include God's creation of his good and ordered universe, creation's corruption by human sin and rebellion, God's gracious

choice of the people Israel to be his very own, his liberation of them from slavery in Egypt, the experiences of sin and salvation at the Reed Sea and Mt. Sinai, the desert journey, and entrance into the promised land.[30]

Meier goes on to include in this "story of the kingdom" the reign of King David, the choice of Jerusalem, the idolatry of Israel, the rejection of the prophets, the destruction of the temple, the Babylonian captivity, the rebuilding of Jerusalem, as also the coming of Jesus—his life, death, and resurrection—and the subsequent community of believers in Jesus.

Such an extensive meaning of the kingdom of God indicates that in many ways there was not a newness in Jesus' preaching of the kingdom. Meier notes:

1. Jesus expected a future definitive coming of God who would rule as king.
2. This hope was so central to his message that prayer should also make it central, i.e., the Lord's prayer: your kingdom come!
3. The coming of the kingdom would bring about a reversal of unjust conditions of poverty, sorrow and hunger.
4. The final Kingdom would bring about a more astounding reversal: inclusion of Gentiles.
5. Even with impending death, Jesus said that he would share in this final banquet in the Kingdom.[31]

At the end of his presentation on the kingdom of God, Meier notes that Jesus expresses the already-now aspect of the kingdom by his "free-wheeling table fellowship with toll collectors and sinners and his rejection of voluntary fasting for himself and his disciples." And "to all of this must be added his—at times startling—interpretation of the Torah."[32] Given what both Sobrino and Meier say, there is clearly a reevaluation of all values in the very reality and meaning of the kingdom of God. As a tensive symbol, kingdom of God clearly involves a radical rethinking of our human values.

With this material on the kingdom of God in mind, let us now review the three sections of the gospels, but with the question: Do these three sections of the gospels make this message of the kingdom of God central or not? In other words, does the same message one hears in the public ministry of Jesus' life, which includes both his preaching and his activity of healing and caring, serve as the centralizing issue in the other sections of the gospels?

The Preexistence and Infancy Narratives

There is a richness of detail in these small but precious sections of our gospels, and I would suggest that the underlying message of these narratives is precisely the same as the preached message of Jesus, namely, that the kingdom of God is at hand, that evil is overcome, that the Spirit has returned, and that the poor or marginalized have the good news preached to them.

Let us begin with John's gospel and his introductory section called the prologue. Light has come into darkness and darkness could not overpower it: put in other terms, one could easily say that the kingdom has begun (light has come), but evil is not the final answer (darkness could not overpower it). The Word was the true light, and therefore the true kingdom is a kingdom of light, not of darkness or evil. To those who accepted the Word, God gave power to become the children of God, a part of God's own kingdom. The Word was made flesh and dwelled among us. More literally, the Word set up a tent in our midst and became like us. The kingdom of God has come; it is to some degree a now event. He lived among us and we saw his glory, the glory of the kingdom. Grace and truth have come through Jesus Christ. Clearly, in the prologue John does not say that the fullness of God's glory is what we have seen in the incarnation of the Logos, nor does John indicate that we already have received all grace and truth simply because the Word became flesh. In this prologue, there is clearly an already aspect, but, as one sees in a reading of the entire gospel of John, there is a not-yet aspect as well. The eschaton has begun, but it is a process that leads to a final stage of the eschaton.

In all of this Johannine material, there is an entry into our world of God's own Word, God's own glory. There was evil in this world and evil resisted the light and the power and the grace, but to no ultimate avail. In the prologue, John does not speak of the Spirit, nor does he mention the poor. He does mention, however, that God's own people did not accept him, but those who did became children of God because they were born of God. In saying this, the author implies that there is an openness to this kingdom, an openness not to those of a certain stock, not to those simply born at the urging of sexuality, not to those born and reared through human will, but to those born of God. In an indirect way, then, the prologue does imply that belonging to the kingdom of God involves those who accept the Word, no matter who "those" might signify. This conclusion must be said in a cautious way, however, since in the gospel of John Jesus' outreach to the non-Jew is very limited.

Nonetheless, one could conclude that the presence of God, the love of God, the compassion of God, the holiness of God—all of which are substitute expressions for the kingdom, realm, or reign of God— have become part of our world. This presence, love, compassion, and holiness is in our midst, and evil will not prevail. Moreover, this presence, love, compassion, and holiness of God is eagerly open to those who receive it. This presence, love, compassion, and holiness of God is not something (someone?) that (whom) one can claim because of race or because of the circumstances in being born. If the preached message of Jesus and the way he led his life during the years of his public ministry form the core of a unified christology, the Johannine prologue clearly reflects this core and in its own way helps substantiate such a unified christology.

When we consider the first two chapters of Matthew, there are even more connections with the threefold description given above. In Matthew's conception/infancy narrative the Holy Spirit plays a major role. The Spirit of God is involved in all of the dreams that Joseph received, and Mary was found with child through the Spirit. The very birth of the child Jesus is seen as the fulfillment of the Torah and the prophets, and with the presence of this child the messianic kingdom has begun. The Magi visit both the child and the parents, and the Magi are gentiles, not Jews. To some of the Jewish leaders of that period they were the non-accepted, and in that sense the marginalized and the poor. Herod rejects Jesus and in this rejection we find a power of evil, but the evil of Herod is not the final word, since the Magi through God's revelatory presence elude Herod. Through the same divine power Mary and Joseph take the child to safety. Even the death of the innocent children does not allow evil to be the final word. Mary and Joseph bring Jesus back to Palestine, and the plan of God continues in spite of the evil killing of innocent children.

The conception and infancy passages in Luke's gospel use different images from those used by Matthew, but the import is the same. The birth of John the Baptist comes about by the active presence and power of God in human life—another way to say that the kingdom of God has begun. The poor are mentioned: Joseph and Mary are surely not presented as wealthy and pretentious people. Mary herself says that God has looked upon a lowly handmaid. The shepherds were shunned by many Jewish people of that time, because too often they came on one's land surreptitiously, watered their sheep, let them graze, and went away without offering any recompense. Simeon and Anna are not presented as major figures, but as marginalized, aged individuals. In the *Magnificat* Mary speaks about exulting the lowly, filling the hungry with good things, and sending the rich away empty. Mary gives birth to the child outside the inn, and she lays him in a manger. In all of this Luke is clearly stating: the poor have the good news of God's compassion, love, presence, and holiness preached to them. One can hardly read this section of Luke's gospel without seeing in it a clear *locus theologicus* for the very meaning of christology. Too often, the virginal conception and therefore the divinity of Jesus are seen as THE *locus theologicus,* but there is far more to fundamental theological source material in these few verses than simply a virginal conception through the power of the Spirit.

Luke clearly mentions the presence of the Spirit. Gabriel tells Zechariah that his son will be filled with the Holy Spirit. To Mary, the angel says that the Holy Spirit will come upon her. At the visitation Elizabeth was filled with the Holy Spirit. Simeon was awaiting the Holy Spirit.

Evil is overcome. The doubting of Zechariah cannot stop the designs of God. Mary's hymn mentions that God has routed the proud of heart. The *Benedictus* is filled with praise for a God who is stronger than evil.

In all of this, what I am suggesting is a unified christology: namely, the meaning of the preexistent section of John's gospel, and the meaning of the birth and infancy narratives in both Matthew and Luke have the same message that the gospel writers portray in a much lengthier way in the preaching and healing of Jesus during his public ministry, namely:

The kingdom of God has come.

Evil is not the final answer.

The Spirit has returned.

The poor or marginalized have
the good news preached to them.

Why does one hear at times not only in various christologies but
also in the liturgies of the advent and Christmas season a different message concerning the preexistence passages and the conception and infancy passages? Why is there at times a changing of gears—namely,
here is the meaning of the prologue as well as the conception and infancy of Jesus, now let us look at his public life? Too often a basic, unifying connection is not made. It is my position that what one hears in
these passages of John, Luke, and Matthew reinforces the message of
Jesus' public life. Even "reinforce" is not the correct word. I believe that
one should bring the same message to bear on these preexistence and
infancy passages as one does on the public life of Jesus. Only when this
is done can we begin to see a unified christology.

Whether one considers the Johannine passage on preexistence and
incarnation or whether one considers the infancy and early life of Jesus
as found in Matthew or Luke, the emphasis is not on Mary, not on
Joseph, not even on the humanity of Jesus. These passages of the New
Testament are ultimately speaking about God's own activity, not a
human action of any kind. They speak to us about the inbreaking of God
into our world, and this is precisely what the symbol *kingdom of God*
means. It is God who is at work in John the Baptist, in Elizabeth, in
Zechariah. It is God who acts in Joseph, in Mary, and in the humanness
of Jesus. The message is about God's compassionate presence and
God's loving action in our human sphere, but the human sphere is of
quite secondary value. The preached message of Jesus was no different:
Jesus was speaking about God's activity: God's action in our lives;
God's action in our sin and evil; God's action of holiness; God's action
in the people whom many judge unclean but whom God judges clean.

Textually there appears to be considerable weight for this. I realize
that these passages do not constitute a major change of message. I realize that these passages are quite amenable to be united organically to
the message of Jesus' public ministry. I do not think that the major problem for constructing a unified christology lies in the linking of the pre-
existence/conception and infancy narratives to the major themes of
Jesus' public message. Consequently, let us now turn our consideration

to an aspect of the public life of Jesus—namely, the arrest, trial, and crucifixion of Jesus—for it is specifically in this area that the most fundamental problems of a disunified christology truly arise.

The Arrest, Trial, and Crucifixion of Jesus

One of the finest summaries of the meaning of Jesus' death according to the New Testament authors can be found in the book *Jesus,* by E. Schillebeeckx.[33] He indicates that there are three motifs which authors of the New Testament make concerning the death of Jesus. (1) Jesus was a martyr-prophet. (2) Jesus was the suffering servant. (3) Jesus atoned for sin. There are textual and contextual difficulties in each of these. After all, since there were very few martyr-prophets, it cannot be seen as a major Jewish theme. Second, the suffering servant in Deutero-Isaiah has no connection with the messiah, and it seems that the uniting of these two disparate images is a product of the early Jesus community. The atonement passages are never center stage, even and maybe especially in the Pauline letters themselves.[34]

Without any doubt, the death by crucifixion of Jesus presented his early followers with an embarrassing situation. Even today, one can almost hear fellow Jews saying to the Jesus followers of that early time: Were Jesus truly the messiah, the expected one of God, why did he die so ignominiously? For Jewish people at that time, some connection to the Torah, the prophets, and the writings was needed to make possible belief in Jesus as the messiah and as one so shamefully crucified. This is why the early followers of Jesus combed these sacred Jewish writings for some clue to and hint of a connection between Jesus as the promised messiah, on the one hand, and the death of such a messiah, on the other.

We realize that in the course of church history, a theology of redemption developed slowly. J. N. D. Kelly rightfully notes:

> The development of the Church's ideas about the saving effects of the incarnation was a slow long drawn-out process. Indeed, while the conviction of redemption through Christ has always been the motive force of Christian faith, no final and universally accepted definition of the manner of its achievement has been formulated to this day. Thus it is useless to look for any systematic treatment of the doctrine in the popular Christianity of the second century.[35]

Kelly goes on to say that "in the third century a marked divergence between East and Western thought on the subject of man and his redemption begins to manifest itself."[36] In the west, Kelly notes, it is the doctrine of original sin that begins to control the way one considered the meaning of the death of Jesus. Since the Eastern churches do not have any doctrine of original sin, a different approach was taken there. Clement of Alexandria, Origen, and Methodius all move in ways quite at odds with their western counterparts on this issue of the redemptive meaning of Jesus' death.[37]

Again, this noted scholar writes:

> The student who seeks to understand the soteriology of the fourth and early fifth centuries will be sharply disappointed if he expects to find anything corresponding to the elaborately worked out syntheses which the contemporary theology of the Trinity and the Incarnation presents. . . . The redemption did not become a battle-ground for rival schools until the twelfth century, when Anselm's *Cur deus homo* (c. 1097) focussed attention on it. Instead he must be prepared to pick his way through a variety of theories, to all appearance unrelated and even mutually incompatible, existing side by side and sometimes sponsored by the same theologian.[38]

Francis Schüssler Fiorenza, among others, indicates that there has never been a defined official statement on the meaning of the death of Jesus.[39] There are indeed the solemn texts from Nicaea, Ephesus, and Chalcedon on the two natures and one person of Jesus, but never during the past two thousand years has a church council or a pope properly using the power of infallibility spoken in so solemn a manner about the meaning of Jesus' death. There are, of course, statements in the various creeds which indicate that Jesus suffered under Pontius Pilate, was crucified, died, and was buried. But these creedal statements simply repeat the brief passages of the New Testament itself.

In the course of theological history, various theories have been theologically elaborated. In *Christus Victor,* G. Aulén notes that the objective atonement theory, which received a strong analysis in the writings of Anselm and Thomas Aquinas, and the subjective theory, which received its theological analysis from Peter Abelard, tended to drown out a third patristic position, namely, Jesus the victor. He uses these three foci, *Christus Victor, Christus Victima,* and *Christus Revelator,* to present his case in favor of Jesus the victor.[40] Jean Rivière, from a Roman Catholic side, studied these various theories, and although he used the triadic format that Aulén employs, he adds a number of subcategories to each of them.[41]

From earliest Christian times down to today, the theological investigation of the meaning of the death of Jesus has taken many paths. *No one path is the standard, official, defined church doctrine, Protestant or Roman Catholic, as regards the meaning of the arrest, trial, and death of Jesus.*

The point I wish to make, however, is this. When we arrive at the death of Jesus, suddenly a number of new messages begin to appear. In the west, the more common is this: Jesus died to atone for all our sins. However, one does not find this in the preached message of Jesus. Such an idea is nowhere the central theme of his teaching. Nowhere does Jesus ever say: I will die to atone for all sins and this is the central issue of my life and my ministry. Rather, Jesus speaks of the kingdom of God already at work, of a diminishing power of evil, of a returned Spirit, and of marginalized people who hear the good news. It is in the linkage between this theme from the life and teaching of Jesus, including as we have seen above his conception, birth, and earliest life, and the meaning of his dying and death that most christological writings become disunified. All of a sudden new themes are at work. More than any other place, it is in this linkage that a changing of gears takes place with the result that one begins to notice schizophrenic forms of christology.

I wish to suggest that in the death of Jesus we see the same four *foci* of the kingdom:

The kingdom of God is at hand.
Evil is not the final answer.
The Spirit has returned.
The poor have the good news preached to them.

In his commentary on the gospel of John, Raymond Brown makes a rather startling statement; he notes that if one wishes to understand what the author intends to say as he moves through the arrest, trial and death of Jesus, one must understand the washing of the feet.[42] In other words, the hermeneutic for the Johannine interpretation of the arrest, trial, and death of Jesus is not found in some "victor" motif, nor in an "atonement" motif, but in the service motif of Jesus washing the feet of his own disciples. "I have come not to be served but to serve."

We will return to this issue of a unified christology, but before any final attempt at christological unification is possible, it is necessary to consider another basic area that has contributed to a divisive or even a schizophrenic form of christology: the issue of a theology of grace and various christological statements. Two sources evidence this second basic area of disunification: first, there is an abundance of influential theological literature on Jesus which over the centuries has contributed and still currently contributes to this disunity; second, there are time-honored liturgical expressions that over the centuries have played and continue to play an enormous role in the way one considers the meaning of the arrest, trial, and death of Jesus.

THE RELATIONSHIP BETWEEN A THEOLOGY OF GRACE AND VARIOUS CHRISTOLOGICAL STATEMENTS

Two ways of discussing the relationship of grace and christology have been operative in our Western Christian expression of christology, whether theologically in monographs and books, or in liturgical prayers and actions. On the one hand, there has been a constant realization in theological writings that the incarnation (section 1: the prologue and the conception/infancy narratives), the public message and life-style of Jesus (section 2: the message and then the arrest, trial, and death of Jesus), and the resurrection (section 3: the many voices in the New Testament on the resurrection) are all moments of God's gift of grace. Never has either Christian theology or Christian worship portrayed the presence of Jesus in our historical existence as a purely natural event or an event that in some fate-determined way had to take place. The Jesus-event has consistently been seen as an extraordinary event—an event of grace.

In the twentieth century the issue of nature and grace has itself been a major theme for theological research.[43] Roger Haight, in his recent essay "Sin and Grace," presents a very clear statement on the basic issues of the Christian theology of grace, and also a brief but clear overview of current Roman Catholic theology of grace.[44] One of the major works in this current research on grace was the volume *Surnaturel,* by H. de Lubac.[45] In the aftermath of *Humani generis* this volume was not placed on the index, but the Vatican authorities instructed seminaries to remove it—along with many other volumes—from the library shelves. It was not a book that those preparing for the priesthood should read. In a later book, *Le mystère du surnaturel,* when de Lubac had been officially to some degree reinstated theologically, he speaks of a natural desire for the supernatural.[46]

A "natural desire for the supernatural" is a dicey way of speaking. De Lubac hedges his words, of course, and states clearly that grace should never be seen as something so extraordinary that "nature" is simply discounted. His intent of uniting grace and nature in as intimate a way as possible, without thereby denying the giftedness of grace, is clear. For his part, Karl Rahner does the same thing in his *Nature and Grace*:

> Grace is God himself, his communication in which he gives himself to us as the divinizing loving kindness which is *himself*. Here his work is really himself as the one communicated. From the very first this grace cannot be conceived as separable from God's personal love and man's answer to it. . . . God's act of love to us, precisely because it is God's and not our act (although of course it frees us not only to have things done to us but to do things), must be thought of as coming before our act of love and faith and making this act possible.[47]

L. Boff, in his small volume on grace, attempts to overcome the two-storeyed world that since tridentine times has prevailed in Roman Catholic theological studies of grace.

> When we talk about grace, we are trying to grasp this phenomenon that breaks down all the narrow barriers which we use to describe realities, dimensions and world. Grace establishes one single world where opposites meet: God and humans, Creator and creatures. Grace is oneness and reconciliation; hence it is synonymous with salvation, with perfect identity between humans and God.[48]

An enormous litany of similar theological statements could be presented, in which the grace or gift aspect of the Jesus-event has been clearly stated by first-rate theologians. Nowhere would one find a theological presentation that sees Jesus as simply a natural event within an evolutionary development of human life. This same litany of theological statements would preclude any presentation of the Jesus-event as simply a predestined or fated part of human existence. Time and time again, the Jesus-event has been clearly seen as a gift of God, a grace of God. In many ways, the theology of grace says the same thing as a theology of the "kingdom" of God. Grace in our Roman Catholic literature is often described as the presence of God, the love of God, the compassion of God, the mercy of God, the power of God, the forgiveness of God, the justice of God, the holiness of God, and so on—all phrases which, as mentioned above, are "substitute expressions" for the "kingdom" of God. Grace in our Roman Catholic literature (and in Protestant literature as well) consistently says that the grace of God is far more powerful than sin—evil is overcome; evil is not the final answer. Again and again, in these same theological documents grace is often described as the act of the Holy Spirit—the return of the quenched Spirit. With fits and starts grace in these same documents is presented as the gift of God's very self to those who are marginalized.[49]

Likewise, the liturgies of the advent and Christmas cycle as well as those of the lenten and Easter cycle continually speak about the grace of redemption, the grace of forgiveness, the grace of the incarnation. Prayer after prayer could be cited in which one clearly sees that the worshiping community celebrates the ineffable grace of God in all these liturgical gatherings.

Again, one could easily develop a dossier of liturgical texts that in no way portray Jesus as a natural development within a natural world. Nor would these text ever indicate that "fate" is the basic reason why Jesus is central to the Christian vision.

If all of this is true—and I surely submit that it is—where would one even begin to find a problematical area that could be interpreted as disunifying christology? Needless to say, my task to do just that is a delicate one, but I strongly believe that a Christian theology of grace and various christological positions are at variance with one another. Greater clarification, greater precision, and greater care in teaching/ preaching are requisite.

Slowly but inevitably the issue of grace and good works became a major theological and spiritual issue for the western church. In the Reformation, or better the many diverse reformations of the sixteenth century, this theme in particular divided the western church.[50] Indeed, this theme, grace/good works, became the central issue for the divisioning of the Christian church. The Council of Trent, in its efforts to respond to the reformers, focused on this issue particularly in its chapters and canons for each of the sacraments and in a most special and centered way in its decree on justification. From the *Acta* of the Council of Trent it is clear that the most astute bishops and most insightful theologians walked very deftly through this area of grace and good works.[51]

We now come specifically to the area of discontinuity. Once again I would like to use a pre–Vatican II theologian of high esteem, I. Solano, who presented what at times almost appears to be the "standard" teaching of the Roman Catholic Church on the suffering and death of Jesus. Solano's christological work appears in the series *Sacrae theologiae summa,* which is one of the better manuals of theology; it was published in 1961 immediately prior to Vatican II.[52] His thesis on the meaning of the suffering and death of Jesus reads as follows: "Iesus Christus sanctissima sua passione nostram redemptionem operatus est" ("Jesus Christ through his most holy suffering effected our redemption").[53]

Solano judges his thesis to be *de fide definita et catholica ex magisterio ordinario* and also *definita ex sollemni magisterio* (Denz. 54 and 831). Defined by the solemn magisterium and part of defined, catholic faith because of the ordinary magisterium is no small theological judgment. I have translated *operatus est* as "effected," since Solano says clearly that redemption signifies freedom from sin through the suffering of Jesus.[54] In a brief scholion Solano clarifies the issue even further, speaking of the work of Christ, which, insofar as it is a good work, pleasing to God, obtains gifts for human beings.[55] The author admits that the primary efficient cause of our salvation is God, but that the human activity of Jesus is the instrumental cause used by God for the salvation of men and women. The divine person offered the sacrifice of the cross since its value was infinite, but the *principium quo* whereby the divine person offered this infinite sacrifice is the humanity of Jesus.[56]

This "standard" approach to the meaning of the suffering and death of Jesus has long been with the Roman Catholic Church and to some degree with Protestant churches as well. In a presentation on grace and good works, no theologian of any standing has ever denied the gratuity of God's grace. The decree on justification promulgated by the Council of Trent makes this officially quite clear.[57] Human good works do not effect grace; rather, grace is always first and human good works are the response to this gift of grace. When one comes to the presentation of christology, specifically in the suffering and death of Jesus, the human good work over and over again becomes effective of grace. Even if caveats such as "instrumentally," not simply "morally" but also "physically," are found in the presentations, the christological statements on this subject imply that to some degree or another the humanity of Jesus "effected" the gift of God's grace.

The usual theological terms to describe the arrest, trial, suffering, and death of Jesus also reinforce this view: atonement, expiation, redemption, salvation, justification, reconciliation. All of these words can be explained and have been explained in ways which indicate that the human actions of Jesus, even his suffering and death, are effective of God's grace. These human acts of Jesus to some degree atone, expiate, redeem, save, justify, reconcile, and so on. The decree on justification again and again states the absolute gratuity of God's grace, a theme that excludes any human activity that might "cause" God to give grace. Second, the decree on justification clearly states that the only efficient cause of human salvation is God. In this decree, the human acts of Jesus are described as "meritorious." But once again, this "meriting" aspect cannot be in conflict with either the absolute gratuity of God's grace or with the statement that God alone is the efficient cause of human salvation. From the eleventh century to the present time some Roman Catholic theologians have attempted to distinguish merit *de condigno* from merit *de congruo*. They made this distinction precisely to indicate that all our human "meriting" does not effect grace except in a way in which God finds the giving of God's own self, God's presence to us, congruous, *de congruo,* because we are creatures of God and images of God. The phrase *de congruo* kept the focus on the absolute gratuity of God's grace. On the other hand, mention is made of merit *de condigno* precisely because of Jesus, and more specifically his meriting salvation for us on the cross. This small step, however, has contributed to the disunity in christology and even at times in a theology of grace itself. The absolute gratuity of God's grace, of God's holy and forgiving relationship to us, must be maintained, whether one is speaking of the humanness of Jesus or of any other creature.

It is hoped that the reader is beginning to see the disunifying issues that various christological statements make, disunifying issues because they can easily be interpreted as contradicting official Roman Catholic teaching on the absolute gratuity of God's grace and the teaching that God alone is the efficient cause of human salvation.

There is clearly no doubt at all that in post–Vatican II christology Roman Catholic theologians have attempted to correct this ambiguous language. At the same time, there is no doubt at all that at this given moment of time, these efforts remain for the most part purely theological;

that is, they are views of eminent and respected theologians, but few of these views or even a movement toward these views are incorporated into the official statements of the Roman Catholic Church. This diversity complicates the formulation of a unified christology.

It is noteworthy, however, to see that in the many sacramental rituals which Vatican II mandated and which were eventually officially adopted a change of language has often taken place. In older liturgical rituals we heard most of the time: "We have been saved by the crucifixion of Jesus." In the newly developed rituals we hear: "We have been saved by the cross and resurrection of Jesus." It is remarkable that this unity of cross/resurrection is seen as the salvific event. No longer can one speak about salvation and refer only to the cross, to the dying, of Jesus. Now one needs to speak about the death/resurrection as the salvific event. I would prefer that we would hear the life/death/and resurrection of Jesus, and maybe this phrasing will come in due time.

This change in liturgical phrasing and the theological reflection on the resurrection of Jesus in our century that have brought this about do raise some rather basic questions. Christian theology and Christian liturgy have spoken rather frequently about the "sacrifice of the cross," but if the resurrection becomes a major component of salvation, does one speak of the "sacrifice of the cross/resurrection"? How does the very term *sacrifice* dovetail with resurrection, particularly if the focus is on expiatory sacrifice, not merely on the sacrifice of praise? A sacrificial resurrection is a most unintelligible phrase.

Robert Daly, who has written extensively on the issue of sacrifice, moves into a newer approach when he speaks of a spiritualization of "sacrifice," a process already begun in the Yahwistic material of the Old Testament, profoundly furthered by the exile and diaspora of the Jews, but given an even deeper significance through the incarnation, since in the incarnation the material elements of sacrifice are now found in the bodily life and works of Christian people and identify—not merely imitate—the dispositions of sacrifice with Christ's self-giving love.

> This alone is the true basis for the Christian use of sacrificial language and imagery in Christology, liturgiology, sacramentology, soteriology, atonement theory, spirituality, asceticism, etc. Taken *strictly* or in the general sense defined in our opening paragraph (which was not of course what Trent had in mind with its defensive "*verum et proprium sacrificium*" [DS 1751]) *Christianity has no sacrifice.*[58]

"Christianity has no sacrifice." What a statement this is, for it tends to shake some time-treasured foundations of our faith. This statement, challenging as it seems, calls us to consider anew the theology of grace with its absolute giftedness-nature aspect, on the one hand, and on the other various christological statements that have been made and are still made about the "sacrifice of the cross" and the "sacrifice of the mass." Can they ever be united in such a way that the problem of the grace/good works issue is not reestablished? Whenever there is a *do ut des* (I give so that you might give) situation, is grace really gratuitous? Can one speak of an "expiatory sacrifice" without presenting it as a good work that Jesus did in and through his humanness? In his humanity Jesus does nothing first *(do)* so that God may do something in return *(ut des)*.

Another major writer in this area is G. O'Collins, who states in his essay "Redemption":

> What is redemption? When and where did and does it occur? Who brought and brings it? The liturgy bears witness, above all, to the utter centrality of Christ (and his Holy Spirit) in the work of humanity's redemption which has brought to humankind justification, adoption as God's sons and daughters, incorporation into the Body of Christ, the gift of the Holy Spirit, and a divinized existence that human beings share in the life of tri-personal God.[59]

O'Collins clearly focuses on the action of God in redemption. The mention of the centrality of Christ is immediately connected to the action of the Holy Spirit, the action of God. His focus in this passage is not on the "death of Jesus" as the sacrifice that redeemed the world. O'Collins speaks of three ways the scriptures, the liturgy, and theology have expressed "redemption": first, Christ as second Adam conquering the power of sin, death, and all evil; second, Christ as the high priest expiating sin; third, Christ as the universal mediator, whose act of reconciliation has brought humanity a new covenant of love with God and with one another.[60] He then goes on to say:

> In these terms Christian visual art, hymns and poetry have persistently interpreted Jesus' Cross as the flag or standard of victory, the means of atonement, and the great sign of divine love toward humankind.[61]

Some of the theological expressions used here do not dovetail well with the first citation from O'Collins, which is his final summarizing statement on the meaning of "redemption." Jesus as conqueror is the Jesus Victor theory; Jesus as high priest is the Jesus Victim theory; the great sign, flag, or standard is Jesus the Illuminator theory. It is true that these three theories have been at play in the history of western theology on redemption. The mere mentioning of all three, at least in equivalent terms, does not bring about a unified christological view.

In both of these essays, the authors are clearly trying to maintain something we might describe as follows: that God alone effects salvation, or that the life, suffering, and death of Jesus is a symbol of God's love, a manifestation of God's presence, an incarnation of God's compassion. However, some important traditional theological statements tend to move in a different direction; these more traditional statements include "means of salvation," and an "expiatory sacrifice."

Francis Schüssler Fiorenza in his essay entitled "Redemption" presents us with a grand historical overview of various interpretations of redemption. In his concluding remarks he stresses the symbolic aspect of the human action, especially the symbol of the cross. He insists that an understanding of the suffering and death of Jesus be seen as a consequence Jesus' proclamation, ministry, and life practice. In other words, Fiorenza is asking for a unified christology; the meaning of the death of Jesus must be intimately united with the life and ministry of Jesus. Second, he stresses that the life, death, and resurrection of Jesus must be seen in a communal, not simply an individual, way. Again, there is an emphasis on a unified christology which is the basis of any unified ecclesial community. Finally, he says that "Jesus' death has to be related to God's gracious love, manifest in creation, reconciliation and redemption. Jesus' pro-existence is at the same [time] a manifestation of God's *pro nobis*."[62] Clearly, Fiorenza stresses the revelatory aspect of the life, death, and resurrection of Jesus: a revelation of the absolute love and gratuity of God's grace. In doing this, he deemphasizes an "effective" aspect of Jesus' life, death, and resurrection, which authors such as Solano so overemphasized but which lingers on in liturgical phrasings and in various traditional christological statements.

John Galvin in his essay "Jesus Christ" clearly states the problem, although he does so along confessional lines:

> While the resurrection has not been a traditional source of division along confessional lines, foundational differences among Catholics

and Protestants on the nature of faith and on the relationship of divine grace to human activity often influence approaches to this topic.[63]

Galvin cites a telling passage from Karl Rahner:

If the fate of Jesus has any soteriological significance at all, this significance can be situated neither in the death nor in the resurrection taken separately, but can only be illuminated now from the one and now from the other aspect of this single event.[64]

Galvin, after presenting positions by R. Bultmann, W. Marxsen, and W. Pannenberg for the mainstream Protestant side and positions by K. Rahner, E. Schillebeeckx, and R. Pesch for the Roman Catholic side, offers his own conclusions. Galvin clearly admits that specifying the meaning of the resurrection is not an easy task. This we have seen in this present volume. Galvin also states that resurrection and its revelation must be distinguished: "The views of theologians on the historicity of the empty grave and of the appearances must be distinguished from their conclusions concerning the resurrection itself."[65]

In agreement with Pesch, Galvin notes that "the context established by Jesus' life and death is an indispensable factor in weighing the foundation of Christian faith that Jesus is risen."[66] This is a clear call for a unified christology. A resurrection, he notes, that signifies a reversal of all that Jesus had done through his life, his preaching, and his death is an untenable position.

If the message and life of Jesus, during his public years, were centered on the view that the "kingdom" of God has begun and therefore evil in principle is overcome; that the Spirit of God has returned and in abundance; and that the marginalized are major players in any understanding of this "kingdom," then my own position would read as follows:

In the arrest, trial, suffering, and death of Jesus we hear once again the message of Jesus' life and ministry:

a. The kingdom of God is present even in the suffering and death of Jesus.
b. The evil of such suffering and death is not ultimate.
c. The Holy Spirit makes every death, even a crucifixion, holy.

d. A marginalized person, such as Jesus, in his suffering and death
speaks in a major way about God's gracious love to those who
are similarly marginalized.

In making this statement, I wish to indicate that it is this centralizing theme: God's kingdom—but taken with all the caveats, substitute
terms, and so on mentioned above—which can, I believe, unify christology. In this approach, one returns to Jesus, hears his message anew,
reconsiders the style of his life, rethinks the prologue and infancy passages, and reinterprets the meaning of resurrection. In each of these
areas, one hears the same theme: the *kingdom* of God is already at hand.
What might occur when one hears this deep within one's spirit and accepts it to some degree at least? The answer is simple: a religious experience. There is an inbreaking of God into my/our life (the gratuity of
grace) and there is my/our response to this presence, compassion, love,
mercy, forgiveness, and liberation which we Christians call the incarnate God.

SUMMARY OF CHAPTER FOUR

The main issues in this chapter can be summarized as follows:

1. Too many formulations of a christology appear to be disunified
and at times even schizophrenic. There is not a clear connection for the
preexistence/infancy narratives of the New Testament, the life and ministry of Jesus together with his arrest, trial, and crucifixion, and the resurrection material. These three areas of New Testament thought need a
clearer unity for a christology to be credible.

2. The preexistence and infancy narrative sections lend themselves rather easily to mesh with the main section of all four gospels:
the public life and public ministry of Jesus. The theological interpretations given to the arrest, trial, and crucifixion of Jesus have, in the
course of Christian history, often been the interpretations that tend to
cause the most disunity, since they introduce themes that one does not
find in the message of Jesus' preaching and the message of Jesus' public life.

3. Besides this lack of integration, the arrest, trial, and death of
Jesus have at times been presented as a "good work" that effects God's
grace. Often such presentations, both in theological literature and in
liturgical phrasings, clash with the decree on justification promulgated

by the Council of Trent. At times christological presentations both in theology and in liturgical celebration seem oblivious of what Trent officially stated in this decree.

4. Since most contemporary biblical scholars and most theologians who have written serious material on christology claim that the core of Jesus' message can be symbolically stated—the kingdom of God is at hand—it would seem that this center, even though it is seen as a tensive symbol, and even though other words could be substituted for "kingdom," would well serve as a unifying thread for a credible christology.

5. Serious Roman Catholic theologians are currently moving in this same direction, and although each does so in a slightly different way, the fact that there is this theological rethinking of the "entire Jesus-event," from his conception to his resurrection, indicates quite strongly that some time-honored christologies as well as some current christologies are disunified. The main effort at present in christological research and writing is to formulate a unified christology.

Notes

Introduction

1. See John F. Noll, *Father Smith Instructs Jackson,* revised by Albert J. Nevins (Huntington, Ind.: Our Sunday Visitor, 1972) nn. 50, 52.

2. J. A. O'Brien, *The Faith of Millions,* 11th ed. (Huntington, Ind.: Our Sunday Visitor, 1938) p. 118.

3. *The Vatican II Sunday Missal,* prepared by the Daughters of St. Paul (Boston: St. Paul Editions, 1974) p. 455.

4. Ibid., p. 456.

1. Contemporary Theological Research on the Resurrection of Jesus

1. Typical examples of this brevity and apologetic use can be found in such widely studied authors as L. Lercher, *Institutiones Theologiae Dogmaticae,* 5th ed. (Barcelona: Herder, 1951) 1:113–21 for the apologetic section; 3:214–19 for the christological section; see also M. Nicolau, "Introductio in Theologiam," in *Sacrae Theologiae Summa* (Madrid: BAC, 1952) 1:371–90 for the apologetic section; I. Solano, "De Verbo Incarnato," in *Sacrae Theologiae Summa,* 3:270–71 for the theological section; see also L. Ott, *Fundamentals of Catholic Dogma,* trans. P. Lynch, 6th ed. (St. Louis: Herder, 1964) pp.192–93.

2. This four-volume work is one of the best because it cites in a very comprehensive way the finest work that other manuals had already produced, and it presents its readership with a clear *status quaestionis* as far as manual theology is concerned.

3. Solano, "De Verbo Incarnato," esp. p. 306. In his statement, Solano notes: "Cum de hoc nostrae fidei dogmate circa Christi resurrectionem abunde in theologia fundamentali actum sit, sufficiat eius momentum soteriologicum efferre."

4. Ibid., p. 297.

5. Ibid., p. 306.

6. Nicolau, "Introductio," esp. pp. 365–66, in which the author focuses on the resurrection of Jesus as a miracle and a fulfillment of prophecy.

7. Ibid., p. 365.

8. A. Tanquerey, *Manual of Dogmatic Theology,* trans. John J. Byrnes (New York: Desclée, 1959) 1:76–81.

9. Ibid., p. 76.

10. See R. G. Collingwood, *The Idea of History* (Oxford: Oxford University Press, 1946) pp. 134ff.; J. Levie, *The Bible: Word of God in Words of Man,* trans. H. Treman (New York: P.J. Kennedy, 1962) pp. 7–60. Another interesting presentation of this situation can be found in V. A. Harvey, *The Historian and the Believer* (New York: Macmillan, 1966).

11. See A. Schweitzer, *The Quest of the Historical Jesus,* trans. W. Montgomery (London: Adam & Charles Black, 1910) pp. 13–26.

12. D. F. Strauss, *Das Leben Jesu* (Tübingen: Osiander, 1835). See also C. Welsh, *Protestant Thought in the Nineteenth Century* (New Haven, Conn.: Yale University Press, 1972) esp. 1:139–69.

13. F. C. Baur, *Geschichte der christlichen Kirche* (Tübingen, 1853; 3rd ed. 1863).

14. Welch, *Protestant Thought,* pp. 147–60; see also P. C. Hodgson, *The Formation of Historical Theology* (New York: 1966); R. S. Cromwell, *David Friedrich Strauss and His Place in Modern Thought* (Fairlawn, N.J.: R. E. Burdick, 1974).

15. See Thomas M. Loome, *Liberal Catholicism, Reform Catholicism, Modernism* (Mainz: Matthias Grunewald, 1979); R. Brown, *Biblical Exegesis and Church Doctrine* (New York: Paulist, 1985); T. Bokenkotter, *A Concise History of the Catholic Church* (New York: Doubleday, 1990) pp. 261–94.

16. J. A. O'Brien, *The Faith of Millions,* 11th ed. (Huntington, Ind.: Our Sunday Visitor, 1938) p. 65.

17. W. Künneth, *Theologie der Auferstehung* (Munich: Claudius, 1933; new ed. 1951); English *The Theology of the Resurrection,* trans. J. W. Leitch (London: SCM, 1965) p. 16.

18. F. Schleiermacher, *Der Christliche Glaube,* ed. M. Redeker (Berlin: Walter de Gruyter, 1960) 2:82.

19. A. Ritschl, *A Critical History of the Christian Doctrine of Justification and Reconciliation,* trans. H. R. Mackintosh and A. B. Macaulay (New York: Scribners, 1900) 2:158; see also James Orr, *The Ritschlian Theology and the Evangelical Faith* (London: Hodder & Stoughton, 1897) pp. 203–4.

20. R. Frank, *Die Christliche Wahrheit* (Erlangen: Deichert) 2:208–9; Ludwig Ihmels, *Die Auferstehung Jesu Christi* (Leipzig: Deichert, 1906); Carl Stange, "Die Auferstehung Jesus," *Zeitschrift für systematische Theologie* 24/4 (1924): pp. 705–40.

21. Martin Kähler, *Christliche Wissenschaft* (Leipzig: Deichert, 1905) pp. 327ff.; Paul Althaus, *Die Letzten Dinge* (Gütersloh: Bertelsmann, 1927); idem, *Theologische Aufsätze* (Gütersloh: Bertelsmann, 1929); idem, *Grundriss*

der Dogmatik (Berlin: Evangelische Verlagsanstalt, 1952) p. 92; Karl Barth, *Die Auferstehung der Toten,* 4th ed. (Zurich: Evangelischer Verlag Zollikon, 1953); idem, *The Epistle to the Romans,* trans. E. Hoskins (London: Oxford University Press, 1933) pp. 115, 150, 222; Emil Brunner, *The Mediator,* trans. Olive Wyon (London: Lutterworth Press, 1934) pp. 563ff.; Friedrich Gogarten, *Ich Glaube an den Dreieinigen Gott* (Jena: E. Diedrichs, 1926).

22. Künneth, *Theology,* p. 18.

23. F.-X. Durwell, *La résurrection de Jesus, mystère du Salut* (Paris: Xavier Mappus, 1963).

24. J. Schmitt, *Jesus réssuscite dans la prédication apostolique* (Paris: Gabalda, 1949); see also idem, *Über die Auferstehung Jesu Christi* (Einsiedeln: Johannes, 1968); Künneth, *Theology;* A. M. Ramsey, *The Resurrection of Christ* (London: Collins, 1946); F. Prat, *La Théologie de Saint Paul,* 20th ed. (Paris, 1930).

25. E. Dhanis, ed., *Resurrexit: Actes du symposium international sur la Résurrection de Jesus* (Rome: Libreria Editrice Vaticana, 1974).

26. G. Ghiberti, "Bibliografia sulla risurrezione di Gesù," in *Resurrexit,* ed. Dhanis, pp. 643–45.

27. G. Habermas and A. G. N. Flew, *Did Jesus Rise from the Dead?,* ed. T. L. Miethe (San Francisco: Harper & Row, 1987).

28. P. Perkins, *Resurrection: New Testament Witness and Contemporary Reflection* (New York: Doubleday, 1984).

29. Ingo Broer, *Der Herr ist wahrhaft auferstanden [Lk 24:34]* (Stuttgart: Verlag Katholisches Bibelwerk, 1988).

30. Two Catholic authors who move in this direction are K. Rahner, both in his *On the Theology of Death* (trans. C. H. Henkey [New York: Herder & Herder, 1961]) and in his article "Dogmatische Fragen zur Osterfrömmigkeit," in *Schriften zur Theologie* IV (Einsiedeln: Benziger, 1960); and L. Scheffczyk, *Auferstehung: Prinzip christlichen Glaubens* (Einsiedeln: Johannes, 1976).

31. See R. Brown, *The Virginal Conception and Bodily Resurrection of Jesus* (New York: Paulist, 1973); J. Meier, *A Marginal Jew: Rethinking the Historical Jesus* (New York: Doubleday, 1991) vol. 1.

32. One must remember that this apologetic approach to the resurrection was taught not only in such instruments as theological manuals for the seminaries and the *Baltimore Cathechism* for Catholic Christians generally but also in such widely read popular books as *Father Smith Instructs Jackson.*

33. Bertold Klappert, *Diskussion um Kreuz und Auferstehung* (Wuppertal: Aussaat Verlag, 1967).

34. An analysis of the approach of these Protestant scholars to the resurrection can be found in G. O'Collins, *Jesus Risen* (New York: Paulist, 1987) pp. 34–76.

35. Klappert, *Diskussion,* p. 9.

36. Ibid., pp. 40–52.

37. J. Fitzmyer, "The Letter to the Romans," *NJBC*, p. 843.

38. J. Sobrino, *Christology at the Crossroads*, trans. J. Drury (Maryknoll, N.Y.: Orbis, 1982) pp. 236 –40.

39. Ibid., p. 241.

40. *The Greek New Testament,* ed. K. Aland, M. Black, C. Martini, B. Metzger, A. Wikgren, 2nd ed. (Stuttgart: Wurttemberg Bible Society, 1968).

41. C. F. Evans, *Resurrection and the New Testament* (London: SCM, 1968).

42. R. Fuller, *The Formation of the Resurrection Narratives* (Philadelphia: Fortress Press, 1970).

43. Kirsopp Lake, *The Historical Evidence for the Resurrection of Jesus Christ* (London: Williams & Norgate, 1907).

44. P. Gardner-Smith, *The Narratives of the Resurrection* (London: Methuen, 1926).

45. Maurice Goguel, *La foi a la résurrection de Jesus dans la christianisme primitif* (Paris: E. Leroux, 1933).

46. R. Brown, *The Gospel According to John* (Garden City, N.Y.: Doubleday, 1970) 2:966–78; also *Virginal Conception.*

47. W. Marxsen, *The Resurrection of Jesus Christ,* trans. Margaret Kohl (London: SCM, 1970) p. 12.

48. Ibid., pp. 18–21.

49. E. Schillebeeckx, *Christ,* trans. J. Bowden (New York: Seabury, 1980) pp. 30–42.

50. Xavier Léon-Dufour, *Resurrection and the Message of Jesus,* trans. G. Chapman (New York: Holt, Rinehart, & Winston, 1974).

51. Ibid., p. xxi.

52. H. Vorgrimler, ed. *Commentary on the Documents of Vatican II,* 5 vols. (New York: Herder & Herder, 1967–1969); G. Philips, *La Chiesa e il suo Mistero* (Milan: Jaca, 1975); G. Baraúna and S. Olivieri, *La Chiesa del Vaticano II* (Florence: Vallechi, 1965); B. Kloppenburg, *A Eclesiologia do Vaticano II* (Rio de Janeiro: Editora Vozes Limitada, 1971; English *The Ecclesiology of Vatican II,* trans. M. J. O'Connell [Chicago: Franciscan Herald Press, 1974]).

2. The Many Voices of the New Testament

1. See D. Harrington, "The Gospel according to Mark," in *The New Jerome Biblical Commentary* [*NJBC*] (Englewood Cliffs, N.J.: Prentice Hall, 1990) p. 596. See also J. Hug, *La Finale de l'Evangile de Marc* (Paris: J. Gabalda, 1978) esp. chap. 1: "Aperce d'histoire de l'exegese de la finale longue de Marc" (pp. 11–32), which is an analysis of the data on the longer ending of Mark's gospel from patristic times down to the present. On the same

issue of the ending of Mark's gospel, there is an earlier discussion by R. H. Lightfoot, *The Gospel Message of Mark* (Oxford: Oxford University Press, 1950) pp. 106–17. An opposing view can be found in *Counterfeit or Genuine*, ed. David. O. Fuller (Grand Rapids, Mich.: Rapid International Press, 1975), which is a condensation of the writings of John W. Burgon on the ending of Mark. See also V. Taylor, *The Gospel according to St. Mark* (London: Macmillan, 1952) pp. 602–15; H. B. Swete, *The Gospel according to St. Mark* (Grand Rapids, Mich.: Eerdmans, 1956) pp. 394–408, a reprint of the work that first appeared in 1898 (pp. ciii–cxiii for authorship, and 394–408 for textual analysis). C. E. B. Cranfield, *The Gospel according to Saint Mark* (Cambridge: Cambridge University Press, 1963) pp. 470–76; R. Pesch, "Der Schluss der vormarkinischen Passionsgeschichte und Markusevangeliums: Mk. 15:42–16:8," in *L'Evangile selon Marc*, ed. M. Sabbe (Louvain: University Press, 1974) pp. 365–409; in the same volume, H. W. Bartsch, "Der ursprungliche Schluss der Leidensgeschichte" (pp. 411–33); K. Aland, "Der Schluss des Markusevangeliums" (pp. 411–33), which gives the textual traditions of the various endings of Mark. These last three articles were papers for the twenty-second session of *Journées Bibliques de Louvain*. See Pesch ("Der Schluss"), who goes into minute detail in showing the interconnection between Mark 15:42–47 and 16:1–8 (15:42–46 finds an echo in 16:1–8). There is a literary correspondence to these details (pp. 367–86) and a form-criticism correspondence (pp. 387–98).

2. See B. Viviano, "The Gospel according to Matthew," *NJBC*, p. 630.

3. Ibid., p. 631. Viviano summarizes the Jamnia-Matthew controversy and gives the most important bibliographical references.

4. See Richard Dillon, "Acts of the Apostles," *NJBC*, pp. 722–23. Dillon summarizes the differing views on the issue of authorship, which are based mainly on differing opinions about the "We-passages" in Acts.

5. See Pheme Perkins, "The Gospel according to John," *NJBC*, pp. 942–47. In this section Perkins draws together all of the contemporary biblical scholarship on the author(s) and dating of this gospel. Of particular value is Perkins's summary of the differences between this gospel and the synoptics (pp. 942–43). She notes also that "the importance of the community's history of faith in shaping the Johannine tradition makes preoccupation with a single Johannine author inappropriate today" (p. 946).

6. See D. Harrington, "Gospel according to Mark," pp. 597, 614–15; also K. Osborne, *Ministry* (New York: Paulist, 1993) pp. 57–60.

7. P. Benoit, *Passion et Résurrection du Seigneur* (Paris: Cerf, 1966) p. 261.

8. R. Brown, "Biblical Geography," *NJBC*, p. 1194.

9. R. Brown et al., *Peter in the New Testament* (New York: Paulist, 1979) p. 71.

10. Ibid., pp. 71–72.

11. Ibid., pp. 58–64.

12. Harrington, "Gospel according to Mark," p. 629.

13. See C. H. Dodd, "The Appearances of the Risen Christ: An Essay in Form Criticism of the Gospels," in *Studies in the Gospel*, ed. D. Nineham (Oxford: Oxford University Press, 1955) pp. 9–35; M. Goguel, "Résurrection et apostolat," *Revue de l'Histoire des Religions* 123 (1941): 43–56.

14. Once again, the relationship between belief in the resurrection and a social dimension—the commission to preach to all creation—should be noted. Almost every apparition of the risen Jesus includes something social; the apparitions are not meant to be private spiritual matters.

15. Mark II appears to be a second-century addition; Mark III must be dated even later.

16. For Mark III and the connection to Mark I, see Harrington, "Gospel according to Mark," p. 629.

17. For Matthew's gospel, see among many others U. Luz, *Das Evangelium nach Matthaus* (Zurich: Benziger, 1985); J. P. Meier, *Matthew* (Wilmington, Del.: M. Glazier, 1981).

18. See R. Fuller, *The Formation of the Resurrection Narratives* (Philadelphia: Fortress Press, 1970) p. 78.

19. D. Senior, *The Passion of Jesus in the Gospel of Matthew* (Wilmington, Del.: M. Glazier, 1985) p. 153.

20. On this issue, see Viviano, "Gospel according to Matthew," p. 673.

21. See Justin, *Dialogue with Trypho* 108; Tertullian, *De Spectaculis* n. 30.

22. It might also be noted that the small detail of sealing the tomb has possible connections with Dn 6:17, which is a messianic section of Daniel.

23. See Senior, *Passion*, pp. 179–80.

24. See R. Brown and J. Meier, *Antioch and Rome* (New York: Paulist: 1983) pp. 23–24.

25. In the State of Israel today, there are Jewish groups at odds with other Jewish groups over a variety of issues, most of them relating to the Palestinian-Jewish peace talks, but also to the secularistic tone of some leaders in the government. Naturally, this intra-Jewish dispute cannot be seen as anti-Semitic. So, too, there was an intra-Jewish dispute that went on between the Jewish Jesus community and other Jewish groups of the post–second-temple time. Indications of this intra-Jewish struggle involving a Jesus community can be found as late as the time of the Johannine letters, in which there is mention of an expulsion from the synagogue. This intra-Jewish struggle cannot be interpreted as anti-Semitic. Clearly, however, in a later period of Christian church history, even as early as the second century, anti-Semitism is evident, and to bolster this anti-Semitism, the gospel of Matthew was on occasion presented in

an anti-Semitic way. However, this clearly does an injustice to the text and context of the gospel.

26. See *Septuaginta,* ed. A. Rahlfs (Stuttgart: Württembergische Bibelanstalt, 1965) 2:914–15.

27. Benoit, *Passion,* p. 377. One must be careful not to overburden this particular passage. The passage clearly indicates that Jesus is the messiah. The connection to Daniel bears this out. To impose a "divine nature" interpretation on this particular passage seems to go beyond both the text and the context. Benoit's description seems to tend in this "divine" interpretive way.

28. See F. J. Schierse, "Die neutestamentliche Trinitätsoffenbarung," in *Mysterium Salutis: Grundriß heilsgeschichtlicher Dogmatik* (Einsiedeln: Benziger, 1967) 2:85, 105. Schierse disagrees with L. Scheffczyk, who believes that there is at least a "Wurzelgrund" for the Trinity in the New Testament. See L. Scheffczyk, "Lehramtliche Formulierungen und Dogmengeschichte der Trinität," in *Mysterium Salutis,* pp. 146–220.

29. On the baptismal formula itself, see B. Neunheuser, *Baptism and Confirmation,* trans. J. J. Hughes (New York: Herder & Herder, 1964) pp. 13–15. See also H. Vorgrimler, *Sakramententheologie* (Düsseldorf: Patmos, 1987) pp. 125–26.

30. For the gradual development of a trinitarian doctrine, see Scheffczyk, "Lehramtliche Formulierungen," pp. 147–87.

31. C. F. Evans, *Resurrection and the New Testament* (London: SCM, 1968) p. 91.

32. See Fuller, *Formation,* p. 81.

33. Ibid., pp. 89–90.

34. Although he keeps the detail from Mark I on the women bringing spices, Luke makes no mention that these spices were to anoint the body. Perhaps he does this because in 23:56 he had already mentioned that the women returned to their homes and prepared the spices and ointments for Jesus' body. However, since the sabbath rest had intervened, they had waited until after the sabbath to come to the tomb.

35. In saying that these two men were sent by God, the inference should be clear. First of all, it is not Jesus who sent these two men, but Yahweh. At this juncture of their lives, the Jewish women would not have believed that Jesus was the messiah or the Son of God. The theophany through these two men was an epiphany of Yaweh, the one God. The indirect reference to Galilee, namely, "as he told you," also indicates that it is not Jesus who had sent these two messengers.

36. Fuller, *Formation,* p. 99.

37. On the Lucan notion of *exodos,* see J. A. Fitzmyer, *The Gospel according to Luke,* Anchor Bible (New York: Doubleday, 1985) 1:166–67.

38. There is some textual difficulty with this entire verse, 24:10, and it is

omitted by A, D, W, and other manuscripts. The majority of the manuscript material, however, includes this verse, even though it does not harmonize with the other synoptics.

39. See R. Karris, "The Gospel according to Luke," *NJBC*, p. 696.

40. The Western text (Beza) omits this verse, as do some other minor manuscripts. The editors of the Nestle-Aland Greek text rated its authenticity at the lowest level possible. Even if this verse is an addition made at some later date to the Lucan material, there still does not seem to be a dependence of the author of this verse on John. It is therefore likely that the two versions share a source.

41. On this issue, see Craig L. Blomberg, *Matthew, New American Commentary* (Nashville, Tenn.: Broadman Press, 1992) pp. 43–46.

42. The Greek word *ekklēsia* is derived from *kalein* (to call) and *ex* (out of). Sometimes the translation of *ekklēsia* as "church" completely distorts the connection of *ekklēsia* to *qahal*. The Jewish meaning is drowned out by the later "Christian" meaning of "church." At this early stage of the Jesus community, some term other than "church" should be used to reflect the New Testament usage of *ekklēsia*. This other term should rather evoke the Jewish framework of *qahal*. The earliest postresurrection disciples of Jesus retained a Jewish identity, and only gradually did this Jewish identity diminish and a "Christian" identity begin to take over. Even then, during this process of transition, the early identity of the emergent Jesus community included a Jewish identity—they were the true Israel. Since the term *Christian* is so freighted with later notions and nuances, I believe it would be much better to retain as long as possible in any historical discussion a term such as "Jesus community," so that the internal identity of Jewishness is stressed.

43. A eucharistic interpretation of this verse may not be the intent of either the text or context; see Karris, "Gospel according to Luke," p. 721.

44. It is important to realize that one cannot speak in some stereotypical and monolithic way about Judaism at the time of Jesus. Indeed, one should speak about the various Judaisms of that time. Each of these Judaisms existed because there were different interpretations of the Torah, the prophets, and the writings. The interpretations of these sacred writings by the early Jesus communities were easily seen, at first, simply as other "Judaisms." Neither the gospel of Luke nor Acts reflects a persecution by Domitian or the severe controversy between the followers of Jesus and the synagogue that developed after the pharisaic reconstruction of Judaism at Jamnia (85–90 C.E.). See Karris, "Gospel according to Luke," p. 676. See also J. Neusner, "Varieties of Judaism in the Formative Age," in *Jewish Spirituality,* ed. A. Green (New York: Crossroad, 1987) pp. 171–97.

45. See X. Léon-Dufour, *Resurrection and the Message of Jesus,* trans. G. Chapman (New York: Holt, Rinehart & Winston, 1974) p. 166.

46. The phrase "they spent all their time in the Temple" (24:53) indicates

that the self-identity of these early disciples remained Jewish. Their self-identity was not "Christian." There was no conversion from Judaism to Christianity. They were Jews who remained Jews and believed that the interpretation of
the Torah, the prophets, and the writings that included Jesus as messiah was the
correct interpretation of such writings and that as a Jewish community who
believed in Jesus, they were the true Israel.

47. Evans, *Resurrection,* p. 96.

48. For Acts, see E. Haenchen, *Die Apostelgeschichte* (Göttingen: Van-
denhoeck & Ruprecht, 1965) pp. 104–19.

49. When the two disciples arrive at the tomb, the relationship between
Peter on the one hand and the disciple whom Jesus loved on the other is heightened. Peter enters the tomb; the other does not. The disciple believes; Peter
does not. Some later authors have interpreted this contrast symbolically, that is,
as a sign of synagogue, on the one hand, and church, on the other. Neither the
text nor the context allows such an interpretation. Historically, at the time of
the writing of John's gospel, such a contrast of synagogue–church would have
made little sense. The self-identity of the Johannnine Jesus community was a
self-identity of being the true Judaism. Other Jewish groups, such as the pharisaic group at Jamnia, were considered by the Jesus community to be groups
that really did not understand Judaism. In a much more Roman Catholic and
apologetic way, other later writers saw in this contrast between Peter and the
"other disciple," a sign of Peter's supremacy over the other disciple, that is, a
supremacy of the pope over all other leadership in the church. Neither the
Johannine text, however, nor the Johannine context allows such a fanciful interpretation. We simply know that the one disciple outran Peter but did not
enter the tomb.

50. R. Brown, *The Gospel according to John,* Anchor Bible 29, 29A
(Garden City, N.Y.: Doubleday, 1970) 2:1009.

51. Ibid: "The stories of the empty tomb emphasize continuity, but the
recognition scenes emphasize transformation."

52. For an overview of the way this text has been used theologically, see
K. Osborne, *Reconciliation and Justification* (New York: Paulist, 1990)
pp. 17–24.

53. See, e.g., K. Rahner, "Theos in the New Testament," in *Theological
Investigations* (Baltimore: Helicon, 1963) 1:79–148.

54. See Brown, *Gospel According to John,* 2:1047.

55. On this issue, see Brown, *Gospel According to John,* 2:1118.

56. See Evans, *Resurrection,* p. 14.

57. L. Cerfaux, *The Christian in the Theology of St. Paul,* trans. Lilian
Soiron (London: Geoffrey Chapman, 1967) pp. 75–102.

58. Ibid.; cf. Gal 1:22.

59. A. Deissmann, *Paulus* (Tübingen: J. C. B. Mohr, 1925) pp. 90–124.

60. J. Lebreton, "La contemplation dans la vie de saint Paul," *Recherches de Science Religieuse* 30 (1940): 83.

61. Cerfaux, *The Christian,* p. 90.

62. Léon-Dufour, *Resurrection,* pp. 57–58.

63. For the position of Dibelius, see Haenchen, *Apostelgeschichte,* pp. 64–81, 99–103.

64. Ibid., pp. 267–83.

65. Tacitus, *Annals,* 11.24; see G. Lohfink, *Paulus vor Damaskus* (Stuttgart: Katholisches Bibelwerk, 1966) pp. 42–44 for the details of Tacitus's approach to historical thought.

66. Flavius Josephus, *Antiquitates, Proemium 3;* see Lohfink, *Paulus,* pp. 42–44.

67. For Luke, see Lohfink, *Paulus,* pp. 42–53.

68. Ibid., pp. 53–60.

3. A Theology of the Resurrection

1. Lao Tsu, *Tao Te Ching,* trans. Gia-Fu Feng and Jane English (New York: Vintage Books, 1972). This is a good translation, although the Chinese itself is more dense. Just as M. Heidegger uses such language as "a thing things," making the noun *thing* into a verb, so too does Lao Tsu use the word *Tao* as a verb, namely: Tao can tao—not unchanging tao; name can name— not unchanging name. So too a resurrection that can be named and described is not the unchanging resurrection. Mystery remains mystery.

2. See K. Osborne, "Alexander of Hales," in *The History of Franciscan Theology* (St. Bonaventure, N.Y.: Franciscan Institute, 1994) pp. 1–38; idem, "Incarnation, Individuality and Diversity," *The Cord* 35/3 (May/June 1995): 19–26.

3. In the past two centuries there has been a flurry of material on the history of various doctrines and dogmas, of sacramental life and liturgical rituals. It is commendable that systematic theologians utilize church history, since often the systematic theologian will see and evaluate things in church history that the professional church historian does not see. In my own book *Ministry* (New York: Paulist, 1993), I have attempted to do this on a rather large scale.

4. I use the term *leadership* deliberately, rather than *bishops.* In so many of the church councils and synods abbots, priests, deacons, and lay people were an integral part of the meetings. In the Roman Catholic Church only Vatican I and Vatican II can be seen as meetings of bishops.

5. See p. 23.

6. J. A. Fitzmyer, *The Gospel according to Luke,* Anchor Bible (New York: Doubleday, 1985) 2:1537.

7. J. Sobrino, *Jesus the Liberator,* trans. P. Burns and F. McDonagh (Maryknoll, N.Y.: Orbis, 1993) pp. 45–46.

8. Even today, statements from the Vatican use the term "intellectual assent" when they press theologians to maintain and teach "official" church positions. This call for "intellectual assent" on the part of theologians and religious teachers clearly continues the nonscriptural approach to understanding the term *faith;* this call continues the neoscholastic understanding of faith, which eventually can only be found wanting. What is needed in the Roman Catholic Church is a renewal of faith, but a faith that corresponds to what the Jewish scriptures and the New Testament mean by "faith." After all, this is the kind of faith that the Jewish Jesus urged on his Jewish disciples, and that is the paradigm for Christian faith.

9. See A. Weiser, "Pisteuo," *Theological Dictionary of the New Testament,* ed. G. Friedrich, trans. G. W. Bromiley (Grand Rapids, Mich.: Eerdmans, 1968) 6:183ff.

10. Chapter 2 of the Vatican II document on the church, *Lumen gentium,* stresses this mission and commisioning that every baptized Christian receives at baptism. What is said in the text above about the social nature of resurrection faith is substantiated in a very magisterial way by *Lumen gentium.*

11. X. Léon-Dufour, *Resurrection and the Message of Jesus,* trans. G. Chapman (New York: Holt, Rinehart & Winston, 1974) p. 20.

12. Ibid., p. 20.

13. In his volume on Jesus (*Institutiones Theologiae Dogmaticae,* 5th ed. [Barcelona: Herder, 1951] p. 174), L. Lercher speaks about an imperfect resurrection and a perfect resurrection: the imperfect resurrection means that one is raised from the dead but to a life in which death will recur; perfect resurrection means that one is raised from the dead to a life in which not only does actual death not occur, but even the necessity or possibility of death is eliminated. One is made totally incorruptible: *penitus incorruptibilis.* Lercher then goes on to say: "Therefore the resurrection of Christ consists in the real reunion of the soul of Christ with the same body, which had fallen through death, and in the glorification of the total composite." One can see in this statement by Lercher that the Greek view of the human structure and death is patently operative. Lercher is interpreting the resurrection of Jesus, as far as his anthropology is concerned, not from a New Testament point of view but from a Hellenistic approach. In doing this, he is not alone, since many other theologians, both Protestant and Catholic have done the same. Their view is certainly acceptable, but only as a theological opinion. In no way can this view of a soul being reunited with a body after death rely on the revelatory Word of God in the bible. To move from this Hellenistic view of death and resurrection to further theological statements about the resurrection of Jesus can only result in a more and more tenuous understanding of what the resurrection is all about. One opinion simply begets or colors another opinion.

14. J. McKenzie, "Aspects of Old Testament Thought," in *The New Jerome Biblical Commentary* [*NJBC*] (Englewood Cliffs, N.J.: Prentice Hall, 1990) p. 1295.

15. The reader will notice that there are overtones of scotistic thought in this presentation: the absolute freedom of God; the total contingency of every created thing, included the humanity of Jesus; the complete gratuity of all God's works *ad extra*.

16. See Thomas Aquinas, *Summa theologica*, 3, a. 23 q. 7, a. 12. Reference should also be made to the decree of the Holy Office, June 5, 1918, *De scientia animae Christi* [Denz. 3645] and to Pius XII in his encyclical *Mystici corporis,* June 29, 1943 [Denz. 3812].

17. J. Sobrino, *Christology at the Crossroads,* trans. J. Drury (Maryknoll, N.Y.: Orbis, 1982) p. 157.

18. Cf. an older but for its time well-documented essay by J. Ternus, "Das Seelen- und Bewußtseinsleben Jesu," in *Das Konzil von Chalkedon,* ed. A. Grillmeier and H. Bacht (Würzburg: Echter-Verlag, 1954) 3:81–237. More recently, J. P. Meier has reviewed the New Testament data on the issue (*A Marginal Jew: Rethinking the Historical Jesus* [New York: Doubleday, 1991] 1:255–78). R. Brown presents in detail the New Testament data on the issue of the knowledge of Jesus (*Jesus, God and Man* [Milwaukee: Bruce, 1967] pp. 39–105). D. Gelpi's book *The Turn to Experience* (New York: Paulist, 1994) also helps to present the value of experience, particularly religious experience, to an understanding of the human Jesus and his own religious experiences.

19. In the rather extensive material on the issue of the knowledge of Jesus, at least in Roman Catholic literature, most of the theologians begin *mediis in rebus,* that is, they begin with New Testament data (Brown) or they begin with a history of this issue within Christian tradition (Ternus) or they begin from a theological discussion (Rahner). In my own view, every discussion of the knowledge of Jesus should begin with a presentation of various philosophical models of anthropology. Certain models find the center of the human person in reason: the human person is a rational animal (Aristotle); I think therefore I am (Descartes); what is reasonable is true and what is true is reasonable (Hegel). Most scholastic theologians accepted Aristotelian anthropology as a given, although Scotus with his emphasis on will might be seen as an exception to this almost uniform scholastic format. Feuerbach accepted Hegel's approach. Kant accepted the Aristotelian/Cartesian approach with his discussion of pure reason and practical reason. In all of these approaches reason is the center. In modern times, it was Marx who offered the first most powerful challenge to this Western anthropology. In Marx reason is not the center. Process philosophy and phenomenology are also two contemporary movements that present a different approach. The psychological thought of Freud

and Jung, with their emphasis on the unconscious, has also challenged the reason-centered view of Western anthropology. It is my view that if one retains a reason-centered anthropology, one must say that Jesus did not grow in knowledge. The hypostatic union must take place at the very center and core of human life. If that center and core are reason/consciousness, then this is the area in which the union is to be found most fully. If, on the other hand, one accepts an anthropology that does not place reason at the center and core of the human person, then there is room for a discussion on the growth in Jesus' knowledge and experience.

20. R. Fuller, *The Formation of the Resurrection Narratives* (Philadelphia: Fortress Press, 1970) p. 35.

21. Léon-Dufour, *Resurrection*, p. 81.

4. The Resurrection and a Unified Christology

1. See, e.g., J. Sobrino, *Jesus the Liberator* (Maryknoll, N.Y.: Orbis, 1993) pp. 36–63; likewise *Christology at the Crossroads,* trans. J. Drury (Maryknoll, N.Y.: Orbis, 1982) pp. 1–39.

2. D. Harrington, "The Gospel according to Mark," in *The New Jerome Biblical Commentary* [*NJBC*] (Englewood Cliffs, N.J.: Prentice Hall, 1990) p. 597.

3. J. D. Kingsbury, *Matthew* (Philadelphia: Fortress Press, 1977).

4. C. H. Lohr, "Oral Techniques in the Gospel of Matthew," *Catholic Biblical Quarterly* 23 (1961): 427ff.

5. See J. A. Fitzmyer, *The Gospel according to Luke,* Anchor Bible (New York: Doubleday, 1985) 1:141–258, esp. 164ff.

6. P. Perkins, "The Gospel according to John," *NJBC,* p. 950.

7. Harrington, "Gospel according to Mark," p. 597.

8. B. Viviano, "The Gospel according to Matthew," *NJCB,* p. 631.

9. R. Karris, "The Gospel according to Luke," *NJBC,* p. 676.

10. Perkins, "Gospel according to John," p. 948. F. J. Moloney says the same thing: "John is the story of Jesus of Nazareth, written to communicate belief in him and in his saving life, death and resurrection. . . . John really is not a story about Jesus, but a story about what God has done in Jesus" ("Johannine Theology," *NJBC,* p. 1420).

11. See the essay on the knowledge of Jesus in R. Brown, *Jesus: God and Man* (Milwaukee: Bruce, 1967) pp. 41–42 n. 6.

12. See, e.g., Sobrino, *Christology at the Crossroads,* pp. 179–235 for a challenging analysis concerning a theological interpretation of the death of Jesus.

13. There are currently some attempts at a noncontextual hermeneutic for the New Testament; for an overview of various methods for New Testament

hermeneutics, see R. Brown and S. Schneiders, "Hermeneutics," *NJBC,* pp. 1158–60.

14. See, e.g., E. P. Sanders, *Paul and Palestinian Judaism* (Philadelphia: Fortress Press, 1977); idem, *Paul, the Law and the Jewish People* (Philadelphia: Fortress Press, 1983); J. Neusner, *First Century Judaism in Crisis* (Nashville: Abingdon, 1975); idem, *Judaism in the Beginning of Christianity* (Philadelphia: Fortress Press, 1984); G. Vermes, *Jesus and the World of Judaism* (Philadelphia: Fortress Press, 1984); J. D. Crossan, *The Historical Jesus: The Life of a Mediterranean Jewish Peasant* (San Francisco: Harper, 1991); J. H. Charlesworth, *Jesus Within Judaism* (New York: Doubleday, 1988); *Jesus' Jewishness,* ed. J. H. Charlesworth (New York: Crossroad, 1991).

15. J. Weiss, *Jesus' Proclamation of the Kingdom of God,* ed. and trans. R. H. Hiers and D. L. Holland (Philadelphia: Fortress Press, 1971) p. 133.

16. C. H. Dodd, *New Testament Studies* (Manchester: Manchester University Press, 1953) 70:63.

17. J. Jeremias, *New Testament Theology,* trans. J. Bowden (New York: Charles Scribner's Sons, 1971) esp. pp. 76–121.

18. Joel and Daniel lived in the same century as well. The dividing point appears to be the destruction of the temple and its immediate aftermath.

19. John 6 is an indication of this, but there are numerous other passages throughout the New Testament in which Jesus' relationship to the Spirit of God is questioned, since an acceptance of the Spirit in Jesus would mean that the messianic time has come and that Jesus is a central part of that return of the quenched Spirit. In general, the various healings of Jesus are also presented in this way: Are they from God and therefore is the Spirit of God working in Jesus? Or are they from Beelzebub, and therefore suspect?

20. See, among many D. Jacobs-Malina, *Beyond Patriarchy* (New York: Paulist, 1992); R. Chinnici, *Can Women Re-image the Church?* (New York: Paulist, 1992); M. Grey, *Feminism, Redemption and the Christian Tradition* (Mystic, Conn.: Twenty-Third Publications, 1990); *Feminist Theology: A Reader,* ed. Ann Loades (London: SPCK, 1990).

21. See, e.g., D. W. O'Dell, *A Post-Patriarchal Christology* (Atlanta: Scholars Press, 1991); E. Bianchi and R. Ruether, *A Democratic Catholic Church* (New York: Crossroad, 1992).

22. This is the way that I believe Meier approaches the material on the kingdom. Meier at first questions the position that the "kingdom of God" is the central message of Jesus (*A Marginal Jew: Rethinking the Historical Jesus* [New York: Doubleday, 1991] 2:237–38), but in his elaboration of the material (esp. p. 241), the "kingdom of God" in his clearly developed description or "story" does become the central message of what Jesus taught and lived.

23. N. Perrin, *Jesus and the Language of Kingdom* (Philadelphia: Fortress Press, 1976). Meier offers two caveats to Perrin's approach to

"Kingdom of God" as a tensive symbol. Both of these caveats are valid. "Tensive symbol" indicates that "the grand story of the kingdom has many twists and turns and not a few alternate endings" (*Marginal Jew,* p. 242).

24. From a theological standpoint, Tillich has probably been one of the most insightful theologians ever to delve into the meaning of symbol.

25. Sobrino, *Jesus the Liberator,* p. 69.

26. Ibid., pp. 105–34.

27. See, e.g., K. Osborne, *Ministry* (New York: Paulist: 1993) pp. 466–72.

28. See, e.g., A. Kosnik et al., *Human Sexuality* (New York: Paulist, 1977).

29. Meier, *Marginal Jew,* 2:237–506.

30. Ibid., p. 241.

31. Ibid., p. 337.

32. Ibid., p. 454.

33. E. Schillebeeckx, *Jesus* (New York: Seabury, 1979) pp. 272–94.

34. For a more lengthy description of this issue of New Testament discussion on the meaning of the death of Jesus, see K. Osborne, *Reconciliation and Justification* (New York: Paulist, 1990) pp. 38–51.

35. J. N. D. Kelly, *Early Christian Doctrines,* 3rd ed. (Edinburgh: T. and T. Clark, 1965) p. 163.

36. Ibid., p. 174.

37. Ibid., pp. 183–88.

38. Ibid., p. 375.

39. See F. Schüssler Fiorenza, "Redemption," in *The New Dictionary of Theology,* ed. J. Komonchak, M. Collins, D. Lane (Wilmington, Del.: Michael Glazier, 1987) pp. 836–51.

40. G. Aulén, *Christus Victor,* trans. A. G. Hebert (New York: Macmillan, 1969).

41. J. Rivière, *Le dogme de la Rédemption: Études critiques et documents* (Louvain: Bureau de la revue, 1931); *Le dogme de la Rédemption chez saint Augustine* (Paris: Gabalda, 1933); *Le dogme de la Rédemption après saint Augustine* (Paris: Gabalda, 1933); *Le dogme de la Rédemption au debut du moyen-âge* (Paris: J. Vrin, 1934).

42. R. Brown, *The Gospel According to John* (Garden City, N.Y.: Doubleday, 1970) 2:558–72, esp. 569–72.

43. Extensive bibliographical material on this Roman Catholic theme of grace can be found in many volumes on the theology of grace: e.g., L. Boff, *Liberating Grace* (Maryknoll, N.Y.: Orbis, 1981) pp. 231–36; P. Fransen, *The New Life of Grace* (New York: Seabury, 1973) pp. 353–69.

44. R. Haight, "Sin and Grace," in *Systematic Theology: Roman Catholic Perspectives,* ed. F. Schüssler Fiorenza and J. P. Galvin (Minneapolis: Fortress Press, 1991) 2:78–85, 108–14.

45. Henri de Lubac, *Surnaturel* (Paris: Aubier, 1946).

46. H. de Lubac, *Le mystère du surnaturel* (Paris: Aubier, 1965).

47. K. Rahner, "Nature and Grace," in *Nature and Grace: Dilemmas in the Modern Church,* trans. D. Wharton (New York: Sheed & Ward, 1964) pp. 128–29.

48. Boff, *Liberating Grace,* p. 4; see also pp. 35–37, 213–16.

49. Boff makes much of this aspect of grace: God's gift to the marginalized.

50. On this matter, see the lengthy discussion on the reformation in my volume *Ministry,* pp. 333–463. The sixteenth-century Reformation was simply one of many reform movements that had been taking place since around 1000 C.E. The issue of grace and good works, often called justification, became the theological heart of the sixteenth-century reformations. On this matter, see my *Reconciliation and Justification,* pp. 137–56. The Council of Trent faced this issue in its discussion of every sacrament, but above all it faced the issue in the decree on justification itself (ibid., pp. 157–97).

51. At times, in the Council of Trent the theological issue under discussion became focused not on the theological issue itself but on the authority of the church, particularly the authority of bishops. This refocusing came about because some of the major reformers claimed that former bishops had "created" some issue, e.g., the sacrament of confirmation or of penance. Whenever, as we see in the *Acta* of Trent, "authority" becomes the refocused theme, the theological issue of grace and good works takes a back seat. However, there were numerous occasions during the many sessions of Trent when the bishops did not move the theme to authority but stayed with the primary theological issue: namely, grace and good works. This is particularly true in the discussion and final statement on justification.

52. I. Solano, "De Verbo Incarnato," in *Sacrae theologiae summa,* 3:13–322. The material pertinent to our present investigation is found on pp. 297ff. Once again I wish to state that I have selected Solano not to single him out specifically, but rather to use his presentation as one of the many so-called standard theological expressions of the meaning of Jesus' suffering and death. Clearly, a host of other such authors who wrote the manual theology books could be cited.

53. Ibid., p. 297.

54. Ibid., p. 298.

55. Ibid., p. 304, scholion 2.

56. Ibid., p. 305, scholion 3. Reference is also made to Solano's interpretation of human instrumental causality as far as the humanity of Jesus is concerned (pp. 134–44). Solano argues for physical, not merely moral, effectivity on the part of the humanity of Jesus in the things that ultimately only God can do. Salvation, for him, is clearly one of these issues.

57. See Osborne, *Reconciliation and Justification,* pp. 185–90.

58. Robert Daly, "Sacrifice," in *The New Dictionary of Theology,* pp. 923–25. Daly, in this same article, cautions one about using the term "sacrifice" in an indiscriminate way. See also his *The Origins of the Christian Doctrine of Sacrifice* (Philadelphia: Fortress Press, 1978).

59. G. O'Collins, "Redemption," in *Encyclopedia of Catholicism,* ed. R. McBrien (San Francisco: HarperCollins, 1995) p. 1090. J. Nilson, in this same volume, under the entry, "Salvation," says: "As human, Jesus makes humanity's complete and irrevocable acceptance of God's gift" (p. 1158). In other words, the acceptance of suffering and death is a response, that is, good work, to the prevenient grace of God. On the other hand, R. McBrien does not quite say enough when he writes: "Jesus' life, death, and resurrection were neither merely exemplary or inspiring, nor (in the case of the resurrection especially) merely divine disruptions of physical and natural laws" (*Catholicism* [San Francisco: HarperCollins, 1994] p. 531). Rightfully, he states that "no explanation, from whatever side of the theological spectrum is consistent with the Catholic tradition if the *redemptive* significance of the life, death, and resurrection of Jesus is denied or ignored" (p. 532). However, McBrien does not attempt to further describe this integration of the life, death and resurrection into a *redemptive* connection.

60. O'Collins, "Redemption," p. 1090.

61. Ibid.

62. Schüssler Fiorenza, "Redemption," p. 849.

63. John Galvin, "Jesus Christ," in *Systematic Theology: Roman Catholic Perspectives,* ed. F. Schüssler Fiorenza and John P. Galvin (Minneapolis: Fortress Press, 1991) 1:301.

64. K. Rahner, *Foundations of Christian Faith* (New York: Crossroad, 1982) p. 266.

65. Galvin, "Jesus Christ," p. 313.

66. Ibid.

Index

Aland, Kurt, 178
Alexander of Hales, 108, 183
Althaus, Paul, 11, 175
Ammonius, 41
Anselm of Canterbury, 161
Aristotle, 185
Assumption of Moses, 91
Aulén, Gustav, 16, 161, 188

Baraúna, Guilherme, 26, 177
Barth, Karl, 11, 15. 16, 176
Bartsch, Hans Werner, 178
Baruch II, 91
Baur, Ferdinand Christian, 10, 175
Benoit, Pierre, 12, 39, 57, 178, 180
Bianchi, Eugene, 187
Blomberg, Craig L., 181
Boff, Leonardo, 13, 19, 27, 150, 164, 188, 189
Bokenkotter, Thomas, 175
Broer, Ingo, 13, 176
Brown, Raymond, 21, 39, 79, 80, 84, 162, 175, 176, 177, 178, 179, 182, 185, 186, 187, 188
Brunner, Emil, 11, 176
Bultmann, Rudolph, 15, 16, 19, 107, 171

Campenhausen, Hans Freiherr von, 12
Cerfaux, Lucien, 93, 94, 182, 183
Charlesworth, James H., 28, 187
Chinnici, Rosemary, 187

Clement of Alexandria, 41, 161
Collingwood, R. George, 175
Cranfield, Charles E. B., 178
Cromwell, Richard S., 175
Crossan, Dominic, 28, 187

Daly, Robert, 168, 190
Daniélou, Jean, 12
Dante, 111
Deissman, Adolph, 94, 182
Delling, Gerhardt, 12
Descartes, Rene, 107, 185
Dhanis, Edouard, 11,176
Dibelius, Martin, 96, 98, 183
Didache, 57
Dillon, Richard, 178
Dodd, Charles Harold, 136, 137, 147, 179, 187
Durwell, Francois-Xavier, 11, 176

Eliot, Thomas S., 111
Enoch, I and II, 91
Esdras II, 91
Eusebius of Antioch, 41
Evans, Christsopher F., 21, 40, 57, 177, 180, 182

Feuerbach, Ludwig, 185
Fiorenza, Francis Schüssler, 161, 170, 188, 190
Fitzmyer, Joseph, 17, 114, 177, 180, 183, 186
Flew, Anthony G. N., 12, 176

Francis of Assisi, 137, 138
Frank, Richard, 11, 175
Fransen, Piet, 188
Freud, Sigismund, 108, 185
Fuller, David O., 178
Fuller, Reginald H., 12, 21, 58, 135, 177, 179, 180, 186

Galvin, John, 170, 171, 188, 190
Gardner-Smith, P., 21, 177
Gelpi, Donald, 185
Geyer, Hans Georg, 12
Ghiberti, Giuseppe, 12, 25, 176
Gogarten, Friedrich, 11, 176
Goguel, Maurice, 21, 39, 177, 179
Gospel of Peter, 50, 88
Graß, Hans, 12
Gregory the Great, 130
Grey, Mary, 187
Gutierrez, Gustavo, 27

Habermas, Gary R., 12, 176
Haenchen, Ernst, 96, 98, 182, 183
Haight, Roger, 163, 188
Harrington, Daniel J., 143, 176, 178, 179, 186
Harvey, Van A., 175
Hegel, G. W. F., 108, 185
Heidegger, Martin, 107, 108, 183
Heim, Karl, 11
Hodgson, Peter C., 175
Hoffmann, Paul, 91
Homer, 111
Hooke, Samuel, 12
Hoskyns, Edwin C., 40
Hug, Joseph, 177

Ignatius of Antioch, 32
Ihmels, Ludwig, 11
Innocent III, 23
Irenaeus of Lyon, 31

Jacobs-Malina, Diane, 187
Jeremias, Joachim, 15, 148, 187
Jerome, 41
John of the Cross, 137, 138
Josephus, Flavius, 99, 100, 183
Jubilees, 91
Jung, Karl, 108
Justin, 53, 179

Kähler, Martin, 11, 16, 175
Kant, Emmanuel, 16, 107, 108, 185
Karris, Robert, 181, 186
Käsemann, Ernst, 16
Kelly, John N. D., 160, 161, 188
Kingsbury, Jack D., 143, 186
Klappert, Bertold, 15, 16, 19, 20, 176
Kloppenburg, Bonaventure, 26, 177
Kosnik, Anthony, 188
Kümmel, Werner Georg, 15
Küng, Hans, 18
Künneth, Walter, 10, 11, 175, 176

Lake, Kirsopp, 21, 177
Lao Tsu, 106, 183
Lebreton, Jules, 94, 183
Leo IX, 23
Leo XIII, 117
Léon-Dufour, Xavier, 12, 24, 93, 95, 125, 126, 127, 135, 136, 177, 181, 183, 184, 186
Lercher, Louis, 174, 184
Levie, Jean, 175
Lightfoot, Robert Henry, 40, 178
Loades, Ann, 187
Lohfink, Gerhardt, 100, 183
Lohmeyer, Ernst, 40
Lohr, Charles H., 143, 186
Loome, Thomas M., 175
Lubac, Henri de, 163, 164, 189
Luz, Ulrich, 179

Maccabees IV, 91
Marèchal, Joseph, 107
Marx, Karl, 185
Marxsen,Willi, 12, 16, 19, 21, 22, 24, 25, 40, 171, 177
McBrien, Richard, 190
McKenzie, John, 127, 185
Meier, John P., 28, 154, 155, 176, 179, 185, 187, 188
Merleau-Ponty, Maurice, 108
Methodius, 161
Metz, Johannes B., 19
Michel, O., 40
Miethe, Terry L., 12
Mohn, G., 12
Moloney, Francis J., 186
Moltmann, Jürgen, 15, 16, 19

Neunheuser, Burkhard, 180
Neusner, Jacob, 28, 54, 181, 187
Nicolau, Miguel, 8, 9, 174
Nietzsche, Friedrich, 108
Nilson, Jon, 190
Noll, John F., 174

O'Brien, John A., 2, 10, 13, 174, 175
O'Collins, Gerald, 12, 169, 170, 176, 177, 190
O'Dell, D. W., 187
Olivieri, S., 26, 177
Origen, 41, 161
Orr, James, 175
Osborne, Kenan, 178, 182, 183, 188, 189
Ott, Ludwig, 174

Pannenberg, Wolfhart, 15, 19, 171
Perkins, Pheme, 12, 176, 178, 186
Perrin, Norman, 149, 187
Pesch, Rudolph, 171, 178
Peter Abelard, 161
Philips, Gérard, 26, 177

Pius XII, 130, 185
Polanyi, Michael, 108
Prat, Ferdinand, 11, 176
Psalms of Solomon, 91

Rahlfs, Alfred, 180
Rahner, Karl, 107, 164, 171, 176, 182, 185, 189, 190
Ramsey, Arthur Michael, 11
Ranke, Leopold von, 100
Reimarus, Samuel, 9
Rengstorf, Karl H., 12
Reuther, Rosemary R., 187
Ricoeur, Paul, 108
Rigaux, Beda, 12
Ritschl, Albrecht, 11, 147, 175
Rivière, Jean, 161, 188
Robinson, H. Wheeler, 117
Russell, David S., 91

Sanders, E. P., 28, 187
Sartre, Jean Paul, 110
Scheffczyk, Leo, 176, 180
Schierse, Franz Joseph, 180
Schillebeeckx, Edward, 22, 24, 107, 160, 171, 177, 188
Schleiermacher, Friedrich, 10, 11, 29, 175
Schmitt, Jean Claude, 11, 176
Schneiders, Sandra, 187
Schweitzer, Albert, 175
Scotus, John Duns, 108, 185
Segundo, Juan Luis, 19, 27
Seidensticker, Philip, 12
Senior, Donald, 52, 53, 179
Shakespeare, 111
Sibylline Oracles, 91
Sobrino, Jon, 13, 19, 20, 27, 115, 150, 151, 152, 155, 177, 183, 185, 186, 188
Solano, Iesu, 8, 166, 174, 189
Stange, Carl, 11, 175

Stefan, Horst, 11
Strauß, David Friedrich, 10, 175
Swete, Henry Barclay, 178

Tacitus, 99, 183
Tanquerey, Adolph Alfred, 9, 175
Tatian, 31
Taylor, Vincent, 178
Teresa of Avila, 137, 138
Ternus, Johannes, 185
Tertullian, 53
Testaments of the Twelve Patriarchs, 91

Thomas Aquinas, 130, 161, 185
Tillich, Paul, 18, 107, 110, 188

Vermes, Geza, 28, 187
Viviano, Benedict T., 178, 179, 186
Vorgimmler, Herbert, 26, 177, 180

Weiser, Artur, 184
Weiß, Johannes, 40, 147, 187
Welch, Claude, 175
Whitehead, Alfred North, 108
Wilckens, Ulrich, 12
Wisdom of Solomon, 91